GARY OWEN: COLLECTED PLAYS

T0315824

Gary Owen

COLLECTED PLAYS

**In The Pipeline • Mrs Reynolds and The Ruffian •
Love Steals Us From Loneliness • Iphigenia in Splott
• Violence and Son • Mum & Dad**

OBERON BOOKS
LONDON

WWW.OBERONBOOKS.COM

This collection first published in 2016 by Oberon Books Ltd
521 Caledonian Road, London N7 9RH
Tel: +44 (0) 20 7607 3637 / Fax: +44 (0) 20 7607 3629
e-mail: info@oberonbooks.com
www.oberonbooks.com

Cover image by Jon Pountney

Visit www.oberonbooks.com to read more about all our books and to
buy them. You will also find features, author interviews and news of
any author events, and you can sign up for e-newsletters so that you're
always first to hear about our new releases.

Contents

IN THE PIPELINE

for the chairman of the board of
Pembroke Power Station Sports and Social Club

My thanks to Gilly Adams for originally commissioning this piece as a radio play. To George Perrin and James Grieve at Paines Plough, for giving it a new life on stage. And to my family in Pembrokeshire for lending me more of their stories.

In The Pipeline was first presented by Radio Wales in April 2005.

Cast

ANDREW, Rob Storr
DAI, Ifan Huw Dafydd
JOAN, Jennifer Hill

Creative Team

Director Gilly Adams
Broadcast Assistant Willa King
Technical Presentation Nigel Lewis, Dyfan Rose

In The Pipeline had its British stage premiere in a co-production between Paines Plough and Òran Mór at Òran Mór, Glasgow, on September 6th 2010.

Cast

ANDREW, Rhodri Lewis
DAI, Grahame Fox
JOAN, Meg Wynn-Owen

Creative Team

Director David Horan
Design Patrick McGurn
Lighting Grant Anderson
Sound Scott Twynholm

Characters

ANDREW

DAI

JOAN

ANDREW: The letter came and it said, we're going to build this big gas plant in Milford Haven. And once we've done that, we'll want a pipeline from Milford Haven to Neath, link up with the main grid.

The letter reassured us that no route had been decided – they were just wanting to know in principle, whether people in our village would mind selling up and sodding off out of the way of vital economic progress.

The great and the gobby of the village were up in arms.

Let's form a committee, was their thought. Let's barricade some bridges, let's show them they can't push us around.

Which is fine, except that they can push us around. And they will, if they want to.

I thought it might be worth seeing what good could come out of the situation. If we took the money. If we went along with things.

The idea had been, I'd get some old wreck of place, and do it up, and in a year I'd've made ten or twenty thousand.

And that would be something. To get me started, again.

For the first month, or the first week, I was at it nearly every night, stripping one thing, painting something else.

But then. I'd come home, and –

– I wouldn't come home, was the thing.

Because my job. It's the best job on the railways, and it's the worst job on the railways.

It's the best job on the railways, because it's dead easy and there's nothing to do. And it's the worst job on the railways – because it's dead easy. And there's nothing to do.

It's just pushing the trolley up and down the train, and selling the tea, the coffee, the crisps. Some days it's not even that. If the train's a bit full, or I'm a bit queasy, I can elect to engage in static sales. Which means I park the trolley up at one end of the train, and the punters come to me.

People say, but you see the country don't you? You get about?

And that's true. You do see a lot of back gardens. You see a lot of washing lines. And what you learn is that, from Pembroke Dock to Crewe, everybody's washing looks pretty much the fucking same.

So after a day of pushing the trolley or just letting the punters come to me, twice up to Manchester and back, or three times up to Shrewsbury and back, or four times to Cardiff – it becomes hard not to make another, unscheduled stop at one of the three pubs on my way home.

I'm not the kind of guy to drink on my own. Not more than two pints, anyway, so even if I end up stopping at all the pubs on the way home, I never have more than six which isn't so bad, but…

I'd gotten into the habit of coming home half-cut and collapsing into the couch, is what I'm trying to say.

I'd meant to have a bit more of a life in the village.

So I made a point of going and sitting in the Red Lion quite a bit when I first moved in, hoping to make an impression. Or some friends. But usually after half an hour someone would come up and ask if I was using that chair and I'd say no, go right ahead, you take it mate.

And then after a while you've become the bloke in the corner that talks to no-one, and no-one talks to, and that's it.

When Alison moved in over the road I thought I had a chance.

Not a chance with her. But a chance to be a bit different, now I wasn't the newest person in the village.

First I thought I'd go over, introduce myself as she was unpacking, maybe lend a hand with the boxes and crates. But I'm not the world's most dextrous person. I drop things.

Plus she had a kid. A little girl, about five or six.

A grown-up will say at worst, that you're looking nice and healthy. A kid will just go – why's that man so fat, mummy?

So I thought best not.

Then one night I come into the Red Lion, having had the full quota of two in the Bull and two in the King's Head, and Alison's there. Sitting on her own. No kid, no boyfriend, no nothing.

And without thinking about it I make myself go up to her. And I say, hiya.

She looks at me a bit funny and I say, sorry – I live opposite you. And she's all yes of course you do, and I go, no, no reason why you should recognise me, I just thought I'd say hello.

Welcome you to the village.

Great, she says. Are you – on your own?

Am as it happens, I say.

Well d'you wanna join me, she goes.

I say, yeah, that'd be nice –

– and as I'm saying it, she goes, you can introduce me to some of the locals maybe?

And of course I can't do that. Cause I don't know any of them.

So I sort of slap on my thigh. And pull out my phone. And stare at it a bit.

I say, sorry, bit of an emergency at work, I'm gonna have to go.

Right, she says. Well perhaps another time.

Yeah perhaps, I go.

Of course what this little exchange tells me is that she's the friendly type. So she's bound to get talking to people, and she'll say who was that bloke who was in here earlier, who went to sit down with me and then rushed out. And everyone in the pub will say – we don't know. He's just this bloke who comes in, half-cut, sits on his own, sinks two pints, and shuffles off home.

I gave up on Alison then. She would smile at me, across the road, but – it was, you know.

And I suppose I gave up on the village. I thought, if they want to build that pipeline right through here, it'll suit me fine. I'll sell up, move on, try again somewhere else.

Then I was on the Manchester train. Coming back, for the second time that day. A guy got on at Swansea with two cats. He sat on the benches, where there was room for his cat boxes, and I had the trolley parked up, doing static sales, and we got to chatting.

Turns out he was from Kilgetty, and he was going back to Kilgetty to drop off his cats with his mum, cause he was off for a month. He had a shop, a record shop in Camden Town, but he was closing up. To go off with his wife. To Australia.

I said to him, yeah I've been doing this two and a half years now, and the money's good but I'm starting to get itchy feet. He says, you must see a bit of the country though. And I say yes, you do. Back gardens, mostly. Washing lines. This old lady stood up. I didn't stop talking to the guy, because the lady looked like she was just on her way over and buy a cup of coffee. But then she gasped.

And she clutched her left arm, close to her body.

And then she fell down.

People started to gather round her. Then they started to look at me. Being the only person present in a uniform.

Train manager was nowhere around.

I called the driver and told him we had a medical emergency. We were five minutes out of Tenby so he said he'd call for an ambulance to meet us there.

In the meantime I should administer whatever first aid I could.

The guy's two cats are mewling. Still no sign of the train manager. And the guy is kneeling over this woman, checking her neck for a pulse.

He says to me, I think she's having a heart attack. He says I'm not sure, but my dad had one once.

And he goes, have you got a defibrillator?

And someone else says, they're supposed to have a defibrillator.

And some other bloke goes, they've got to have a defibrillator, that's the law.

So I go into the train manager's cabin, and there in the big first aid kit is one of those things with the pads that you put on someone chest and go 'clear' and you shock them. And those things are of course called defibrillators.

I fetch the defibrillator, and bring it back to the little huddle of people around the old lady.

I hold out the first aid kit, to give it to someone. But the huddle of people parts, to let me through.

So I kneel down, by the guy with the cats. By the old lady's side.

And everybody's looking at me. Because I'm in uniform.

The uniform of a trolley operative.

I'm reading the instructions, on the side of this defibrillator thing.

And someone is going on that it's the treatment a victim receives in the very first minutes that determines the survival rate.

The instructions say it's important to place the pads exactly as shown in the picture.

If a clean contact with the skin is not made, an effective shock will not be delivered.

My job is to push the trolley up and down the carriage, selling coffee, tea and crisps.

When I was a kid, if I made a model plane, or anything, it would just fall apart.

So I hold out the box and pads.

The guy with the cats takes them from me. He rips off the cover of the box. The defibrillator starts talking to him, in a calm American voice. He rips open this old lady's blouse. And her bra, and everything, and he slaps the pads on. The American voice says not to touch the patient. Then it says it is analysing. Then it says it recommends delivering a shock. The guy presses a button on the defibrillator, and the voice tells everybody to stand clear, and we do.

There's a crack. The woman's body shudders. The American voice recommends administering CPR and so the guy asks if anybody knows CPR because he'll give it a go, but if there's anyone trained…

By then we've pulled into Tenby. A couple of paramedics in green overalls charge into the carriage. And they, of course, know how to do CPR, so the guy backs off, we all back off.

The paramedics give her heart massage, and the kiss of life, and they find out her name from her purse, and start talking to her.

I think that's it then, she's a goner.

But the old lady starts talking back.

She opens her eyes, and starts talking back to them.

They give her aspirin, and tell her to lie still, and they put her on a stretcher, and take her away.

Me and the guy with the cats sit there. And don't really look at each other. We get to Kilgetty and he picks up his catboxes, and says, well.

I say yeah, thanks. And thanks for helping out. With the old lady.

The bloke says, you do what you can.

We pull out from Kilgetty. And then after that, it's Penally, Manorbier, Lamphey, Pembroke, and finally Pembroke Dock. Where the service terminates.

Walking home that night, I stopped at every pub along the way. I thought I deserved it.

I don't quite know why I thought that.

When I got to the Red Lion, it was packed. There was no table free, so I had to sit at the bar, and nod at people as they brushed past me to get their drinks.

I'm coming to the end of my second pint, when a voice says, oh hello you.

It's Alison. I say, hello, and she looks at me and goes, are you alright, you're pale as a ghost.

And I say, yeah, I'm fine.

And she goes, alright then, and turns her attention back to getting served.

I say, I'm fine I just had somebody nearly die in front of me today.

Alison goes no, how's that? I tell her, this old lady collapsed on the train. Massive heart attack.

Alison goes, what happened?

And I tell her.

I tell her how I fetched the defibrillator from the train manager's compartment.

How the huddle of people parted before me.

How I knelt at the old lady's side.

How for a moment I didn't know what I was doing, and almost panicked.

And then how I pulled open the woman's blouse. How I made sure I had placed the pads exactly as was shown in the diagram. How I got a good clean connection between the pad, and the woman's skin. How I administered a shock, and then began to perform CPR.

And all this after instructing a young man with some cats to phone ahead and have a paramedic team meet us Tenby.

Alison goes, how come you knew to do all that? Are you trained?

I say, I'm trained to sell tea and coffee, love.

Which is odd, because I'm not the kind of person to call anyone 'love'.

She was lucky you were there, Alison goes.

Well, the machine pretty much tells you what to do, I say.

And Alison looks at me, and I look away, and when I look up again Alison's still looking at me. I smile at her.

A little smile. Nothing too flashy.

I don't see her for about a week or so after that, and then one night there's this banging at my door.

I open up and there she is. Alison, and in her arms, her little girl. Louisa.

And Louisa's face is all blue.

And Alison's face is all teeth clenched, and everything held very tight.

Alison goes, she's swallowed something, she's choking on something, and I don't know what to do.

And I'm not dressed. I'm not in my uniform. I'm in my dressing gown.

Alison stands there going, my daughter's suffocating, what am I gonna do?

And what she means is – what are you going to do?

DAI: I can't remember when, but you started hearing people say there were no more jobs for life.

We were all gonna have to get off our backsides, and get on our bikes, and get into the marketplace.

We were gonna have to sell ourselves.

We were gonna have to go after the work, because the work was not gonna come to us.

It wound me up because the people who went on a lot about getting out there in the marketplace were the same people who went on a lot about family values.

And family values are great. I'm all for them.

But it's not so easy to be a responsible loving father in a ten minute phone call home every night from your… meat-packing job in Aberdeen.

I think what also used to wind me up was that whole idea of selling yourself.

Pushing yourself forward all the time. Saying, no give me the job, not him, I'll be great, I'll be better than he will.

I mean.

When I got the job at the power station, I thought I might be safe from all that.

People are always gonna want electricity, aren't they. At least until civilisation collapses.

When I started I was an auxiliary plant operator. After a couple of years, I moved from being an auxiliary plant operator, to be a plant operator, which meant I ran a generating unit – the engine which made the steam, which drove the turbine, which spun the generator, which made the electricity.

By this point, we weren't a base load station any more: we weren't generating all the time. Oil had gotten more expensive, and so they just brought us on line to cope with peak demand.

It had been that peak time was first thing in the morning, when all the smelters and furnaces and productions lines fired up for the day. But by the time I was running a unit, peak time was about 7.45 at night, during the ad break in

Coronation Street, when 12 million people, as one, got up and switched their kettles on.

In the space of 15 years, we'd gone from being a nation of steel makers, to a nation of tea drinkers.

Obviously we had always been tea drinkers. You know what I'm getting at.

Then they separated us off from the grid, and the grid would always be playing funny buggers, trying to save a penny wherever they could.

I remember one night, one November demand dipped for a bit and they were on the phone, telling us to shut down a unit. We said, are you sure. They said yes. We said, are you sure you're sure? And they were. And so we shut down a unit.

And I swear to God, not three minutes later – three minutes, now – and they were on the phone again. A unit had gone off-line somewhere else on the grid. And demand was going up – which was apparently a shock to them, on a cold, wet, windy winter night. Could we get our spare unit back on line please?

But of course you can't just switch a generator on and off like a kettle. Or – a toaster.

There's an awful lot of dangerous stuff involved.

There's oil burning.

There's metal heating.

And metal expands as it heats. You have to give it time.

But there we were. The great British public needed their lights on and their three bar fires aglow.

Our unit had to be gotten up to be speed.

We did it in forty-five minutes.

And that is a record.

It's not the kind of record Norris McWhirter would've been interested in, even when he was alive.

And all you'll know about our record-breaking achievement is that your lights, and your telly, and your three bar fire, and your fridge, and your kettle, all kept working that freezing November night.

We were good at what we did.

And as much as our new bosses might try to mess us around, we knew that what we were doing mattered.

We could tell by the note of undisguised panic that would enter their voices whenever things looked like they were going wrong.

And we knew because –

– you know we had to train to be firemen?

What with the oil, and the hydrogen, and the chlorine and God knows what else we had stashed around the place, if a fire started with us, it had to be dealt with. Fast.

People would say, don't you worry you might have to tackle some huge blaze and if you get it wrong you might die and also there might be a horrible disaster with thousands killed or injured?

And I'd say yeah it does worry me.

But actually it didn't.

I liked it. I liked having the responsibility.

But obviously you'd have to say it worried you, cause otherwise you'd just look a bit of a git.

And then we'd get the SAS coming down.

They'd come to practice blowing a power station up.

Each group of SAS would come down to the station twice while they were being trained. Once at the start of their training, and once at the end.

The first time, when they were new, they were just there to learn where to place the charges. And so you'd see them, wandering about.

The second time, when they were trained, you wouldn't see them at all.

Just suddenly their instructors would walk in, and point out to you the little charge that had appeared, on the turbine shaft.

We had motion-sensitive cameras, the lot.

The motion alarms would trip, you'd go down and look, you'd see nothing.

There'd be a guy in the control room on the intercom, telling you the alarm is tripping right now and you'd be staring right where the camera was pointing, and – nothing.

In the end the only thing that would ever get them was the sheep.

In all the fields around the station, they grazed sheep and sometimes when the SAS were sneaking in suddenly the sheep would stand up and all look in the same direction and start baa-ing and making a fuss.

The SAS. Foiled by sheep. But not by us.

I say you wouldn't see them.

I saw one of them, once.

I saw a shadow move and I thought better safe than sorry and I went to phone the control room.

Actually what I thought was – we'll get 'em this time.

And as I picked up the receiver I felt something behind me.

I turned round and there was a figure.

I couldn't see his face I could just see, in his hand, a blade.

He said – put. The phone. Down.

So I did.

He was this tiny bloke.

He was carrying a rucksack the size of a small mountain, all sorts of kit hanging off it.

As he went, he did not make a single sound.

I think the quiet unnerved me more than the knife.

There was almost something witchy about it.

And I suppose all this business with the SAS was another thing that made me think that at the power station we were safe.

If we made a mistake, the nation ground to a halt. If there was a war, people would try and blow us up. I thought we were safe, because what we did mattered.

And then one day we came into work and they told us they were closing the station down, and getting rid of us all.

Which just goes to show how wrong you can be.

ANDREW: So I take Louisa, and I lay her down on the couch.

She's spluttering, trying to push me away with her hands. Alison's trying to calm her down.

I prise open her jaw – I have to, cause she's clamping it shut – and I can't see anything down her throat.

But I can hear this – squelchy rattling noise.

And I realise it's not coming from her throat, it's coming from her nose.

I run and get tweezers – I'm the kind of person that gets a lot of splinters, so I've got tweezers all round the place – and with Alison holding her face still as she can, I carefully, carefully, slide these tweezers up poor Louisa's nose and grab.

And whatever it is I've grabbed, I feel it give way under the tweezers' jaws. And I pull, and for a second I'm sure I'm gonna pull – something I shouldn't, some part of Louisa, out through her nose –

– but what comes is, a runner bean.

Plus a certain amount of mucus and blood.

They've had runner beans for tea, and Louisa hadn't wanted to eat them, and Alison had said she had to, and then the beans started just falling off her plate. Diving onto the floor, of their own accord. And finally, Louisa reckons, this one jumped up her nose.

I say to her, if you'd told me it'd run up your nose, I'd've believed you. She looks at me, and I go, because it's a runner bean, isn't it. And Louisa says, don't be stupid. It doesn't actually run, just because it's called a runner bean.

And Alison offers me a beer.

And I find myself sitting in Alison's lounge, playing with her daughter, drinking a can of lager.

And I stay there till Louisa goes to bed. Then me and Alison sit, and have a drink, and watch a bit of telly.

And then I say I think I should go, and Alison doesn't stop me, but she says, Louisa likes you. We should do this again.

So I say but hopefully without your daughter nearly suffocating herself at the start of the evening.

And Alison says well in an ideal world, yeah.

And so it becomes a thing that I go over to Ally's, and sit round there, and – I make Louisa laugh. Without really intending to, I mean – not by being funny. She just laughs at me a lot.

Which is fine. Which is better than her for example crying at me. Or ignoring me altogether.

And then Louisa will go to bed, and me and Alison will sit.

And then I'll go, back across the road. Back to my house.

Then one night Ally phoned, and told me to come over, and I found her there, with a mate. And Ally noticeably at least a little bit dressed up.

And it occurs to me what's happened. I've been groomed for baby-sitting duty.

Which is fair enough. A mum on her own needs a night out, every now and again.

But then Ally kisses Louisa, and tells her mate she'll be back by eleven, and says to me, come on then.

And we walk down the Red Lion. And sit.

And sitting there, in the pub, people looking at us, suddenly a couple or apparently a couple, and we can't find anything to say. So we sit, in silence. Not the lazy silence we have in front of the telly after Louisa's gone to bed, but – a silence that makes you sweat.

And it's so horrible that in the end Alison says look shall we just go?

And I say yeah might as well.

We walk back home, and don't speak, and as we get to our houses, Ally says look I'm sorry about all this, and I say no that's fine –

– and she stamps her foot and says why couldn't you just have kissed me, you idiot, and gotten it over with weeks ago?

She stands there, for five, ten, twenty seconds, and then realises I'm not gonna do anything.

I'm not even going to try.

She turns away.

And once she's not looking at me, I can move.

I go after her. She hears me coming, she slows down, and I catch her and spin her round, and I kiss her, there, in the middle of street.

And after a bit, she says, d'you want to go back down the pub, and try again?

I say no, let's go in, let's see Louisa before she goes to bed.

So we become a couple. Ally starts coming over the road to mine. Gradually we begin doing all the work on the house I've been putting off. We sand, and plaster, and paint, together.

And it occurs to me that maybe I don't want to let them to bulldoze this place to make way for the pipeline. Because we're making something here, me and Ally and Louisa. We're making a home.

And so one day we're talking about what colour might do for the spare bedroom and I say, Louisa likes blue, doesn't she.

And Ally says, yes she does.

And I say, right, blue for that room, then. For Louisa's room.

Ally walks over and puts her arms around me and we stand like that for a minute and then Ally goes, and speaking of she who must be obeyed, where is the little spawn of Satan?

And we both realise that that house is quiet.

Downstairs we find my front door open. And looking across the road, so is Ally's. Which is reassuring because it means Louisa must have crossed the road safely, and frightening because it means Louisa has wandered out and crossed the road, on her own.

We run round Ally's house, but Louisa's nowhere to be found.

And –

– the mistake we made was, we panicked. We panicked and all we could think about was the road. Because people slow down for the village, but they're back on the throttle again as soon as they're round the corner and there's no pavement or verge or anything.

So we split up, and we ran in different directions to see if we could find her.

I must've kept going for twenty minutes, which was stupid because Louisa'd been gone for five minutes at the most. If I was gonna find her, I'd've found her straight off.

But I couldn't bear to turn back, was the thing.

Of course in the end I had to.

I got back to the house, and Ally was crying on the front lawn.

I took her in and we went into the kitchen and I remember it just hitting me there was something wrong in the garden.

I looked again, and I realised, the back gate – which Ally never used – had been opened. There were dandelions with their stems all bent, where the gate had pushed them over.

We ran out into the garden, and opened the gate. The pathway behind the houses was all overgrown, and we could see people'd been down there.

So we followed and their tracks came out at this field that the kids call the park, cause there's a tyre-swing hanging off one of the trees.

The place was deserted.

We went back to the house. We phoned the police, and phoned all Louisa's friends, and we went door to door and people came out to help.

Eventually the police said it was best we went home, in case Louisa came back of her own accord. And so they'd know where to get hold of Ally, if they needed her for anything.

We knew they meant if they needed her to make some sort of appeal. Or some sort of identification.

I tried to get Alison to eat. She wouldn't.

We sat there.

And there was a point when it occurred to me that Louisa wasn't coming back.

It was awful but also it was a relief.

Because then I could start thinking, what will we do, how will we go on, how will we cope with this.

I could see that for ages – months, a year – everything would be pure pain.

And then after that it wouldn't be that we'd forget, or the pain would lessen: but there'd be other things in our lives as well. At first just all the mundane business of staying alive. And then gradually, occasionally, there'd be moments of light. We might laugh at something on the telly.

And for that second we'd be doing something apart from missing Louisa. And that would be the start, of healing. And living again.

And I said to Ally, I won't leave you, you know.

She said, what?

I said to her, this has happened, and it's awful, and it's the worst thing ever – but I won't leave you. We'll get through it. I promise.

And Ally looked at me. She said, nothing has happened.

I said, no I know, but –

Ally said, nothing at all has happened to my daughter.

We sat there in silence. For maybe an hour an a half.

Then the phone went.

And as Ally got up to answer it, a police car pulled up outside.

They'd found her.

She was fine.

She'd gone off with some kids, and gone wandering in the woods and they'd found some old abandoned mill and gone exploring. And the stairs had collapsed and left Louisa trapped upstairs.

These kids had gone home, and said nothing, cause they were scared they'd get in trouble.

They kept Louisa in hospital for a couple of days, just for observation. She was cold, and hungry, and dehydrated, but basically alright. She hadn't even panicked, particularly – she said, she knew someone would come and find her.

When Louisa came out of hospital Alison said it was probably best if we stayed at our own places for a night or two, so she could give all her attention to Louisa. And I thought yeah, good idea.

Then they went off to stay with Ally's parents for a fortnight, just for a bit of a break.

And I thought yeah, fair enough.

But then when they came back, Ally didn't come over to see me, didn't even call.

When I saw her I said, what's going on, and she said, you gave up on my daughter.

And then she went inside her house, and pulled the blinds.

Weeks went by and she just ignored me and I thought, that can't be good for the child, can it.

Months went by, and – I suppose I gave up hope.

Then Ally turned up at my door one evening.

She said – apparently, my daughter misses you.

But by then it was too late.

Cause I'd already signed the contracts, and sold my house to the gas people.

I was already moving on.

DAI: So they decided they were closing the power station and they didn't need us anymore.

Of course they did need us. For a bit.

They needed us to take the station to bits.

Obviously it's not a cheery task, dismantling your own place of work.

I've gotta say, we didn't exactly rush.

We stripped out everything that could be sold, or used on another site.

The SAS popped down, took away a few bits and pieces they could practice blowing up.

There was just a shell left.

Some engineers came, demolished that.

We cleared up the rubble.

And that was it.

Those of us who were left then – those of us who hadn't taken redundancy – they seconded us out.

To a security firm.

And we were put to guarding those 590 concreted-over acres, that had been our place of work.

I was doing that for two years.

There's not much to say about it.

I don't mean to just skip two years, and give the impression the time just flew by.

Because it certainly did not fly by.

If we were lucky, on a night shift, a badger would come snuffling out of the woods, and we could watch him on the CCTV.

That was quite interesting.

Happened about – once a month.

The pay cut wasn't much fun either.

I wouldn't say we went down to minimum wage, because at the time there was no minimum wage.

That's one thing we can thank Uncle Tony for –

– you know they say for every five months you spend working shifts, you lose a month off your life?

I'm not sure how they figure stuff like that out.

But I think I probably believe it.

I certainly think we lost something, sitting in that gatehouse. In the dead of night. Watching nothing happen. For hours.

But at least we weren't redundant.

Anyway.

I stuck that for two years and then I could get early retirement.

So I took it, and I got a little pension.

I had become a pensioner.

It wasn't enough to live on, so I looked round for something else.

There wasn't much to be had.

And of course I was too old.

Not that anyone would ever say that.

I started doing little jobs for people, just to fill up time.

Bit of gardening, putting up shelves, that sort of thing.

I'd do someone a bit of painting or plastering and they'd say, oh my brother needs a tree taking down, you should give him a call.

And when they were paying me for materials, they'd chuck in a few quid for my trouble.

Bit embarrassing really.

But after a while, all these little jobs were taking up most of my days.

The car was getting in a state, cement and brushes and all sorts of rubbish on the seats.

I went to the bank, and they gave me a loan, and I got a van.

Which made sense but it was pressure then. The loan had to be paid off, whether I got work or not.

And about the same time, we decided to buy out the club.

Cause they'd given us what was left of the lease on the power station sports and social club.

A nice gesture, they said.

And first we thought we'd just let the lease run out and then pack it in.

What was the point in having a power station club, if you didn't have a power station?

But then we thought no.

This was when we were doing the security guard thing, and we had a lot of time to chat, and we started talking about how we might keep the club afloat.

How we might make it a going concern.

So we got together a business plan. Got one loan from the brewery, another from the bank, and made an offer on the freehold.

And after a bit of faffing about, they sold it to us.

The club was ours.

We ran it through a committee of members.

And you know they say a camel is a horse designed by a committee?

Well I think that's quite an insulting thing to say.

Insulting, to the camel.

Because actually a camel is extraordinarily well put together. Very few things are better at living in the desert than a camel is.

Our committee was like most committees. Ask it to design you a ship of the desert, and it would come up with a ship, floating in a huge great big tank of water, on wheels, pushed around by a jet engine.

It would not come up with a camel.

So while it was nice having the club, it stopped being somewhere I could go for a couple of pints and a game of skittles and just relax.

28

Cause everytime I went down there, people had complaints. Shouldn't we be doing this, this way? Shouldn't we be doing that, the other way?

All for the good of the club, of course.

But it was a pity, cause I could've done with having somewhere just to go to relax.

Cause having to pay off this loan on the van was starting to get to me.

I mean more than it should.

Work always turned up but I could never be sure that it was gonna turn up, from week to week.

So I put in a tender to do all property maintenance and gardening on a new development.

It'd be a long term contract, regular money, a bit of security.

They asked me to come in and have an interview.

So I'm driving there, in the van.

I've gone down the back lane, turning onto the main road in Milton.

And a bloke smashes into me.

Bloke in a Mondeo.

He gets out and and I say we'd best exchange details then and he goes all shifty.

And then gets back in his Mondeo and drives.

I've got his number plate, of course, and the police pick him up past Stepaside, but guess what, he's got no insurance.

The van is a wreck.

The RAC tow me home, and – it's a wreck.

Bev says who cares about the van, thank God you're alright.

I think, I care about the van, cause wrecked or not it needs paying for.

Bev starts on that I should go to casualty, get myself looked at.

But I've still got this interview, so I phone them, warn them I'm gonna be late and jump in the car.

Bev yelling at me that if I drop dead of a brain haemorrhage then I'll be getting no more than I deserve.

I'm pushing it a bit on the way over, enough to get flashed by a speed camera, but still when I get there the bloke I need to see has gone.

And I ask if I can arrange another time but apparently he doesn't wanna see me now.

He needs to be able to rely on his staff. If I can't bothered to turn up on time for an interview, then…

I go home and Bev's still on about going to hospital.

And for a quiet life I tell her no, I'm not going to sit around in casualty for hours, but I will go to the surgery.

The doctor gives me the once over, and tells me I'm alright. Says I look a bit red in the face, though.

I tell him it's been that kind of day.

He says he wants to check my blood pressure, and the first time he says he thinks the machine must be broken.

So he goes and gets another machine, and checks again. Twice.

And it turns out the machine wasn't broken. I've just got unbelievably high blood pressure.

He writes me a prescription for beta blockers and says, if you wanna live to see sixty, you're going to have to make some changes.

No more booze, no more fags, no more salt, no more fatty foods, no more stress.

I say yeah great no problem.

As I'm leaving I get a call. Can I come out to a job in Lamphey.

I say not really no but the bloke's desperate. He can smell something foul from his drains and he's afraid sewerage is going to explode into his bathroom.

Please, he says. My neighbour gave me your number. Said you could be relied on.

What's happened is the wind has driven the water out of the trap in his waste pipe. So I just run the taps, fill the trap up again, and that does the trick.

He says cheers mate, you're a godsend.

And then he looks at me and goes, are you alright?

I say not really no. And I tell him about the van getting written off, and missing out on this contract, and how I'm going to need to get a new van to carry on paying for the old one, so that'll mean twice the repayments, and twice the pressure, and I'm not allowed to get stressed, but I can't even have a pint or a fag to calm myself down.

And he gets out a couple of cans and says, you can have one, can't you.

And he listens to me go on.

And I calm down a bit.

We have a bit of a chat.

He's a nice enough bloke.

And he mentions he's moved to the area cause he's going to be a manager at the new gas plant in Milford.

I say to him, you couldn't give me a job there, could you.

And the shutters come down.

He puts on this face.

This corporate face.

The face they wear when they tell you that while they value the contribution you've made to the company over the years, you are as of now surplus to requirements.

He says well you're welcome to apply, of course…

He doesn't go on to say – but you're too old.

So I say no, that's fine, you're right, it's all over for me. I'm just gonna go home, get out my shotgun, and put both barrels through my skull.

When I get home I'm exhausted from – the day. And I've got pins and needles in my arms and legs, which the doctor said the beta blockers might do, so I go straight to bed. And I'm flat out.

When I open my eyes again, I have that moment of confusion, when I'm not sure what day it is.

I hear a noise, downstairs.

It sounds like Bev, shouting.

I get up and I'm a bit unsteady on my feet.

I walk down the stairs – and I see Bev being dragged out the front door by these blokes in black.

And I can see one of them's got a gun.

Like a little – submachine gun.

There's a noise from garden and I go to look.

And then my phone rings, and the landline rings, both at the same time.

I hear a voice, through a tannoy, from out the front.

Then more noise out the back.

So I creep to the back door, and I can hear whispering. Men's voices.

They try the back door.

It's locked.

More whispering.

Some shuffling about.

I take a deep breath.

And I turn the key and open the back door and this huge bloke in black comes charging past me, trips on the step, and goes crashing onto the kitchen floor.

The bloke gets to his feet. Brushes himself down.

I say are you alright, mate?

He says, I'm fine. Now: armed police. Put your hands up.

I say, you want some tea after your trip?

His mates all laugh.

He says I'm serious, armed police. Put your hands above your head.

I go and fill the kettle up. I'm not saying I wasn't scared. It's just: I've been stalked by the SAS. Once you've had the best, the rest don't really measure up.

The commander explained, they got phoned in what seemed a credible threat of someone going psycho with a shotgun.

And I think to be honest the local armed response unit hadn't had chance to get dolled up in their flak jackets and gas masks for months.

This bloke in Lamphey. He thought he could say no, you're too old – and that would make me go and shoot myself.

The power these people imagine they have.

Once the police have made their apologies and gone, I don't know what to do with what's left of the day.

So I say to Bev jump in the car.

I drive us down Freshwater West.

And we go for a walk.

JOAN: It gets to about five and neither of us've spoken.

Will fills up the kettle. Puts it on the stove.

I say, Will. If you don't go and look at it all now, there'll come a day when you'll wish you had.

And so.

We get wrapped up, layers, thick socks, wellies.

Will gets a torch. Just in case.

And we head down the hill, to walk round the wood.

In lots of places, everything's changed.

All the little paths we used to run along, overgrown.

The badger paths and the fox trails are still there, and still where I remember them. But our paths are gone.

A clearing we used to play in has gone as well: a beech, and a couple of rowans have sprung up right in the middle of it.

Well, not sprung up. They'll've grown over… decades, I suppose.

I say how much I like the rowans and Will says, we'll have one for the garden, shall we?

And then leans on me, and takes off his left welly.

I say what are you doing now?

And he's got his foot in a carrier bag, as extra lining against leaks.

He takes the bag off his foot, puts his welly back on, then finds a sapling, and gently works round its roots with his fingers, till it comes up.

That's probably against the law, I tell him, digging up wild things.

Probably is, he says, putting the sapling in his grimy carrier bag. But it's my land. For tonight.

We wander past the fort. I can never remember if it's Roman, or Iron Age, or if they're the same thing.

When we get there it's a bit of a shock.

Kids from some conservation group came down a couple of years back, and they said there were going to clear some of the lower branches off the trees, so you could see the shape of the mound better.

And we said, fine, good idea, go ahead.

Course they've not been back since, and with the extra light coming through all the brambles have gone mad.

They've covered the place.

You can barely see the shape of the fort at all.

So I decide I'm going to phone the conservation people in the morning, and see if they feel like a return visit: I can't imagine the new owners will begrudge me doing that.

We head along then to have a look at the spring.

The watercress has gone from the stream, but when we lift the cover, the water is clear as ever.

I get a little chill when I think, the Romans drank from it, and we still drink from it today.

I remember when we were little, we had to come down every morning to get water, and if we were unlucky, again in the evening as well.

It was odd because I loved going down the woods, but if I had to go down for water in the evening, it would scare me.

Like the ghosts were watching me, cause I was doing the same as they'd've done, thousands of years ago.

It was a relief when they fixed a pump, to bring the water up to the house.

I can't remember when that was. Nineteen sixty-five, I think.

Will jumps into the stream that comes off the spring.

He starts pulling branches and muck out from it.

Great, he says. There's a leak in this pipe.

And he lifts the pipe out of the stream, and you can see water trickling from it.

But we're still getting water up in the house, I say.

Yes, he goes, but half of it's river water, isn't it.

I say I'll go back to the house and call someone but he says no, he'll do it himself.

He'll see if he can prop the pipe up so the leaky bit's out of the stream. Then he'll come back and get his tools and some pieces of pipe, and see if he's got one that'll fit.

In the meantime, he tells me to go back to the house and get a decent fire going, cause he's gonna be soaked by the time he's finished.

And so I set off, my new little rowan tree in my bag.

But then I think, no.

I haven't seen the badger set.

So I don't head back to the house.

I wander further into the forest.

And I find the slope where the badgers live.

There's not much to see, of course.

Just holes in the ground to most people.

But I know, some of the holes have been there for –

– they were there when my mum was young, so eighty, ninety years at least.

The badgers've been there all that time.

All the while our family's been at the farm.

The set has spread since I was down here last. There are new holes.

Freshly dug earth piled up outside them.

Bits of grass the badgers've dropped when they're bringing in fresh bedding.

It comes to rain, so I turn for the house.

Go through a ditch, that used to be a quarry.

When we were little everyone said that was where fairies came up to the world, from a hole under a rock.

They'd come into town, and buy things, and always pay with the right money.

If you tried to follow them back to fairy land they'd curse you, and you'd fall asleep.

Then when you woke, you'd look around you, and recognise the land, but not recognise how everything looked.

And what would've happened was, you'd've slept for five hundred years, and as soon as you touched anyone, you'd crumble and turn into dust.

I get to the path again, and just as I'm crossing the stream, I see something in the wood.

A big orange shape.

I step towards it, and I realise there's twine strung across the trees in front of me. At about shoulder height.

The twine goes in ring, around this orange shape. There's about thirty, forty foot of it, threaded through the trees.

And it's held together with a tiny silver padlock.

I come a bit closer, and it occurs to me the orange shape is a tent.

Now obviously this bit of twine isn't going to keep anybody out.

It must be there as some sort of warning.

To who I'm not sure.

I grab the twine and give it a bit of a tug. It pulls on the branches. And a voice from in the tent says, who's there?

A girl's voice.

I say, it's me.

And a girl's head sticks out of the tent.

The head is very wet.

She says, what're doing in my camp?

I say, what're you doing, camped in my wood?

Oh, she says: it's your wood, is it?

I say, well yes. It is for now.

The girl gets out of the tent. Comes and stands opposite me, just the other side of the twine.

She's a tiny thing, but with one of those faces, she could be thirteen, she could be thirty.

She says to me, well I'm only camped here for now. I'm not doing any harm.

I'm sure you're not, I say. But, you look a bit damp, and the rain's getting up – would you like to come to the house for a cup of tea, and to dry off?

As we're walking up to the house, I ask her where she's from. She says she's from not far away, she's had a bit of scrap with her dad, and she just walked out.

I say oh, you moved in recently, then, have you? But she says no, they've been here ages. And I say it's just I don't recognise you.

The girl says, well, we don't get into town as much as we did.

When we get to the house, I give her a towel for her hair, and put the kettle on the stove.

I put out bread, cheese, and blackberry jam that Judith gave us, and jam tarts that I'd made the day before.

This girl falls on the food.

She finishes all the bread, and all the jam tarts but the last one. Which she leaves, sitting lonely on the plate.

I say go on, you have that last tart, and I'll cut some more bread.

If you're sure, she says. We've got bread to spare, I tell her.

I watch her gobbling her food down, and I say, lucky I came along. You obviously needed a good feed.

She says, yeah, it was.

And then she looks at me, and says – bit of an odd night to be wandering in the woods, on your own. Hardly weather for a walk.

And then she says nothing.

Just looks at me.

And I can hear the clock in the kitchen, and the clock in the living room, ticking and tocking, each just out of time with the other.

The rain on the porch roof.

The crackling of the fire taking hold in the grate.

I say well no the thing is it's the last day that bit of wood is properly ours. They want to build this pipeline to carry the gas from Milford and they said we could rent them the land or sell it outright, and we thought, sell it, cause then we get the money, and half the time these things never get built, and they'll end up selling it back to us for half the price.

Very wise, she says.

And the wood will be there whatever happens. It's not like they're going to cut it down. They're just gonna build this pipe, and bury it.

They'll have to cut some of the wood down, she says. You don't mind them doing that?

I say, well. That's the way the world is going, isn't it.

She says, you're right there.

And something in her tone makes me want to get up.

So I do. I go into the living room and poke the logs.

Then I head back towards the kitchen.

But I don't go in straight away.

I stand for a second at the door.

And then I think, what, am I afraid to go in my own kitchen?

So I just go in and say, your dad, won't he be worrying about you?

Don't you think you should let him know you're alright?

She says, yes I probably should.

I say, and will you, then?

She goes, yes I will.

Right, I tell her. The phone's in the living room. I'll just go upstairs, see if I can find something dry that'll fit you.

So I go upstairs, and find a jumper and an old pair of jeans, and wait for a bit to leave her use the phone in peace.

Then I hear the door slamming.

I go downstairs, and the girl's gone.

On the kitchen table, there's a note.

It says, thank you so much for my tea. This is to cover the cost of feeding me.

Next to the note is a pile of coins.

Which comes to three pounds sixty-eight exactly.

I go out, and see her walking off down the lane, back towards the wood.

I shout after her, but she keeps going.

So I run after her. And I'm just catching her, and I slip.

And as I'm going over, she turns.

And she reaches out – and she catches me.

She says, oh God, I'm so sorry, I really didn't mean to do that.

And then I wake.

There's a badger, snuffling at my face.

I sit up, and it runs away.

And I find I'm sat up in the lane, exactly where I fell.

I've got no idea how long I've been out, but it must've been a while because the rain has stopped, and the air is dry and warm.

I go to get up, but it takes a while. I'm stiff as anything.

Finally I make it to my feet.

I'm breathing really hard, and – the air tastes different. Like that washed clean taste it always gets after a decent bit of rain but – different again.

I walk up the lane, back toward the house.

I get to the top of the hill, and then I come to a complete stop.

Because it occurs to me what's different.

It's the sky. It's full of stars.

Everywhere you look, dots and smears of light, blazing down.

There's no moon and I can see where I'm going by starlight alone.

Except I'm not going anywhere.

I'm standing and gazing at the sky.

I look and gradually I can see the stars are all different colours. They're white, and yellow, and blue, and almost pink.

Some shine steady and clear. Some are twinkling. Some are only there when you're not quite looking at them.

It's like all the most precious jewels from every museum and treasure house in the world have been nicked and thrown up to hang there in the night, so that everybody can see them.

And I remember I've seen the sky like this before.

The sky always used to be like this, when I was little.

Before there were lights from town all through the night, before they lit up the dual carriageway.

And I look over towards the dual carriageway, and it's dark.

I look over towards Narberth, I can't see anything there.

So I think I'll go into the house and switch on the little radio for news of when the power might come back on.

And the house isn't there.

It's a ruin, overgrown with moss and ferns. And a wild cat, peering out at me from the shadows.

The lawn is a mess of brambles and stinging nettles. And rising tall above them, a single rowan tree.

I listen, and I realise I can't hear any cars. There's no music, no planes overhead. No tank fire echoing from the range at Castle Martin.

Just badgers snuffling, foxes braying, bats swooping overheard, grasshoppers chirruping in the hedges, owls shrieking through the forest.

And then I open my eyes, and I wake up properly, and Will is there, standing above me, and I'm lying in the mud of the lane, and the rain is still pouring down.

What on earth are you doing, he goes.

Just pick me up, I tell him, and he half-carries, half-drags me about three feet till I decide I'll do better under my own steam.

And I'm sat on my bed, in my wet and muddy clothes, with this baby rowan tree in a plastic bag.

And all can I think about is the sky.

That beautiful, blazing sky.

And all the badgers, and foxes, and cats and owls just carrying on with their business.

But no people to stop, and look around, and see how beautiful it all is.

It seems such a waste.

MRS REYNOLDS AND THE RUFFIAN

Mrs Reynolds and The Ruffian was first performed at Watford Palace Theatre from 15 April to 8 May 2010 with the following cast in order of appearance:

CASSIE, Annie Hemingway
JAY, Morgan Watkins
MRS REYNOLDS, Trudie Goodwin
KIERAN, Ricci McLeod
MEL, Suzie McGrath

Director, Brigid Larmour
Designer, Ruari Murchison
Lighting Designer, Mark Jonathan
Sound Designer, Adrienne Quartly

Author's Note

This play owes much to a number of different sources.

First, To Kill A Mockingbird by Harper Lee gave me the germ of a story: an encounter between an old lady and a young boy, which means very different things to each of them.

Second, Camila Batmanghelidjh's brilliant and disturbing book 'Shattered Lives' taught me something of the damage that can be done to children by persistent abuse and neglect, and raised the possibility that such damage might eventually be healed.

Third, Professor Peter Raynor of the University of Wales,

Swansea talked to me about restorative justice, and pointed me towards a wealth of research material on such schemes around the world. I drew in detail on Lawrence W. Sherman and Heather Strang's report for the Smith Institute, 'Restorative Justice: the evidence'. It's worth saying that while the restorative justice process in this play is based on actual schemes, the ways that both Jay and Mrs Reynolds abuse the process should be taken as examples of dramatic licence. I certainly don't mean to suggest that actual restorative justice schemes lay their participants open to being similarly manipulated.

Finally, this play owes most of all to the young people of the Prince's Trust XL Group at Pethybridge Youth Centre, and the young people of Sherman Cymru's Acting Out group, both of which are in Cardiff. They are the inspiration for everything that is good and brave and hopeful about Jay, and this play is for them.

Gary Owen, March 2010

Characters

CASSIE

JAY

MRS REYNOLDS

KIERAN

MEL

Act One

1

An interview room. A table.

On opposite sides of the table are JAY and MRS REYNOLDS.

JAY is in his late teens – he's a bit nervy, on edge, but with a ready smile.

MRS REYNOLDS is late fifties, early sixties, and harassed.

At the head of the table is CASSIE, a bright young professional woman in her twenties.

Some distance away, a WPC.

CASSIE takes up her notes.

CASSIE: Jay, you acknowledge that

    (Reading briskly.)

    Mrs Reynolds had put many hours' work
    Into her garden, all of which was lost
    As a result of your actions –

JAY: *(Interrupting.)* Yes I acknowledge that.

CASSIE: I'll just – read it all? And you can say yes or no at the end?

JAY: Oh okay.

    CASSIE continues to read – JAY greeting each point with a nod, or a 'yeah', but not breaking into her speech.

CASSIE: Mrs Reynolds felt insecure in her own home, never knowing
    When it might be attacked again.
    You acknowledge this was the result
    Of your actions.
    And while having her house broken into
    Was a traumatic experience for Mrs Reynolds,
    It was the destruction of her garden
    – an act of deliberate and purposeless vandalism –

Which caused Mrs Reynolds most distress.
You acknowledge that this was the result
Of your actions.

(She looks up from the paper.)

Do you agree to all that?

JAY: Yeah yeah yeah yeah, no problem.

CASSIE: Mrs Reynolds you've said

(Reading again.)

That as a result of meeting Jay
You feel less threatened and vulnerable –

MRS REYNOLDS: Not threatened at all by that little ruffian.

JAY: *(Jovial, not vicious.)* Ruffian? Where'd you get her,
Antiques Roadshow?

CASSIE: *(Reading again.)*

Understanding that the incident
Was random, not specifically targeted,
Has left you feeling much less
Victimised.

(She looks up.)

Mrs Reynolds.

MRS REYNOLDS: Hello.

CASSIE: Understanding the incident was random and not
specifically targeted at you has left you feeling much less
victimised?

MRS REYNOLDS: Yes alright.

CASSIE: *(Back to the document.)*

In order to rectify the situation, first
Jay will formally apologise to Mrs Reynolds
For the damage done. Second,
Jay will undertake Community Payback –

MRS REYNOLDS: Sorry, Community Payback?

CASSIE: It's what they used to call Community Service, but then they decided – doing service to the community, sounds like it might have some sort of dignity about it, so they changed it to Community Punishment. But then if it's just a punishment what is the community getting out of it? So now they've gone for Community Payback.

MRS REYNOLDS: *(Beat.)* Right okay.

CASSIE: Jay will undertake Community Payback.
He will make himself available
At a time convenient to Mrs Reynolds
And he will do such work around her garden
As she specifies.

She looks up from the paper.

CASSIE: Okay so – do we all agree, what I read accurately represents the outcome of this meeting?

MRS REYNOLDS: A fairly sanitised version, yes.

CASSIE: Jay?

JAY: Totally yeah.

CASSIE: Great stuff. *(To the WPC.)* Debbie if you wouldn't mind? *(The WPC goes off.)* . Debbie will sort us out some tea and biscuits, which I think we've all earned. I'll pop next door, run off a couple of copies and then we can sign.

She leaves.

A moment.

And then JAY looks up and beams at MRS REYNOLDS. His demeanour has completely changed. He's swaggering, sprawling, full of attitude – and himself. He gets out a lighter and a pack of cigarettes.

MRS REYNOLDS: I doubt you're allowed to smoke in here.

Jay looks round.

JAY: I'm not seeing any signs.

Jay lights up.

JAY: Glad to hear you're feeling less victimised now. Cos of the *(Mimicking Cassie.)* 'random nature of the incident.'

MRS REYNOLDS: *(Of his cigarette.)* Each one of those is ten minutes off your life.

JAY: Pity it wasn't.

MRS REYNOLDS: Sorry?

JAY: I walk along your street every other day.
I see you, in your garden.
You always look so pleased with yourself.
It wasn't random. I did it on purpose.
And you should feel victimised. Because you are a victim.

CASSIE pops her head in.

CASSIE: Everything alright?

JAY: Just having a lovely little chat. About gardening.

CASSIE: Won't be a sec.

CASSIE is gone.

JAY: And if you repeat a word of what I just said, and I get put away – well that would not be too clever.

MRS REYNOLDS: You little / sod –

JAY: / You just, you be careful what you say now, cos I'm a lot of fun, I'm a fun kind of guy, but about this I am deadly serious. I got people. I got a strong support system. I know you're fired up now and you want to have a go at me but – don't bother. Just suck it up. Sign the paper, say you are happy. Because if you don't –

CASSIE returns.

CASSIE: Can't smoke in here.

JAY: Sorry. You should put up some signs.

2.

The front garden of MRS REYNOLDS' house.

JAY is lounging around, finishing a packet of crisps. He flattens the packet, tips the crumbs directly into his mouth.

Then he scrunches the packet up, tosses it away.

MRS REYNOLDS emerges with a mug of tea.

JAY: What, no tea for the worker?

MRS REYNOLDS: Haven't seen you lift a finger.

JAY: Maybe you need your eyes fixing.

MRS REYNOLDS: If you think you can just loaf about, you've got another think coming.

JAY: Nah. I haven't.

MRS REYNOLDS: I'm not frightened of you…

JAY: Yeah you are. You're terrified.

MRS REYNOLDS: I know you think you're this ruffian –

JAY: I'm starting to really like that. 'Ruffian.' *(Echoing the Justin Timberlake song.)* I'm bringing ruffian back…

MRS REYNOLDS: If I make you some tea, then will you think about doing some work?

JAY: *(Beat.)* Milk and three sugars, please.

MRS REYNOLDS moves off.

JAY relaxes in the garden.

Sings a snatch of an incredibly offensive or insufferably irritating song (Something like the charming "I Wanna Fuck You" by Akon.) But he can sing a bleeped version, so he puts in a bleep where there should be an f-word.

Mrs Reynolds returns with a mug of tea.

MRS REYNOLDS: *(Forced cheer.)* There you go.

JAY takes a sip.

JAY: You trying to poison me?

MRS REYNOLDS: You said, milk and three sugars.

JAY: In my coffee. I never drink tea.

MRS REYNOLDS: You said to me, tea for the worker.

JAY: The eyes aren't the only thing on the way out. Your memory's going, love.

MRS REYNOLDS: I know what I heard.

JAY: When I was five a teabag burst and I swallowed a whole load of tealeaves and nearly choked to death. Since that day I've never touched tea in my life. I know I'm not your favourite boy in the whole wide world but – using my childhood traumas to get to me? That is cold, Mrs R.

He tips the tea away into the flower beds.

MRS REYNOLDS: You said you'd do some work if you got some tea, so now / let's see

JAY: / No no no, you asked me to think about doing some work.

MRS REYNOLDS: Oh for goodness' sake…

JAY: And I'm still thinking. I'm still thinking. I'm thinking – that there's something you forgot.

MRS REYNOLDS: What?

JAY: A tiny little word, that gets you what you want.

MRS REYNOLDS: I haven't got a clue what you're wittering on about.

JAY: 'Please'.

MRS REYNOLDS: Will you get to work on my garden as you promised you would. Please.

JAY: Wasn't so hard, was it? Where d'you want me to start?

MRS REYNOLDS: Just – do some weeding in those beds.

JAY: You're the boss.

JAY offers her his empty mug.

MRS REYNOLDS takes it, heads off.

JAY takes a look at the beds.

Puts on some gardening gloves.

Then walks up to a rose bush, grabs it by its lowest stems, just above the ground, and heaves away at it.

MRS REYNOLDS: What the bloody hell are you doing?

JAY: Oi oi oi! Language! Mind my delicate ears…

MRS REYNOLDS: That's a rose bush you're pulling up.

JAY: Is it?

MRS REYNOLDS: You'll've torn half the roots.

JAY: So weeding's not my thing.

MRS REYNOLDS: You'll've killed it.

JAY: Just doing what you told me.

MRS REYNOLDS: This is a joke to you, isn't it.

JAY considers, solemn. Then smiles.

JAY: Pretty much, yeah.

CASSIE enters.

CASSIE: Hello all, sorry I'm late. Targets meeting at HQ. There are targets, we're missing them. How're you two getting on?

JAY: Yeah, we're good.

CASSIE: Mrs Reynolds – happy? Happ-ier?

MRS REYNOLDS: He's hardly put it back like it was.

CASSIE: I think one of the things we established was that the damage Jay did was irreparable, in terms of your time, and your care for your garden; and so he's not going to be able to put that back, is he?

MRS REYNOLDS: Well no.

CASSIE: I mean – by definition.

JAY: Try to keep up, Mrs R.

CASSIE: What we're doing here today, it is practical I hope but it's a recognition that there's a debt to be paid and that Jay is willing to pay it. *(Beat.)* And do you feel he has?

MRS REYNOLDS: Sorry?

CASSIE: Do you feel Jay has recognised he owes you a debt?

A look between JAY and MRS REYNOLDS.

JAY: Take your time, Mrs R.

MRS REYNOLDS: Shall I put the kettle on?

CASSIE: *(Beat.)* Okay, yeah, do that. Have a little think about what I've said. And I'll have a chat to Jay.

MRS REYNOLDS goes inside.

CASSIE: So how's it been? Not strained yourself?

JAY: Sorry?

CASSIE: By working too hard.

JAY: Not really no.

CASSIE: No, thought not.

JAY: D'you know what –

(He's looking at Cassie.)

That's really interesting.

CASSIE: What is?

He turns away, picks a flower and gives it a sniff.

JAY: That's nice that is. Smells like air freshener.

CASSIE: What's really interesting, Jay?

JAY: She –

CASSIE: – Mrs Reynolds –

JAY: – well, obviously, yeah.

He stops, blinks.

CASSIE: What?

JAY: It's gone all up my nose.

He sneezes. CASSIE produces a packet of tissues. JAY takes one.

JAY: Cheers.

He blows his nose. Inspects the tissue. Then throws it away.

CASSIE: Jay!

JAY: What?

CASSIE gingerly picks up the scrunched up tissue and finds somewhere to put it.

JAY: Grandma Reynolds – round you she's like a mouse. Why is that?

CASSIE: We all relate to different people in different ways.

JAY: And some people we don't relate to at all.

MRS REYNOLDS brings out three teacups on a tray.

CASSIE: Mrs Reynolds, I'd like to chat to you about −

MRS REYNOLDS: Oh and biscuits, I meant to bring / biscuits

CASSIE: / I don't know if we'll have time for biscuits…

MRS REYNOLDS: They're just in the kitchen, won't take two seconds…

And MRS REYNOLDS goes in again.

CASSIE: Okay, I'll come with.

CASSIE follows her.

JAY gets up, fetches himself a cup of tea from the tray, then sits back down where he was.

He sips from the tea − then puts the cup down.

He gets up, walks back over to the tray, leans down, and dribbles spit into each of the two remaining cups.

Then goes back to where he was, sits back down, and resumes drinking his own tea. Grinning broadly now.

MRS REYNOLDS comes back out, carrying a plate of biscuits, CASSIE at her heel.

CASSIE: But there have been some positives from this morning?

MRS REYNOLDS: I suppose while he's here he's not causing mischief elsewhere.

(She puts down the biscuits.)

Help yourself.

JAY: I always do.

JAY takes two or three biscuits. One of them is a custard cream and he sets to work demolishing it by stages − nibbling off one half of the biscuit, then licking up the cream filling.

CASSIE: So do you think we can say −

JAY: How's your tea, Cass?

CASSIE: It's fine.

JAY: Makes a lovely cup of tea, doesn't she – our Mrs R.

CASSIE: Usually I'm a slave to the charms of the double shot latte but this really is hitting the spot, thanks.

MRS REYNOLDS: Just teabags, milk and water – it's hardly rocket science.

CASSIE: As I was saying, the point of this morning was for Jay to go some way towards rectifying the situation. How do we feel that's gone?

JAY: Brilliant. Couldn't've gone better.

CASSIE: And Mrs Reynolds?

MRS REYNOLDS: Well I –

She breaks off, lifts the cup to her mouth. JAY is watching carefully.

Then without taking a sip she continues speaking.

MRS REYNOLDS: I don't know if his heart's really in it.

JAY: Oh that's harsh, Mrs R.

CASSIE: And what makes you say that?

MRS REYNOLDS: Just a feeling.

CASSIE: And what gives you that feeling?

MRS REYNOLDS: The way he behaves.

CASSIE: What sort of behaviour, specifically, gives you the feeling Jay's heart isn't in it?

MRS REYNOLDS: And not just what he does. What he says as well.

CASSIE: What sorts of things does he say, Mrs Reynolds?

JAY: Yes, Mrs R, what have I said?

CASSIE: Specifically.

JAY: Be specific, Mrs R. Cause you're really upsetting me now. I'm really hurt.

MRS REYNOLDS: Well I don't know –

Again she lifts the cup to her mouth. Again JAY is on tenterhooks. And again she doesn't drink.

MRS REYNOLDS: His attitude.

CASSIE: Sometimes attitudes are difficult to judge. Say when people come from different backgrounds to us sometimes we can misinterpret the signals that are being given off. Do you think that's what might have happened today, possibly?

MRS REYNOLDS: I don't know.

JAY: You don't wanna misinterpret me, Mrs R.

CASSIE: Jay, shut up. *(To Mrs Reynolds).* I have a sense there are things you're not saying.

MRS REYNOLDS: Well I –

She lifts the cup to her mouth. JAY on tenterhooks again. MRS REYNOLDS stops. Looks into the cup. Looks up at JAY.

She throws the tea towards the root of the rosebush.

MRS REYNOLDS: It just seems – last Christmas kids came along and painted, you know graffitied –

CASSIE: Yes, I know.

MRS REYNOLDS: – the whole street. Every house along this side. And the council wrote to us. Said the "appearance of our houses was detrimental to the area". Said we had to clear it up, or else.

CASSIE: Well that's – that's horrible.

MRS REYNOLDS: Cost me a hundred and fifty quid to get a man. And cars get smashed up or stolen – all the time. Sheila down the road's given up having one now. Doesn't bother. Too much hassle. D'you see? If you live in this street, you can't even have a car. Cause *(At JAY.)* they won't let you. If we were rich someone would stop it but – and now he waltzes along here for an hour – and he's just let off?

CASSIE: I understand your frustration, and I don't know what went wrong with the graffiti incident, that just sounds like

59

a horrible, horrible mistake somewhere – but that was nothing to do with Jay. And we're here to deal with what Jay did to your garden. So – do you feel Jay hasn't done enough? He could come back another day and do more. But would you want him to come back?

JAY: I could come back, Mrs R. With some friends maybe. Do a proper job.

MRS REYNOLDS: No I don't want that.

JAY: No I thought not.

CASSIE: So we'll say – you're content?

MRS REYNOLDS doesn't answer.

CASSIE: Everything I've learned, everything I've seen in this job tells me, if Jay goes to prison, it will not help. He'll come out worse.

At this MRS REYNOLDS seems to soften a little. But then –

JAY: Imagine that. Imagine me – but worse.

CASSIE: And it's a real pity your flower displays will be a bit depleted this summer but – there's always next year?

MRS REYNOLDS: *(Beat.)* Yes of course.

MRS REYNOLDS looks out over what remains of her garden – it's just a tiny moment.

MRS REYNOLDS: You're right. He's turned up, he's done his best. I'm satisfied.

CASSIE: I'm really pleased to hear that.

JAY: I am too, Mrs R. Pleased and relieved. For the both of us.

CASSIE: Some people find they want to shake hands at this point.

MRS REYNOLDS: Do they.

CASSIE: You might find it helps you reach a point of closure –

JAY: I'll shake. No problem.

JAY extends his hand.

CASSIE: The courts take it as quite a big symbolic thing, if the victim and offender shake hands.

MRS REYNOLDS: Say we did then.

CASSIE: You're perfectly free not to shake hands with Jay. If that's how you want the record to stand.

JAY: Is that, how you want the record to stand, Mrs R?

MRS REYNOLDS steps towards JAY, takes his hand. They shake.

JAY: Nice we can part as friends.

JAY holds the handshake for longer than MRS REYNOLDS wants to. She slightly snatches her hand away from him.

MRS REYNOLDS: I'll get your coat.

MRS REYNOLDS leaves, quickly.

CASSIE is watching JAY.

JAY: What?

CASSIE: Just.

JAY: Just, what?

CASSIE: Don't make me regret… you know.

JAY: Regret what?

CASSIE: She could've gone either way.

MRS REYNOLDS returns with JAY's jacket.

MRS REYNOLDS: Here you go.

CASSIE: What I can do, Mrs Reynolds, is give you the number of Victim Support, they might be able to offer you counselling in relation to the various offences you were talking about…

MRS REYNOLDS holds the jacket out so JAY can put it on.

JAY: Very kind.

JAY goes to put the jacket on. As he does so, something falls out.

CASSIE: Think you dropped something there.

CASSIE bends and picks up a pearl necklace. She holds it for a moment.

MRS REYNOLDS: My pearls. How did they get in your coat?

JAY: Not a clue.

MRS REYNOLDS: You tell me to give him a chance, so I give him a chance, I let him into my home – and the little thug steals from me!

CASSIE: I don't know what to say…

JAY: *(Re Cassie's speechlessness.)* Every cloud, eh.

MRS REYNOLDS: This was a present, from my husband.

JAY: I don't know how it got there, alright?

MRS REYNOLDS: Our thirtieth anniversary…

JAY: How stupid do you think I am?
Anything goes missing while I'm here
Then I'm in the frame.

MRS REYNOLDS: Sounds like you've given it some thought…

JAY: It's obvious!

CASSIE: Were you wearing it today? Could it've fallen from your neck?

MRS REYNOLDS: *(To Cassie.)* He's got you believing him already!

CASSIE: I just want to make sure of every possibility.

MRS REYNOLDS: I can't remember the last time I wore it. It's worth money. He's been into my bedroom, gone through my things.

JAY: I haven't even been in your house!

MRS REYNOLDS: You have, you went to the toilet.

JAY: Okay, yeah, but apart from that –

MRS REYNOLDS: I remember thinking you were taking your time.

JAY: What was I supposed to do, piss in a bottle?

MRS REYNOLDS: You see he lies, he lies at every step.

JAY: I forgot about that, alright?

MRS REYNOLDS: You look me in the eye and you swear you didn't steal from me.

JAY: I swear –

He hesitates, struggles, cannot help but break into a smile.

JAY: I'm sorry, I'm sorry –

MRS REYNOLDS: He can't do it. He can't look me in the eye.

JAY: It's just you're being so deadly serious and – over nothing.

CASSIE: Jay, this is not nothing. This is a really serious abuse of trust.

JAY: Let me guess, you're not angry
You're just really really disappointed.

CASSIE: Actually it's exactly the opposite.
I'm bloody furious.

CASSIE gets out her phone.

JAY: What are you doing?

CASSIE: I'm calling the police.

JAY: You're turning me in?

CASSIE shrugs.

JAY: Is that it? You're just –
– shrugging at me?

CASSIE: Should've thought of that before.

JAY: This is a set-up!

CASSIE: *(On phone.)* Yes hello, I'd like to report a crime.

(Beat.)

No it's not an emergency.

(Beat.)

Yes I'll hold.

MRS REYNOLDS: What will happen, when the police come?

CASSIE: I don't think his application for bail will be looked on too kindly this time.

MRS REYNOLDS: He'll go to jail?

CASSIE: He'll be on remand.

MRS REYNOLDS: But locked up?

CASSIE: Oh yes.

JAY: *(To Mrs Reynolds.)* You are loving this, aren't you?

MRS REYNOLDS: Loving that you came into my house and stole from me? No, I don't think so.

CASSIE: *(On phone.)* Yes I'm still holding.

JAY: I didn't steal from you.

MRS REYNOLDS: Only because you got found out. *(To Cassie.)* Even now, and he won't admit what he's done…

JAY: I hate to keep coming back to this boring, you know, FACT, but I didn't do it!

CASSIE: *(On the phone.)* Yes hello? Hi. Yes I'd like to report a – yes I'll hold.

MRS REYNOLDS: If that's your attitude, then locked up is the best place for you.

JAY: No, it's not, it's the worst place, I swear to God.

MRS REYNOLDS: Not so full of yourself now, are you?

JAY: Do you want me to lie, and say I did it?

MRS REYNOLDS: No.

JAY: What then?

MRS REYNOLDS: I want you to tell the truth. And say you did it.

CASSIE: *(To Mrs Reynolds.)* They're sending a car now.

JAY: Alright! I admit it!

MRS REYNOLDS reaches out to CASSIE.

CASSIE: *(On phone.)* Um – would you mind holding for a second?

CASSIE lowers the phone, hand over its microphone.

MRS REYNOLDS: Tell us what you did.

JAY: I snuck into your bedroom, I went through your jewellery, saw the necklace, thought, right, I'll have that.

MRS REYNOLDS: Then what?

JAY: Then I heard you coming. I slipped it in my jacket pocket.

MRS REYNOLDS: That's the truth?

JAY: *(Beat.)* And nothing but.

MRS REYNOLDS: Cassie, maybe we can sort this out between ourselves.

CASSIE: *(On phone.)* Hi. Actually – it's fine. False alarm. Sorry for wasting your time.

She ends the call.

CASSIE: What exactly are you saying, Mrs Reynolds?

MRS REYNOLDS: The second he thinks he's really going to jail, He's terrified.
We're making progress.

3

A little way from MRS REYNOLDS' house, in a small paved area created to stop joyriders using the street as a ratrun.

There's a fairly big raised bed, into which a young tree was once planted. All that remains of it is a metre or so of thin trunk sticking up from the bed.

To one side of the bed, a bench. Scrawled across it in white marker is the legend 'The Adeline Street Sherry Bench.'

Behind the bench, a brick wall. Long-rusted barbed wire loops across its top, carrier bags caught on the barbs. Lots of graffiti on the wall. Prominent amongst it – certainly visible to the audience – is the legend 'Natille is a slag and a prostitute.'

MRS REYNOLDS arrives, carrying a couple of jute bags in one hand and a watering can in the other.

JAY follows her.

MRS REYNOLDS stops, puts down the bags and watering can. Looks round her – and then expectantly, to JAY.

JAY: What?

MRS REYNOLDS: Look at this.

JAY: What about it?

MRS REYNOLDS: It's horrible – isn't it?

JAY: Dunno.

MRS REYNOLDS: Oh it is horrible, Jay. You're just being your usual kind self in not saying so. What happened was, kids were stealing cars and tearing up and down the street, so they paved this bit off. Put in a bench. This little planter. Stuck a tree in it. *(Beat.)* The tree lasted three days. Look you can see – they snapped it off at the trunk. Must have taken quite an effort. Council haven't bothered to replace it – why would they?
– and the bench has now been christened *(She reads.)* 'The Adeline Street Sherry Bench'. Which is lovely.

JAY: *(Beat.)* And?

MRS REYNOLDS: And I am sick of looking at this horribleness.
We are going to make it beautiful. Or,
I tell the police you tried to steal from me and tonight
you'll be sharing a landing with some very rough men
indeed.

JAY: This is so not fair.

MRS REYNOLDS: It's so not – what?

JAY: Forget it.

MRS REYNOLDS: No, go on – say it again. I love it. I love
hearing you complain about things being 'not fair.'

JAY stays silent.

MRS REYNOLDS: No? Let's get to work, then. First we need to
clean up a bit – well, I say we…

*From her bag she produces a folded up bin bag, and offers it to JAY.
He takes it, goes over to the planter.*

MRS REYNOLDS: There's broken glass and general nastiness
in there *(She means the planter)*. You should probably have
some gloves.

*JAY walks back to MRS REYNOLDS. She hesitates, enjoying the
moment – then gets from her bag a pair of pink rubber washing up
gloves. She holds them out to JAY.*

JAY: Very funny, Mrs R.

MRS REYNOLDS: Now you can start to wonder – did I happen
to have pink rubber gloves in a man's size lying about the
house, or did I go out to buy some, just to make you wear
them.
What's your verdict?

JAY looks at her.

MRS REYNOLDS: Little bit of the tough guy stare – but
you're learning to keep your trap shut, which is a vast
improvement. So snap on the marigolds, and step to it.

*JAY does as he is told. MRS REYNOLDS takes a small sheet of
sandpaper from her bag. Sits on the bench, and begins to sand away*

at some of the graffiti. JAY snaps on the gloves, starts picking up rubbish from the planter.

After a very short while – only thirty or forty seconds – MRS REYNOLDS has to stop sanding. She stretches her fingers to loosen them up, and tries again. It's no good. She switches hands.

JAY: So we gonna be long?

MRS REYNOLDS: We'll be as long as it takes.

JAY: I've gotta sign on.

MRS REYNOLDS: I'm sorry?

JAY: Sign on? At the dole?

MRS REYNOLDS: Oh of course. Jay the gangster. Queueing up at the social, filling out his forms.

JAY: So what?

MRS REYNOLDS: You think you're some kind of outlaw. You couldn't survive five minutes without the law.

JAY: S'alright. I'll tell 'em I was late cos the old lady who's blackmailing me wouldn't let me come in on time.

MRS REYNOLDS: Mmm. You still said 'old lady' though. Not 'old cow'. Or 'old bitch'. Which is obviously what you were thinking.

JAY: Can't stop what goes on in my head, Mrs R.

MRS REYNOLDS: I couldn't care less what nastiness goes on in your vile little head. I just don't want it to impinge on me, ever. And it looks like I'm getting my way.

JAY gets back to picking up rubbish from the planter. MRS REYNOLDS sits, kneading her knuckles.

JAY: Alright I'm finished.

MRS REYNOLDS: Wonderful.

JAY: So can I go?

MRS REYNOLDS: Is this place beautiful? No it is not. Can you go? What d'you think?

MRS REYNOLDS picks up one of her bags, and walks over to the planter.

MRS REYNOLDS: I told Sheila down the road I was going to tidy up this bed, and she said she had a few spares. We have two rudbeckia, three lobelia, and – I don't actually know what those are, but beggars can't be choosers.

She offers him a pot.

JAY: Where do I stick it? *(Quieter.)* Apart from up your arse…

MRS REYNOLDS: What was that?

JAY: Nothing, Mrs R.

MRS REYNOLDS takes the pot back from him.

MRS REYNOLDS: You don't stick anything.
First you observe.
We water the plant, thoroughly.
We dig a little hole, removing non-organic debris, and stones.
We loosen the earth at the bottom of the hole
So it's easy for the roots to spread.
We get the loose earth nice and wet.
We lift the plant from its pot – it pops out,
Thanks to having been watered so thoroughly,
Just moments before.
We loosen the rootball.
We place the plant in the hole.
We push the earth we dug out, back in.
Then we tamp the earth down,
Gently but firmly around the plant.

JAY: Gently – but firmly at the same time?

MRS REYNOLDS: Yes, that's right.

JAY: *(Beat.)* Whatever.

MRS REYNOLDS: As one might be gentle but firm with a lover, for example.

JAY: Oh my gosh, I do not need to hear this…

MRS REYNOLDS: Do you think you can manage that?

JAY: What-ever.

JAY and MRS REYNOLDS both get to work planting, MRS REYNOLDS keeping an eye on JAY's progress.

MRS REYNOLDS: Don't forget to loosen the earth at the bottom of the hole.

JAY: Yeah, I know…

A moment of planting activity.

MRS REYNOLDS: Very nice woman, Sheila.

JAY looks at her.

MRS REYNOLDS: Who gave us the plants?

JAY: Oh right.

MRS REYNOLDS: Mmm. A lesbian, I believe. *(Beat.)* A lot of it about these days – lesbianism.

JAY: Hey, how can you tell a lesbian bar?

MRS REYNOLDS: I don't want to know.

JAY: Not even the pool table's got balls.

MRS REYNOLDS: Sometimes I wonder why that is. Why so many of the young women are lesbians these days. And then I look at a young man like you, and I think – well it's no wonder at all, is it?

JAY doesn't rise to it. He just picks up another plant.

MRS REYNOLDS inspects his work.

MRS REYNOLDS: That last one's not bad, you know. See it's standing up nice and straight. Done a good job there.

JAY: Yeah, right.

MRS REYNOLDS: I'm serious, look at the first one you did – and then look at that last one. Can you can see the difference?

JAY: No.

MRS REYNOLDS: You've learned how to plant something.

JAY: Couldn't give a toss.

MRS REYNOLDS: *(Beat.)* Fine. Off you go, then.

MRS REYNOLDS turns away from him, begins packing up tools and plant pots.

JAY: On the bus, I'm gonna make spitballs. Like bits of paper,
     That you chew up with spit?

MRS REYNOLDS: Yes, I know.

JAY: I'm gonna pick someone.
     An old bloke. Or some fat woman.
     Some prick with big glasses and a haircut.
     I'm gonna sit behind them.
     I'm gonna chuck spitballs
     At the back of their head.
     And one they'll think it's just nothing.
     Then the second, the third,
     They'll know there's something going on.
     But still they'll sit there.
     They'll just take it.
     Because they always do.
     So I'll keep chucking them.
     Till finally they've got to turn round.
     And I'll throw a lovely ball of my flob
     Right in the face of the fat bint. Or the old bloke.
     Or the poor mum with all her kiddies.
     And I will smile.
     And that smile – will be for you, Mrs R.
     And I'm gonna do that every day.
     I'm gonna pick on someone,
     Terrorise them,
     Every day you make me come here.

MRS REYNOLDS: I hope they smack you in the mouth.

JAY: They do, I'll get the law on them.

MRS REYNOLDS: Oh yes, the law – the hoodie's best friend.

JAY: You're a player, you play the system.
     Course you could stop it, Mrs R.
     You could save all those innocent people

From being terrorised,
If you just let me be on my way.

MRS REYNOLDS: Course if you just sat on the bus, minded your business,
No-one would even notice you existed.
But you sprawl across the seats,
Music blaring out your phone,
Swearing and cursing and being foul –
Everyone sees you then. Everyone notices.
And that's what you want.
You want people like me, to even notice you exist.
Well I noticed. We all did.
We were just ignoring you, hoping you would go away.
But I know now you won't.
And I can't ignore you any more.
Cause you, have got to be stopped.

4.

Same as before: the planter, the wall covered in graffiti. But the flowers JAY planted have been ripped up. Their remains are scattered across the stage.

JAY arrives first, carrying a watering can. He takes in the destruction. And is delighted.

JAY: Oh, yes…
That is fantastic work.

MRS REYNOLDS follows, carrying bags and a watering can.

JAY: Morning, Mrs R. And how are you, this fine day?

Mrs Reynolds looks about her.

JAY: Now look, I am dying to get busy with the watering can but – what is there to water?

MRS REYNOLDS: Yes, I see your problem.

JAY: So what, I'll be off then, shall I? If there's nothing for me to do here.

MRS REYNOLDS: Jay: d'you think this is a disappointment for me? A shock?

JAY: You made me plant the flowers, I'm guessing you wanted them to stay planted…

MRS REYNOLDS: Oh no, I knew some little thugs would tear them up.

JAY: What was the point making me doing it then?

MRS REYNOLDS: How does it feel, looking around?

JAY: How does what now?

MRS REYNOLDS: How does it feel, seeing your work ruined.

JAY: Couldn't give a toss.

MRS REYNOLDS: All your effort.

JAY: Yeah I didn't put that much effort in though.

MRS REYNOLDS: It doesn't bother you, that everything you've done has been spoiled?

JAY: I never wanted to do it – why'm I gonna get worked up about it?

MRS REYNOLDS: Fair point.

JAY: So like – can I go?

MRS REYNOLDS: 'Fraid not, no.

She gets from her bag a sunflower – a young plant, with no flowers as yet.

JAY: Oh, what is this?

MRS REYNOLDS: This is a Russian Giant.

He looks at her – what the hell is that?

MRS REYNOLDS: A sunflower. Spare from my garden.

She offers the plant to him.

MRS REYNOLDS: Come on. You know the drill.

JAY: But what's the point?

MRS REYNOLDS: The point is that a bright and beautiful sunflower will cheer up everyone who passes.

JAY: Except it's gonna get pulled up. Just like the others. And you know this. You're just doing it to torment me.

MRS REYNOLDS: Not to torment you, no.

JAY: And what then? When we come back tomorrow and this one is gone?

MRS REYNOLDS: Then – we plant something else. *(Meaning the sunflower.)* Put it close to the trunk, and then we can use that to give it support.

JAY: Yesterday, you had loads of plants. Today, we're down to one. That whole thing, just one flower in it? You're running out. Tonight they'll tear your Russian Giant to bits, tomorrow – you'll have nothing. They're gonna beat you, Mrs R.

MRS REYNOLDS: That's right, Jay. We're trying to make things better, and the thugs and vandals are beating us.

JAY: It's not me that's trying. It's you. I don't give a toss.

MRS REYNOLDS: I know it's hard for you.
You're young, and young people
Don't believe in change,
Having not lived long enough
But believe you me,
You will have people you care about,
People you love, and
The thought of anything happening to them –
JAY: The ones I love, I protect with my life.

MRS REYNOLDS: You can't be everywhere.
You can't be there, all the time.

JAY: I'll do my best.

MRS REYNOLDS: You'll fail.

JAY: I won't.

MRS REYNOLDS: Yes you will. We all do.

JAY: Not me.

MRS REYNOLDS: All you can hope for is
That the world is kind to the ones you love.

JAY: Not much chance of that.

MRS REYNOLDS: And by being such a selfish, nasty, ignorant toe-rag
You make the world a little bit less kind every day.
The way you act will come back, not just on you
But on the ones you care about.

JAY: Couldn't give a toss.

MRS REYNOLDS: You will.

JAY: But I don't

MRS REYNOLDS: But you will.

JAY: So what?
I don't care
What I will care about.
I only care
What I care about now.
And what I care about now –

MRS REYNOLDS: – is your own sweet self, and sod all else.

JAY: Mrs R – you're starting to get me. I love it. What a beautiful hands-across-the ocean moment.

MRS REYNOLDS: Alright –

JAY: *(Cheery, sensing victory.)* You're giving up? I knew you would…

MRS REYNOLDS: *(The sunflower.)* Plant that. I'll be back.

JAY: Whatever you say, Mrs R…

JAY gets to work planting the sunflower.

MRS REYNOLDS heads off.

Once she's gone, JAY sits on the bench, stretches.

After a bit he hears MRS REYNOLDS returning. He jumps up and gets back to the planter.

MRS REYNOLDS enters, carrying a big paintbrush and a tin of white masonry paint.

JAY: Nearly finished.

She puts down the paint, goes over to the wall.

MRS REYNOLDS: 'Natille is a slag, and a prostitute.' Natalie spelt incorrectly – but prostitute spelled right.

JAY: Can spell your name how you like.

MRS REYNOLDS: You can – doesn't make it right. Just means you've chosen to have your name spelled wrong, for the whole of your life.

JAY: Says you.

MRS REYNOLDS: Yes I do.

MRS REYNOLDS puts the paint and brush at his feet.

JAY: You want me to paint over it?

MRS REYNOLDS: You're going to paint the whole wall.

JAY: What for?

MRS REYNOLDS: I don't want to look at – any of this, ever again.

JAY: But there'll just be more graffiti up tomorrow.

MRS REYNOLDS: Will there?

JAY: Well, duuuh.

MRS REYNOLDS: Well, duuuh, then you'll come back tomorrow, and you'll paint over it a second time.

JAY: And there'll be more again the day after.

MRS REYNOLDS: And you'll come back that day. And you'll come back the day after that. The boy that runs the shop on Carlisle Street, I knew his dad, he'll chuck cans of white paint my way as long as I like.

JAY: What's the point painting over graffiti when there's gonna be more up tomorrow?

MRS REYNOLDS: Because every day for seven years I have been reminded that 'Natille is a slag and a prostitute', and I have had enough.

She gathers herself.

MRS REYNOLDS: I'll finish that *(Planting the sunflower)*. You get started on that wall.

JAY: Jesus, what did your last slave die of?

MRS REYNOLDS: Exhaustion: why d'you ask?

JAY fiddles feebly with the paint tin.

JAY: Can't get the lid off.

MRS REYNOLDS: Bring it here.

JAY does as he's told. MRS REYNOLDS tries to prise the lid off with her fingertips. Fails. She looks round the planter.

MRS REYNOLDS: Pass me that stone.

JAY moves.

MRS REYNOLDS: No, the flat one.

JAY passes MRS REYNOLDS a stone. She slots the stone under the rim of the lid and tries again. Still no good.

MRS REYNOLDS shakes her hands.

MRS REYNOLDS: Well – you're not going till the job's done.

She hands the tin back to him, returns her attention to the sunflower.

JAY stares daggers at her.

Then lifts the lid off the paint tin, easily and without any fuss.

He begins to paint the wall – his back to MRS REYNOLDS.

After a moment MRS REYNOLDS stops what she's doing, watches him.

MRS REYNOLDS: My husband would've knocked you into the middle of next week for even looking at me the way you did just then.

JAY: *(Not really turning to look at her.)* What's he gonna do, bash me with his zimmer frame?

MRS REYNOLDS: Mr Reynolds has passed on.

JAY: *(And now he looks at her.)* Passed on? You mean he's wormfood?

MRS REYNOLDS: Worked every day from sixteen to sixty-five. Saw to it his kids went for nothing.

Hundreds turned out for his funeral.
He did more good in a morning than you'll do your whole life.

JAY: *(Beat.)* Who even gives a toss?

MRS REYNOLDS controls herself – but Jay knows he's found a weak spot.

JAY: Where are your kids then? Don't notice them coming around to keep you safe from *(Enjoying the word.)* ruffians like me.

MRS REYNOLDS: Ben lives in Glasgow and Rhiannon has a family in Australia.

JAY: Bloody hell, Mrs R. Good mum, were you?

MRS REYNOLDS: I'm very proud my children are independent enough they can go anywhere they want and make new lives for themselves.

JAY: No you're not. Course you bloody aren't.

MRS REYNOLDS: I speak to my grandchildren over the internet two or three times a week, more than when they lived here.

JAY: Maybe it wasn't you. Maybe it was Mr R. Did your little Rhiannon ever get a bit nervous, around him? Say after she started to 'blossom'? I mean I used to run away, but only down the end of the street. Australia though. You can't run much further than that, can you?

He turns away, returns to painting.

MRS REYNOLDS: You useless little piece of shit.

JAY: *(Turning back to her.)* Easy Mrs R…

But there is such fury in her that his nerve deserts him.

There's a moment when he's too frightened to speak, and she's too angry.

JAY: Look. You know, this is pointless. You know that.

MRS REYNOLDS: You're still going to bloody do it. For however long I like.

JAY: Right you sweep up the pavement in front of your house. Why'd you bother?

MRS REYNOLDS: It won't sweep itself.

JAY: It's the pavement. It's not yours.

MRS REYNOLDS: It's in front of my house.

JAY: So?

MRS REYNOLDS: If the pavement in front of my house is filthy – it upsets me. When people drop crisp packets, and cigarette packets, and let their dogs defecate right in front of my house, I hate it.

JAY: When kids do graffiti, they're doing the same as you, when you sweep the pavement.

MRS REYNOLDS: Sorry?

JAY: The pavement.
    It's not yours,
    But it's part of your life
    So you try and make it yours.
    You sweep it up.
    You keep it clean.
    If you're a kid, you've got nothing.
    Not a house, not a garden.
    You've got the street you walk along.
    The bit of wall by the shop.
    The bus stop.
    Nothing really.
    But what you've got
    You try and make it your own.
    You sign your name. You tag,
    Everywhere you go
    And soon the city
    Is your home. It shouts your name
    As you pass.

    (Beat.)

It's the same:
  What you do,
  What they do.

MRS REYNOLDS: It is a little the same, I suppose.

JAY: What, are you listening, finally?

MRS REYNOLDS: What I do – sweeping up broken glass, hosing down dog crap – makes the world better, for everyone. Foul language scrawled everywhere you look, makes things worse. So they're not the same at all.

JAY: It's not foul language.

MRS REYNOLDS: Clearly it is.

JAY: That's just how we talk.

MRS REYNOLDS: I'm sick of you how you talk. We all are.

JAY: I can't win, can I…

  JAY gets back to painting.

MRS REYNOLDS: But d'you know what you did there?

JAY: *(Infinitely weary.)* No…

MRS REYNOLDS: It wasn't threats, it wasn't excuses, it wasn't lies. You tried to reason with me. Like a civilised young man.

JAY: Lot of good it did me.

MRS REYNOLDS: You're right: progress should be rewarded.

JAY: Like how?

MRS REYNOLDS: You say there's no way this wall will be graffiti-free in the morning.

JAY: It's like a whatchamacall, a blank –

MRS REYNOLDS: Canvas?

JAY: Yes! You're asking people to tag it.

MRS REYNOLDS: Prove yourself wrong. Keep this wall clean for one night, and we'll call it quits.

JAY: What, I stay here? All night?

MRS REYNOLDS: It's warm. It's not going to rain. And don't tell me you've never stayed up all night before.

JAY: And then I can go? You'll sign my report, and you'll never hassle me again?

MRS REYNOLDS: Oh I love it. In your head, I'm 'hassling' you…

JAY: But that's the deal?

MRS REYNOLDS: If I can walk down my own street, just one bright morning, and not be faced with filth and foul language – yes. If you do that for me, we're even.

JAY: Shake on it.

JAY offers his hand.

MRS REYNOLDS takes it.

They shake.

5.

Later in the day.

JAY is sitting on the bench, listening to music from his mobile.

Light begins to fade.

JAY gets bored of music. Begins playing a game on his phone.

It's getting darker.

JAY's battery runs out. He puts the phone away.

Tugs his jacket tighter around himself.

Darker still.

JAY gets out a cigarette. Smokes it.

Settles.

Starts to doze.

KIERAN: Mate.

JAY comes awake.

KIERAN: 'Sup?

JAY: Nothing.

KIERAN approaches; they shake.

KIERAN: Coming into town?

JAY: In a bit.

KIERAN: What you doing?

JAY: Not much.

KIERAN: Not much?

JAY: *(Beat.)* Sitting.

KIERAN: So… you coming then?

JAY: Yeah, no I'm just gonna hang here a bit.

KIERAN: Hang here?

JAY: Yup.

KIERAN looks around, trying to find the attraction of 'here'.

KIERAN: Why?

JAY: What the fuck d'you care?

KIERAN: Mate, I don't. I'm just –

Stung by JAY's reprimand, KIERAN has pulled back a bit. Out of the corner of his eye he notices – the wall.

KIERAN: – oh my gosh.

He gets up.

KIERAN: Have you seen this?

JAY: What?

KIERAN: This wall.

JAY: *(Meaning: what are you getting excited about?.)* It's a wall.

KIERAN: It is a pure, pristine, beautiful, white wall.

JAY: So've you seen Damian? We was going down Apollo's and he jibbed out last minute.

Kieran pulls out a marker pen.

KIERAN: It is my pristine, white wall.

He pulls off the top of the marker. Gives it a little sniff for luck.

JAY: Oi oi Kieran.

KIERAN: What mate?

JAY gets up.

JAY: Alright, come on, let's head into town then.

KIERAN is considering the wall – where he should start, and with what.

KIERAN: In a second mate.

He chooses his spot. He's just about to write on the wall –

– and JAY grabs his hand.

JAY: You can't.

KIERAN pulls free.

KIERAN: You what?

JAY: You can't touch it.

KIERAN: Yeah, I can…

JAY: You do, I will fucking end you mate.

KIERAN looks at him. Smiles.

KIERAN: Come again?

JAY: You heard me.

KIERAN: Is this – are there cameras? Are we on TV?

JAY: It's not a joke.

KIERAN: What then?

JAY: *(Beat.)* Can't say.

KIERAN: What, is it secret? Is it top secret? Are you like, a spy, and keeping this wall clean, is your secret mission?

JAY: Don't take the piss, mate.

KIERAN: Don't you take the piss, then.

Beat.

KIERAN: Is it your community service?

JAY says nothing.

KIERAN: Is it! What – they got you to paint the wall – and now they're making you stand guard?

JAY: Something like that…

KIERAN: They can't do that mate! You've got rights! They can't have you standing out here all night. Anything could happen.

JAY: Don't I know it.

KIERAN: That's got to be dodgy, though. You should tell your solicitor. Have you told your solicitor?

JAY: No.

KIERAN: You should mate.

JAY: Yeah I will.

KIERAN: I could punch you and then you can sue. Say you were attacked.

JAY: Can't afford to sue anyone, can I.

KIERAN: No win no fee, mate. Your legal costs will be paid by the insurers of the third party, innit.

JAY: You are not gonna punch me, and that is the end of it.

KIERAN: Alright, alright…

JAY goes back to the bench.

KIERAN: So what, you gotta keep anyone from graffiti-ing this wall?

KIERAN looks at the wall. Still has the marker in his hand.

JAY: 'Sright.

KIERAN: Gotta keep it perfect?

He's reaching out towards the wall with the pen.

JAY: Kieran.

JAY not looking at him. He doesn't need to.

KIERAN: What?

JAY: Come here, sit down.

KIERAN does as he is told.

KIERAN: So… you're gonna stay here all night?

JAY: Yup.

KIERAN: *(Beat.)* No you ain't.

JAY looks at him.

KIERAN: Come on mate, as if.

JAY: Laugh it up.

KIERAN: You know what you're like though.

JAY: What'm I like, mate. You tell me.

KIERAN: Don't be a little bitch…

JAY looks at him: looks away.

KIERAN: By the way, saw your sister earlier. She said, what was it…

JAY: She said, Kee, do you have any idea how annoying you are?

KIERAN: Oh yeah, she said 'Give it to me Kieran, give it to me hard, like the slut I am.'

JAY: When'd you see my sister?

KIERAN: When did I – shag your sister? Last night. Tried to call you so you could listen in.

JAY: Well I was busy, shagging your mum.

KIERAN: I was shagging your nan.

JAY: I was shagging yours.

KIERAN: My nan's dead.

JAY: I thought she was a bit quiet. And smelly.

KIERAN: I loved my nan, mate.

JAY: And I did. Three times a week, twice on Fridays.

KIERAN: *(Beat.)* You're really just sitting here, all night?

JAY: That's what I said.

KIERAN: I'm going by KFC, why don't you come with?

85

JAY: Cause I'm staying here!

KIERAN: Gonna need a feed, maintain your energy levels.

JAY: I'm as energetic as I need to be, mate.

KIERAN: I'd bring you some, but I'm off to Boycey's.

JAY: I'll be alright, mate.

KIERAN: Get a coffee, few Cokes, keep you going. Be gone half an hour tops.

JAY: Nah, I'm good.

KIERAN: *(Beat.)* Boycey'll have a bit of speed tucked away somewhere. If you're staying up all night.

JAY looks at him – doesn't answer.

KIERAN is triumphant.

KIERAN: On your feet, soldier.

KIERAN springs up.

JAY: Straight to Boycey's then.

KIERAN: KFC first.

JAY: KFC, Boycey's for the speed, then I'm coming right back.

KIERAN smiles.

KIERAN: Course you are, mate.

6.

The next morning.

The sunflower is ripped up.

On the wall has been scrawled 'Stacey lyks cock'.

MRS REYNOLDS is sitting on the bench, waiting.

JAY arrives in the same clothes he was wearing last night. He's haggard and bleary.

MRS REYNOLDS: You're here. Wonderful. Now, this is worth taking a look at…

She gets up, goes over to the wall.

MRS REYNOLDS: Because there are people who say, does spelling really matter? So long as you can get your message across, who cares if words are spelled how a stuffy old dictionary says they should be. *(The graffito.)* But see – someone is trying to tell us something about Stacey. Is it that she likes cock? Or that she licks it? I can't be sure. And why not? Because of poor spelling.

JAY: See – that, that is bad luck.

MRS REYNOLDS: Is it?

JAY: That can only've happened like, five seconds ago, cos I was here the whole time.

MRS REYNOLDS touches the graffiti.

MRS REYNOLDS: Ink's not wet.

JAY: Half an hour ago then, tops. I was here all night, popped off to get a coffee – just my luck, that's when some little vandal wanders past with his marker pen…

MRS REYNOLDS: Where is your coffee, then?

JAY: Drank it.

MRS REYNOLDS: I looked out half eleven last night, you were nowhere to be seen.

JAY: Half-eleven? I was seat of pants to seat of bench. Did you have your specs on?

MRS REYNOLDS: I came out half twelve, you were gone.

JAY: 'Bout half-twelve I might've stretched my legs, walked up and down the street, but…

MRS REYNOLDS: I knew you couldn't do it.

JAY: *(Beat.)* Did you?

MRS REYNOLDS: One hundred per cent certainty.

JAY: Did you think I was gonna sit up all night? Who, in the world, would do that?

MRS REYNOLDS: Have you ever seen – the sea, Jay?

The tiniest hesitation before he answers.

JAY: Course.

MRS REYNOLDS: You know nothing about the world, but hark at you telling us all how it is…

JAY: I know more than you, sat in your nice little house. The real world – is a jungle.

MRS REYNOLDS: Oh that's brilliant. It's a jungle. And what are you, Jay? A lion? A tiger? No – Jay the Jaguar, stalking the streets of the urban jungle. That's marvellous.

JAY: Is it.

MRS REYNOLDS: Oh sorry – a jaguar is a big cat, bit like a leopard or a panther. Just in case you didn't know.

JAY: *(Controlled.)* You know it really pisses me off when you laugh at me.

MRS REYNOLDS: There he goes – Jay the Jaguar, stalking down to the dole office, to sign on the line and get his pocket money…

JAY: A player plays / the –

MRS REYNOLDS: / the system, I know… I've heard it before. I've heard all your excuses, and I am sick of them.

She looks at him.

MRS REYNOLDS: When my kids were little, a sliver of mercury above ninety-eight and I'd sit up with them all night.

JAY: *(Beat.)* I don't know what that means.

MRS REYNOLDS: If they had a hint of a temperature.
We measured it in Farenheit.
I would watch them.
I would count every breath,
From the moment they laid down their head
Till light filled the room
And their eyes opened.

(Beat.)

I bet no-one ever did that for you.

JAY shakes his head.

88

MRS REYNOLDS: No. And I'm not surprised.

JAY: What?

MRS REYNOLDS: My children were angels. You – I dread to think.

JAY: You don't wanna hear what it was like when I was little.

MRS REYNOLDS: Mummy not buy you a Gameboy? Aw, poor baby…

JAY: You couldn't take it.

MRS REYNOLDS: You have no idea, Jay, what I can take.

JAY: Bollocks.

MRS REYNOLDS: I sat with my husband
For three days after his heart attack.
Counting every breath.
Watching the numbers on the machines.
Nothing in Farenheit by then –

JAY: So what – he died, in hospital, nurses and doctors looking after him, you by his side?

MRS REYNOLDS: Yes.

JAY: Sounds nice.

MRS REYNOLDS doesn't answer.

JAY: Got no comeback for that? I'll say it again – sounds nice.
Sounds like an alright way to end a life.
Here's how I started mine.
When I was little, all I remember is
My mum, always sick
And me worrying about her all the time.
She had doctors coming every day
To give her medicine.
Except it wasn't medicine.
And the men weren't really doctors.
And sometimes she didn't have money.
So she'd pay for 'her medicine' in other ways.
There was this one bloke
She called him Holliman

89

I walked into the lounge one day
Found mum on her knees, in front of him.
I didn't know what it meant.
After that, mum put a lock on my door
On the outside.
They used to lock me in – for my sake.
Stop me seeing things I shouldn't.
But they'd get so wasted, they'd forget I was there.
One time I had to shit in the corner of my own room.
I couldn't help myself.
I was seven. It was hurting my belly. Holliman
Rubbed my nose in it.
Held my face down
And rubbed my nose in my own shit.
Said that would teach me.
He would bring men round,
Let them use my mum.
Before they locked me in, mum
Would give me a pot noodle
And the kettle, so I could feed myself.
I would eat every mouthful and think –
See? My mum loves me, really.
One time I heard her screaming.
I kicked the door till the lock gave way
Holliman was standing over her, his foot
On her throat.
I stabbed him in the leg with my penknife.
And she –
– she threw me out.
I was thirteen.
And I don't look to her for nothing these days.
I just thank her.
For everything she taught me.
For how strong she made me.

JAY looks at MRS REYNOLDS.

JAY: Sorry, I didn't catch that.

MRS REYNOLDS: I didn't say anything.

JAY: No, you didn't.

MRS REYNOLDS: I think, this should all stop now.

JAY: Yes.

MRS REYNOLDS: So that's – it's all finished. The stuff about you stealing my necklace –

JAY: The stuff about you framing me, for stealing your necklace?

MRS REYNOLDS: We can forget that.

JAY: Oh can we? That's good to know.

MRS REYNOLDS: And we can just stop all this, you coming here, working for me.

JAY: I knew I'd win.
And I have, haven't I?
Mrs R.

MRS REYNOLDS: Yes you've won.

JAY: I think I deserve
Some compensation
For the way you've treated me.
I'm talking about in cash terms now.
That is if you want me to go.

From one of her jute bags, MRS REYNOLDS gets out her purse.

JAY: Don't bother to count it,
I'll just take everything you've got.

MRS REYNOLDS offers a few notes.

JAY: Oh, very kind, thank you, don't mind if I do.

MRS REYNOLDS: Will you go now?

JAY: What's your name?
Like your first name.

MRS REYNOLDS: Anna.

JAY: Anna? Sounds like a retard's name.
No wonder you were such a fucking spastic all your life.

JAY goes.

MRS REYNOLDS sits down on the bench.

Rests her head in her hand for a moment.

Then gets up, suddenly stiff, like a much older woman.

Begins to tidy up the remains of the sunflower.

Loses heart, throws the bits of plant back in the flower bed.

Sits, slumps on the bench.

As she sits –

A lighting change. Day fades into night.

JAY comes back on. He's pacing, talking on his phone.

JAY: Kee? I've called you
Twenty times mate, come back at me.

(Dials again.)

Steve-o. Coming out?
Come on.
No?
No no, fair enough.
Alright mate.

(Hangs up: dials again.)

Naz mate, it's me.
You in town?
Fancy a quick one?
Forget about that, do it tomorrow.
Come on mate just one and I'll –
Yeah, no, don't worry about it.

(Hangs up: dials again.)

Boycey! What you up to?
What?
Well sod you then.

(Dials again.)

Trev. Trevor mate.

(Beat.)

Mate I can't understand you.
Mate you need to slow down…
No, no I don't know what that is.
Mate turn the music down and −
No there is music mate, I can hear it,
I can't hear you is the problem.
Trev, what've you had?
Trev stop calling me dad.
I'm not your dad, Trev −

(Hangs up; dials again.)

Damian!
You in the mood for a cheeky couple?
No? When d'you ever say no?
− don't you hang up on me, you little…

(But Damian has hung up. JAY hesitates, dials again.)

Hey Ricky.
It's Jay.
Jay.
Jay Kieran's mate.
Jay that hangs round with Boycey.
Jay that plays pool with Trev.
Jay from that time when you and Damien −
No I didn't.
No, I did not.
Then he's a liar, isn't he −

(Dials again.)

Kieran, mate, this is like
The fiftieth time, it's been
A nightmare of a day, I just −
I need −
I need you to pick up, man,

JAY dials again. A number he has to punch out with some care this time.

He waits. The pacing has stopped. He's still now: as is MRS REYNOLDS, on the bench.

There's an answer.

JAY: Yeah it's me.

Don't hang up.

Don't, please please please please.

I just wanted to –

– you okay? Yeah?

That's good. That's great. I'm fine.

Look I was thinking

Maybe I could come round.

No no no nothing like that.

Just for a day.

For an hour or two.

It's your birthday soon.

I could bring you a present.

Anything you want.

Or money yeah.

Money, if that's what you want.

If I could just come round.

Just for a cup of coffee.

Just for ten minutes.

Please. Can I.

Please.

Please.

Please,

Mum.

To black.

7.

MRS REYNOLDS' front garden.

MRS REYNOLDS emerges, begins potter around – pulling off diseased leaves, squirting at infested plants with a spray bottle of soapy water, rooting out weeds.

JAY arrives. Says nothing. Initially MRS REYNOLDS has her back to him.

Then she turns.

MRS REYNOLDS: What do you want?

She's half-expecting an attack.

JAY: You know that money you gave me?
    I spent it.
    I need some more now.

MRS REYNOLDS: I haven't got any more money for you.

JAY: That's the problem, see –
    You pay someone off,
    They're gonna want paying again.
    You have to stand up to people,
    Or if you don't they basically fucking own you.
    And d'you know what's annoying me,
    About you?

MRS REYNOLDS: I just think –

JAY: *(Suddenly snarling.)* What? What?

    MRS REYNOLDS recoils.

MRS REYNOLDS: I want you to go.

JAY: No.

MRS REYNOLDS: Please.

JAY: What you gonna do, call the police?

MRS REYNOLDS: I can't help you, Jay –

JAY: Of course you can't –
    – help me?
    How would you,
    Help me?

MRS REYNOLDS: Because you're not just
    A naughty little boy
    Who's gone astray.

JAY: Oh, I am very naughty…

MRS REYNOLDS: You're broken.
    You were never made right.

    MRS REYNOLDS gathers up her things.

MRS REYNOLDS: Please don't bother me any more.
    I'm asking nicely.

She goes inside.

Shuts the front door behind her.

JAY doesn't move.

JAY: I'm still here.

(Raising his voice.)

I'm still here, Mrs R.

(Beat: then, really yelling.)

I got no other pressing appointments to be at.

In a flurry of movement, the door opens and MRS REYNOLDS comes out again.

She has a phone in her hand.

MRS REYNOLDS: Alright then.
I'll call the police.

JAY: Go on.

MRS REYNOLDS: I will.

JAY: Have me chucked inside,
With all the scum,
Cos that's where I belong.

Stand-off.

JAY: Isn't it.

She lowers the phone.

JAY: I'm not going away.

MRS REYNOLDS: I don't know what to do with you.

JAY: Just tell me something.
Give me something to do.
What were you doing?

MRS REYNOLDS: I was dead-heading the roses.

JAY: Then tell me to do that.

MRS REYNOLDS: I was dead-heading the roses, Jay.
You could help me with that.

JAY: Alright.
Alright then.
We're getting somewhere.

JAY comes into the garden, and gets to work on the rosebush.

MRS REYNOLDS watches him.

Act Two

1

Music, and the quality of the daylight changes. We're moving into summer.

The flowerbed. There's litter everywhere, and the wall is fairly well covered with graffiti. It's mostly tags, declarations of love and hate, but there is also a prominent and skilfully painted flower, in a flower pot.

MRS REYNOLDS comes on with a bin bag, and gets to work on the litter.

JAY appears from the other side of stage at a run.

JAY: Sorry I'm late, again…

> *Runs straight off in the direction MRS REYNOLDS appeared from.*

MRS REYNOLDS: You're not, you can –

> *JAY reappears, now with a tin of paint and a brush.*

MRS REYNOLDS: You can turn up when you like.

JAY: Nah, ten's good. I mean I say that and then I'm late every day but – ten's good as a target, like.

> *MRS REYNOLDS watches him for a bit as he begins to paint.*

MRS REYNOLDS: Looks like someone's joining in.

JAY: Sorry?

MRS REYNOLDS: We're trying to grow flowers in the flower bed, someone's drawn a flower on the wall. Almost a pity to paint over it.

JAY: Then – don't. Leave the flower. If you like it – why not?

MRS REYNOLDS: Because it's vandalism.

JAY: But – you like it.

MRS REYNOLDS: Well, more than the other stuff.

JAY: It makes the place better.

MRS REYNOLDS: Well I suppose it does.

JAY: So let's get rid of everything else, and leave the flower up.

MRS REYNOLDS nods. JAY paints, skirting round the flower. MRS REYNOLDS watches him for a while, and then leaves.

Time shifts while JAY finishes the painting. Summer reaches its height. The flower surrounded by white, JAY leaves the stage.

Music, and the lights shift. There are a couple more pictures on the wall.

Jay returns, with a bin bag and one of those grabbing devices that allow you to pick up rubbish without bending.

He moves around the stage, listening to music on headphones, nimbly picking up bits of litter with the grabber.

MEL enters.

MEL: Hi.

JAY: Alright.

MEL: Hi, I was wondering if you could help me out?

JAY: *(Taking off his headphones.)* Sorry?

MEL: Yeah I've just moved in over the road and the front garden, there's just a lot of bin bags and old chairs and a fridge and an ironing board and – *(Realises she's babbling.)* all the usual rubbish. You probably don't need to know… every single item.

JAY: Right.

MEL: And I was wondering if you could… help?

JAY: *(Meaning the grabber.)* With this?

MEL: No, no, sorry, no, I meant maybe you could – radio to base?

JAY: I'm not sure / what you

MEL: / Cause you do pick stuff like that up, don't you?

JAY: Not – no.

MEL: It says you do on your website.

MRS REYNOLDS arrives.

MRS REYNOLDS: Oh hello, I know you, don't I.

MEL: I don't think we've met…

MRS REYNOLDS: You're the young lady who's just moved in across the road.

MEL: Well yes okay then, I am.

MRS REYNOLDS offers her hands.

MRS REYNOLDS: I'm Mrs Reynolds.

MEL: Mel.

MRS REYNOLDS: How are you finding things so far, Mel?

MEL: I was just hoping our friend here might help me shift a few things from the front garden, but, he doesn't seem too keen.

MRS REYNOLDS: Oh wonderful, cause it's a real eyesore, isn't it. I mean I'm not blaming you. It's a shared house and you've only just moved in, but still –

MEL: No, I know.

MRS REYNOLDS: But I don't think Jay'll be able to do much. You need to ring the council. They'll collect all that stuff, which makes it all the more bloody annoying people just leave it to sit there…

MEL: Doesn't he – oh God – doesn't he work for the council?

MRS REYNOLDS: Jay? Good grief, no!

MEL: Sorry, I just saw him clearing up, and –

(Realising she's talking about JAY while he stands there.)

I just walked up and started ordering you about. What must you've thought?

MRS REYNOLDS: I'm sure he thought, here's a lovely young woman coming to speak to me – and he will have been very happy about that.

JAY: I can talk, you know.

MRS REYNOLDS: Now, let me get you the number for the waste disposal department…

MRS REYNOLDS leads MEL off.

MEL: Nice to meet you, Jay. And sorry for – you know.

JAY watches the women leave. Once they are gone –

JAY: Absolutely no problem at all. Mel.

He puts back on his headphones, gets back to picking litter.

Time starts to shift again. Music. Summer ripens towards autumn.

MRS REYNOLDS and JAY survey newly scrawled messages on the wall.

MRS REYNOLDS: Well, that can go. That can go. That can definitely go.

JAY: What about this?

MRS REYNOLDS: *(Reads.)* 'Steve and Ali – true love – four years of love.' I like that. We'll keep it.

JAY: Passes the Mrs R taste and decency test?

MRS REYNOLDS: The day these so-called 'graffiti artists' start asking permission to spray in my street, then I'll start consulting on what I whitewash.

JAY: Oh you're painting these out yourself, are you?

KIERAN enters.

KIERAN: Alright.

JAY: Alright mate.

They shake.

MRS REYNOLDS: Good morning, Kieran.

KIERAN: Is it?

MRS REYNOLDS: Oh well done, very good.

KIERAN: Just asking a question.

JAY: So what you up to, mate?

KIERAN: Fuck all.

MRS REYNOLDS: Gosh, that sounds exciting.

JAY: Mrs R…

MRS REYNOLDS: Yes, Master J?

JAY: Just…

Mrs R takes the hint; backs off slightly.

KIERAN: You hanging here, are you?

JAY: For a bit.

KIERAN: How long's this going on for?

JAY: Hard to say, mate.

KIERAN: So: how many hours'd they give you?

JAY: Like… hundreds.

KIERAN: You been doing it for months…

JAY: Yeah but she only wants me a half hour a day sometimes, so it takes forever to make up the time.

KIERAN: Stupid cow.

JAY: Tell me about it…

MRS REYNOLDS: If you're going to lurk, Kieran you could make yourself useful.

KIERAN: Yeah, right.

MRS REYNOLDS: Jay says you're a dab hand with a spray can. Why not fill up all the blank spaces on that wall?

KIERAN: If you want…

MRS REYNOLDS: Not with filth. With…

KIERAN: Pretty flowers?

MRS REYNOLDS: If you like.

KIERAN: And how much do I get for it?

MRS REYNOLDS: Get for it?

KIERAN: No pay, no play.

MRS REYNOLDS: You might do it just to make the place look a little better.

KIERAN: *(Beat.)* Are you mentally retarded?

JAY: Kee…

MRS REYNOLDS: Jay's happy enough to help out for free.

KIERAN: Jay 'helps out' cause the filth make him.

MRS REYNOLDS: *(Beat.)* Well of course there is that.

KIERAN: *(To JAY.)* Laters, man.

They shake, and KIERAN goes.

JAY gets on with white-washing.

MRS REYNOLDS: You tell your friends you help me because you have to.

JAY: I don't tell them nothing.

MRS REYNOLDS: But they assume. And you don't correct them.

JAY: And?

MRS REYNOLDS: And –

(Beat.)

And that's fine.
Look: I wanted to give you these.

She gets an envelope from her pocket, gives it to JAY.

He looks inside.

MRS REYNOLDS: They're seeds. From the first sweet peas.

JAY: The ones with the smell?

MRS REYNOLDS: Plant them now or keep them somewhere dry over the winter and sow them in the spring.

JAY: I haven't got no garden.

MRS REYNOLDS: Your nan's flat: you said she's got a little balcony. Plant them in pots, grow them up the railings. Bet she'd love that.

JAY: Yeah. See when I say, I live at my nan's, I do – but it's more I sleep there? Like I can't come in before eleven, and I crash in the lounge, and I've gotta be gone before she gets up? Which is alright actually cause she never really surfaces before midday…

He hands the seed packet back.

JAY: So probably best you keep them.

2.

Time has passed. Now we're well into autumn.

MRS REYNOLDS: Jobs in September are
    Pruning, cutting back dead growth,
    Planting bulbs for spring, then
    Dressing the soil with compost
    Or richly-rotted manure, which
    The frost will break down for us
    Over the winter.

JAY: If we get any frost.

MRS REYNOLDS: And if we don't, you can dig the manure in
    come New Year.
    So. Bulbs.

JAY: They go in the ground.

She shows him a bulb.

MRS REYNOLDS: You see this side?
    That's where the shoots come from.
    So you plant it with that side up. Then
    On the bottom, these little straggly things
    Are the roots.

JAY: And you put them face down.

MRS REYNOLDS: That's right.

JAY: Look a bit like onions, don't they.

MRS REYNOLDS: I wouldn't eat them, though.

JAY: They poisonous?

MRS REYNOLDS: No, because if you do, I'll give you a clip
    round the ear.

MEL walks by.

MEL: Hello.

MRS REYNOLDS: Lovely morning.

MEL: Gardening again.

MRS REYNOLDS: Yes we are!

MEL: Sorry – obviously you are. I mean I saw you, on my way
– I was in the grocers just now, they had these plants they
were just giving away and I thought you might want them.

MRS REYNOLDS: That's very kind of you, but I don't think
I've got an inch of space.

MEL: Oh no I meant – for the flowerbed, down the road. I've
seen you, looking after it.
And then I've seen kids destroying it. Must be costing you
a bomb to keep buying new plants –

MRS REYNOLDS: You've seen kids vandalising the flower bed?

MEL: Well… yeah.

MRS REYNOLDS: And you… shouted at them? Called the
police?

MEL: I didn't see them, really – I was in my flat. I saw them
through the window. I didn't think to –

MRS REYNOLDS: Do anything?

MEL: Well… no.

MRS REYNOLDS: Of course not. Why on God's earth would
anyone do anything…

JAY: Mrs R.

MRS REYNOLDS: What?

JAY looks at her.

JAY: She brought you some plants. Remember?

MRS REYNOLDS: *(Beat.)* Sorry. Ignore me. Pounding
headache. Just nipping inside for some aspirin.

MRS REYNOLDS puts down her tools and goes.

MEL: Bit fierce, isn't she.

JAY: She has her moments.

MEL: "It's Mrs Reynolds' street, the rest of us just live here."
That's what I was told.

JAY: Who by?

MEL: I don't dare say, don't want to get them in trouble.
   Seems to like you, though.

JAY: I'm a likeable guy.

MEL: Are you, really?

   JAY looks at MEL. MEL holds his gaze. JAY looks away.

JAY: Anyway I'd best be getting on…

   MEL offers up the bag.

MEL: So these plants…

   JAY takes the bag from her.

JAY: Yeah sure. *(He takes a look.)* Yeah the thing with these is
   they're what you call summer bedding plants? You put
   them in say the spring, the start of the summer?
   But now it's –

MEL: – the end of the summer?

JAY: Which, to be honest, is probably why they were giving
   them away.

MEL: Cause they're no good.

JAY: Stick them in your garden, never know, they might grow
   again in the spring.

MEL: Yeah, I might. *(Beat.)* I wouldn't know how though, I'd
   kill them straight off.

JAY: Soak the plant in the pot,
   Dig a hole, loosen the earth
   In the bottom,
   Pull the plant out of the pot,
   – it'll come easy 'cos you soaked it –
   Loosen the root ball,
   Stick it in the hole,
   Firm the earth around it
   And water in well.

MEL: Okay…

JAY: Easy really.

   MRS REYNOLDS enters.

JAY: Mrs R, I was just saying, she might as well stick these in her garden, see if anything comes up in the spring.

MEL: I was explaining to Jay I wouldn't have a clue how to do that.

JAY: And I was just saying to her, it's the simplest thing…

MRS REYNOLDS: I see…

MRS REYNOLDS is very aware of the way MEL is looking at JAY.

MEL: And I would give it a go but our garden's split between the three flats you see so no-one really bothers and it's all over-grown with massive brambles and nettles and things, so… be a bit of a waste, really.

JAY: No problem at all.

JAY picks up a billhook and offers it to her.

JAY: Billhook'll sort that out for you.

MEL: Right…

MEL takes the billhook, hefts it. Looks to MRS REYNOLDS.

MEL: Well, thanks for that. I'll get it back to you *(The billhook.)* soon as I can.

MEL goes.

JAY gets back to work.

MRS REYNOLDS: Not your type, then?

JAY: What?

MRS REYNOLDS: Mel. Who was clearly angling to get you to come round and give her a hand.

JAY: I know, cheeky bitch.

MRS REYNOLDS: No, not because – good God, how does the race perpetuate itself? She likes you.

JAY: *(Beat.)* Oh yeah I know that.

MRS REYNOLDS: Oh for goodness sake…

MRS REYNOLDS gets on with some little task, so she's not looking at JAY.

JAY: No no I mean – I knew she did, obviously. Just – good to get a female perspective.

MRS REYNOLDS: *(Still without looking at him.)* You going to then?

JAY: If Mel wants a little sugar from the Jay-meister
Who am I, to deny?

MRS REYNOLDS stops what she's doing and looks at him.

JAY: What?

MRS REYNOLDS shakes her head, gets back to her task.

3.

MEL's garden.

JAY, flushed from hacking back weeds. Carrying a billhook. MEL enters, with some cans.

JAY: That's the worst of it done.

MEL: You want a drink?

JAY: Please.

MEL offers him a can of lager.

JAY: Cheers.

JAY cracks open the can, and drinks deeply. MEL watches.

MEL: Hit the spot?

JAY: Oh yeah.

He drinks again. MEL watches again. JAY becomes aware of her watching.

JAY: What?

MEL: Thirsty then?

JAY: Thirsty work.

MEL: You shouldn't quench a thirst with booze. Bad for you.

JAY offers the empty can.

JAY: I haven't. Still parched.

MEL offers him another can.

JAY: Anybody'd think you were trying to get me drunk…

MEL: You're full of yourself.

JAY: It's all a front.

MEL: No it isn't.

JAY: *(Beat.)* Nah, it's not.

MEL opens a can.

MEL: I remember the first time I saw you.
I remember thinking – what an idiot.

JAY: Oh, cheers…

MEL: No no, it was cause you were painting over graffiti
And I thought, why's he bothering with that?
Kids'll just come do more, the little bastards.
And all those plants you stuck in the flowerbed?
They all got pulled up and ripped to shreds
I remember getting annoyed with you.

JAY: I annoyed you, before you even knew me?
That might actually be a record.

MEL: Exactly, you were just – some guy
On the street, who I didn't even know
And you were so pissing me off.
I remember thinking
Just stop it, just stop even trying
Why are you wasting
All that effort, all that time –

JAY: – all those plants.

MEL: There was once
It must've been you planted seeds
Rather than sticking plants in,
Because they came up, slowly,
Little buds at first then a few leaves…

JAY: The nasturtiums.

MEL: And they actually survived for ages,
    It was like 'cause they grew, gradually,
    The kids didn't notice them, not
    Till they got quite big and then –

JAY: Then the kids did notice them.

MEL: I came past one morning and
    There were all the leaves and stalks
    Just thrown around. I was so sad.
    Then you came out, gathered all the bits up.
    Not annoyed. Not angry.
    Just started again.
    Just planted new seeds.
    I was watching you from my window.
    I remember thinking –

    (Beat.)

    And then I saw you helping Mrs Reynolds
    With her garden as well and I thought,
    What a sweetheart, helping that –

JAY: Grumpy old bag?

MEL: Helping that grumpy old bag
    With her garden. What a star.

JAY: It's just now and again.

MEL: It's every day! I see you, every bloody day.

JAY: Spend a lot of time watching me, then?

MEL: S'pose I do, yeah.

JAY: That's a bit weird, isn't it?

MEL: Is it weird? Or is it, just…

JAY: What?

MEL: Just, when I was younger
    I was into troublemakers, you know,
    Bad boys. And now – a guy like you.

JAY: A guy like me what?

MEL: Now… I'm into a guy like you.

JAY: Are you?

MEL: You know it. You do.
  And this is maybe the moment to say
  You might be into
  A girl like me, too.

  MEL waits for him to say something. He just takes a drink.

JAY: Some people would tell you
  I'm a troublemaker.

MEL: Oh yeah you definitely look it,
  Picking up litter and hanging out
  With old ladies.

  JAY says nothing.

MEL: What I really like about you
  Is that you keep coming back.
  Day after day.
  You're not full of shit,
  In the way most guys, you know,
  Really really are.

  (Beat.)

  And any time you feel like
  You want to come over here
  And kiss me, then,
  You should probably just do that.

  JAY looks at her. And smiles.

4.

The flowerbed. Later the same night.

KIERAN is at work. He's sprayed the letters 'F' and 'U', and is working on a 'C', making them big enough that the finished four-letter word will cover the whole wall.

JAY enters, walking home from MEL's. He watches for a while, silent.

JAY: Alright, mate.

KIERAN: Jesus Christ, I nearly shat myself then.

JAY: What you up to?

Kieran *(Beat.)* What's it look like?

JAY: You know she'll make me paint over that.

KIERAN: She can't make you do anything.

JAY says nothing.

KIERAN: Where you been?

JAY: Only on an actual real-life date.

KIERAN: What?

JAY: Dinner, and wine, and the whole shebang.

KIERAN: I thought you looked chuffed with yourself.
You do the deed?

JAY: Might've.

KIERAN: That's a no then.

JAY: Just playing it slow.

KIERAN: And who is the lucky blind girl?

JAY: You know that Mel?

KIERAN: Just moved in over there?

JAY: That's the one.

KIERAN: Are you shitting me?

JAY: What?

KIERAN: Mate, she has been round the place like a rash.

JAY: Piss off.

KIERAN: Parachute Mel, everyone gets a jump.

JAY: You've got her mixed up, mate.

KIERAN: She's done Robbie, she's done Trev, she's done Naz,
she's done Naz's little cousin.
She's done Will, she's done Brett.

JAY: No way.

KIERAN: Oh my God: she's done Steve Olson. I've seen the
photos on his phone.

JAY says nothing.

KIERAN: And I mean, he's a sick bastard.
    You know the stuff he does.
    Imagine that. Going with a girl
    After he's had her.
    It'd be like you were
    Steve Olson's bitch.

    (Beat.)

    Seeing her again?

JAY: Shut it, Kee.

KIERAN: Maybe take her to a movie?
    Maybe take in a show?
    Treat her real nice.
    After Steve-o's treated her
    Like meat.
    Or maybe Steve-o'll be taking her out.
    And you'll be sitting home looking after her kid.

    (Beat.)

    She did tell you that, didn't she?
    Of course she did:
    On your actual date.
    She's got a kid,
    And she gave it up.
    I mean you did know that, didn't you mate?

JAY: *(Beat.)* I'll see you – mate.

JAY moves off abruptly. For once they part without shaking hands.

KIERAN: See you, Jay.

KIERAN stands. Picks up his aerosol, gives it a shake.

Gets back to spraying.

5

Next day. The flowerbed. JAY is whitewashing the wall.

MRS REYNOLDS is struggling to pick up litter with the grabber.

She gives up. Stretches her fingers.

MRS REYNOLDS: Do you want to swap?

> *She offers him the litter-grabber. JAY doesn't respond.*

MRS REYNOLDS: Jay?

JAY: *(Snapping.)* What?

> *MRS REYNOLDS looks at him.*

JAY: I've known him since I was three.

MRS REYNOLDS: You're telling me Kieran's never lied to you?

JAY: Not about anything that matters.

> *MEL enters.*

MEL: Morning all.

MRS REYNOLDS: Ah, right. We'll get this sorted out now.

MEL: Oh God, what've I done?

MRS REYNOLDS: You've done nothing, my love. But someone else has been feeding Jay's head with stories.

JAY: Mrs R…

MEL: What stories?

JAY: Seriously, drop it.

MRS REYNOLDS: Best these things are out in the open.

JAY: Maybe not out in the street, though.

MRS REYNOLDS: Will you just – trust me? For once?

MEL: You're panicking me now.

MRS REYNOLDS: It's nothing to fret about. Just a silly little friend of Jay's getting a bit jealous, spreading a bit of muck.

MEL: What sort of muck?

MRS REYNOLDS: Let's just say he was besmirching your reputation.

JAY: He said you had a kid. But you gave it up.

MEL: Right.

MRS REYNOLDS: It's almost sweet, him trying
    To come between you 'cause
    He wants Jay all to himself.
    Mel?
    Mel says nothing.

MRS REYNOLDS realises she's put her foot in it.

MRS REYNOLDS: Oh… bollocks.
    Right, I'm going to pop back to the house…

MRS REYNOLDS vanishes.

A pause.

MEL gets out a photo.

MEL: That's him. Mikey.

JAY: Cute, yeah.

JAY hands the photo back, returns to whitewashing the wall.

MEL: After he was born,
    Things weren't easy.
    I got into a bit of a mess.
    I just wanted to be a good mum
    And I couldn't.

JAY doesn't respond, just keeps on painting.

MEL: The doctors said
    It was post-natal depression.
    I couldn't look after him, 'cause
    I was in such a state myself.
    My mum and dad took him.
    We decided they'd have him
    Till I was back on my feet.
    That was two years ago, now.

JAY keeps working.

MEL: Is that even the bit that bothers you?
    I bet it's not.
    I bet it's the other stuff.

JAY stops what he's doing.

MEL: Well whatever your mate told you.
    It's probably true.
    When I was feeling bad
    When I was feeling such a complete failure,
    I'd go out, and knowing I could pull,
    I could make some man want me,
    Well it helped. It kept me going.

    (Beat.)

    Or at least to start with.
    After a bit it made me feel
    Like I was giving my self away.

JAY gets back to painting.

JAY: *(Without looking at her.)* Yeah well you were.

MEL: And you've hardly been
    A choirboy, have you?

She watches him.

MEL: I'm complete disaster
    As a mum, that you can swallow –
    – but what actually bothers you is
    I've shagged some blokes
    You might see down the pub.
    You're thinking about it now:
    Who they were.
    What I did with them.
    Well the answer is – I did
    Pretty much everything, to anybody.
    And I'm not happy about it.
    I'm certainly not proud.

And now the wall is completely white again. But JAY still cannot look at her.

MEL: Do you even like me?

JAY: Why would I give a toss, if I didn't like you?

MEL: I like you, as well.

JAY: It's different, with boys,
　　　When another boy's had your girl,
　　　It's too much.

MEL: Then be a man.
　　　Be a man, and tell me
　　　None of that stuff matters.

　　　Finally he turns to her.

JAY: Look at you.

MEL: What? What?

JAY: You're lovely.

MEL: Am I?

JAY: Yeah. Yeah you are.

MEL: That's nice to hear.

JAY: What you doing Saturday?

MEL: Hanging out with my son.

JAY: Okay.

MEL: You could tag along.
　　　If you wanted.

6.

MRS REYNOLDS' front garden. Night. Several weeks later.

MEL walks up to the front door, knocks.

No response.

MEL: Mrs R?

　　　Was there a noise inside?

MEL: Mrs R was that you?

　　　MEL listens carefully. She pushes open the letterbox.

MEL: Mrs R are you alright?

(Beat.)

Oh my God! Mrs R…

The door opens.

MRS REYNOLDS: I'm fine, I'm fine.

MRS REYNOLDS is looking dishevelled.

MEL: What happened?

MRS REYNOLDS: Just need a bit of air.

When she moves, we see she's limping.

MEL: What've you done?

MRS REYNOLDS: Nothing!

(Beat.)

Sorry.

MEL: That's alright.

MRS REYNOLDS: It's my own bloody fault. I never bother
    with Christmas and I thought, this year, might as well,
    and I remembered stuffing decorations up on top of the
    wardrobe, I was reaching to get them –

MEL: You should use the step-ladder when you're reaching /
    for things

MRS REYNOLDS: / I bloody was. I'm not an idiot.

(Beat.)

Sorry. Again.

MEL: It's alright. Again.

MRS REYNOLDS: I was using the step-ladder. My leg gave way.

MEL: But you're okay? In yourself?

MRS REYNOLDS: *(About to snap.)* Yes, I'm –

MRS REYNOLDS catches herself.

MRS REYNOLDS: I'm fine. Thank you very much for your
    concern.

MEL: No problem.

MRS REYNOLDS: Serves me right, fussing around with decorations when it's just me on my own…

MEL: It's nice to make a bit of an effort.

MRS REYNOLDS: I did think… maybe you and Jay and Mikey could come round for Christmas dinner, if you're / not

MEL: / No, I'd like that. And Jay – it'd be free food, so…

MRS REYNOLDS: Well that's lucky 'cause to be honest I've already ordered the turkey – oh. You wanted something, didn't you.

MEL: Not really –

MRS REYNOLDS: And hark at me, rabbitting on…

MEL: You've had a shock.

MRS REYNOLDS: What can I do for you?

MEL: Jay was supposed to be round at seven and –

MRS REYNOLDS: And you wondered if I had him stuck here doing jobs for me?

MEL: I wondered… if you'd seen him, is all?

MRS REYNOLDS: I haven't, as it happens, not today. Have you tried –

(She pulls up.)

Yes, of course you've tried phoning.

MEL: A couple of times, I don't want to hassle him but…

From off, the sound of JAY singing 'We Wish You a Merry Christmas'.

MRS REYNOLDS: Ah. Somebody's had an early dose of Christmas cheer…

JAY staggers on, still singing. One hand under his jacket.

MEL moves towards him.

MRS REYNOLDS: Does no-one know any proper carols any more? That's all you ever hear, 'we wish you a merry Christmas', on and on, what about the old songs, / Good King Wenceslas…

MEL: / Look at the state of you.

JAY: And look… at the state of you too.

MEL: You are a wreck.

JAY: You are gorgeous.

MEL: Where've you been?

JAY: *(Beat.)* On adventures.

MEL: With who?

JAY: Mates.

MEL: I phoned all your mates.

JAY: I was out – with new mates. Who were not mates at the start of the night. They are now.

MEL: I said I was going to cook.

JAY: Brilliant, I'm starving.

MEL: I was going to cook for seven o'clock.

JAY: Alright, Mrs R?

MRS REYNOLDS: Oh I'm fine.

JAY: *(To Mrs Reynolds.)* You wanna get in, it's freezing out here.

MEL: I was cooking for seven. It's quarter past ten.

JAY looks at her for a long time. Then, almost excitedly –

JAY: Is it?

MEL: Yeah.

JAY: No way.

MEL: And what's that on your trousers, is it piss or vomit?

JAY looks down at his trousers. He considers. Then announces, with huge dignity.

JAY: Neither of the above.

MEL: You've had such a great time with your mates, you get back to them –

JAY: Mel –

JAY extends his hand towards her, tries to cup her cheek. She pushes him away.

JAY: Don't be like that…

MEL: Get lost.

MEL realises there's something wet on her cheek, where JAY touched her.

MEL: Urrr, what the hell is this?

She dabs at her cheek. Sniffs her fingers.

MEL: Jay…

JAY: Come on, let's be nice. Don't you wanna be nice?

MEL: What's happened to you?

MRS REYNOLDS: What is it?

JAY: Can we go in please cause I'm really freezing.

MEL catches JAY's hand.

MEL: Oh my God that's blood. Jay.

MEL opens his jacket. The bottom half of his shirt is drenched in blood.

JAY: I might have to sit down.

JAY slides to the floor.

MRS REYNOLDS: I'll get an ambulance.

MRS REYNOLDS heads inside to phone.

JAY: Just gonna lie down for a bit…

MEL takes off her coat, lays it over him.

MEL: No, listen, you can't.
You can't sleep, baby.
You have to stay awake.
Jay. You have to stay with me.

To black.

MRS REYNOLDS' living room. Something of a spread on the table.

MRS REYNOLDS leads MEL and JAY in.

JAY straight away heads to the table and starts picking.

JAY: *(Of the spread.)* This is a bit much, isn't it.

MRS REYNOLDS: Christmas leftovers. All got to be eaten before it goes off.

JAY: You really go to town, don't you.

MRS REYNOLDS: Not normally. This year… I was planning to have people round.

JAY: Anyone I know?

Mrs Reynolds looks at him.

JAY: Oh right me.

MEL: Who else d'you think?

JAY: *(To Mel.)* Her kids could've been coming home.

MRS REYNOLDS: It was going to be you, and Mel, and Mikey.

JAY: Alright, sorry to ruin everyone's plans by selfishly getting stabbed…
(Off MEL's look.) What? *(To MRS REYNOLDS.)* I'll see what I can do to get rid of this little lot now. And, you know, there's always next year.

MRS REYNOLDS: *(Beat.)* Yes there is.

A knock at the door.

MRS REYNOLDS: I'll go.

JAY: Who's that?

MEL: Dunno.

JAY: *(Sensing something is up.)* Really…

MEL: Let me have a look at your dressing.

JAY: My dressing's alright.

MEL: So what's it matter if I have a look?

JAY: No.

MEL: Jay…

They stare at each other. Then with huge weariness –

JAY: Alright…

JAY pulls up his shirt – a big bandage taped to his stomach, tape winding right round him to hold it on.

MEL: That looks fine. Don't know what you're making such a fuss about…

MRS REYNOLDS enters. And with her, CASSIE.

JAY: Looks like I've been set up again…

MRS REYNOLDS: I asked Cassie to come here / today…

JAY: *(To MEL.)* / You were in on this, weren't you?

MEL: You got stabbed, Jay.

MRS REYNOLDS: And we don't feel you're taking it seriously enough.

JAY: Don't we, really.

MRS REYNOLDS: Oh / for goodness' sake…

MEL: / Jay…

JAY: *(To CASSIE.)* You got anything to say for yourself?

CASSIE: Yes. As it happens.

MRS REYNOLDS: And actually listen.

JAY: Will you give me a break for one second?

CASSIE waits for silence.

CASSIE: You might remember, we talked about how hard it is for people to get out of offending behaviour once they're involved with the criminal justice system.

JAY: You might've talked about that, don't think I did.

JAY is aware that MEL and MRS REYNOLDS are deeply unimpressed by him right now.

JAY: Okay, get on with it.

CASSIE: You start with the best intentions in the world but you're walking the same streets, seeing the same people –

JAY: I'm not seeing the same people.

MRS REYNOLDS: You got stabbed.

JAY: Yeah. That's right.
Someone stabbed me.
Not me doing the stabbing.

CASSIE: So there's someone out there now who stabbed you.

JAY: And perhaps he should be getting your attention.

MEL: So it was a he?

JAY: *(Beat.)* Yeah. I'm guessing.

MEL: You said you couldn't remember a thing.

JAY: It wasn't anyone I knew.

MEL: How do you know that, if you can't remember a thing about what happened?

MRS REYNOLDS: Would you remember his face if you saw him again?

JAY: They're never gonna catch him, are they?

CASSIE: But if you saw him, you'd recognise him.

JAY: Might do.

MEL: So if you saw him down the pub you'd know his face.

JAY: Maybe.

CASSIE: And what then, Jay?

MEL: What'll you do
When you see this guy again?

JAY: Nothing.

CASSIE: Nothing?

JAY: Just mind my own business.

CASSIE: You'd let him get away with it?

JAY: Alright – I'd dial 999. Is that what I'm supposed to say?

CASSIE: You're not supposed to say anything.
	I'm asking you to think about
	What you would actually do,
	And what the consequences of those actions
	Might be.

JAY: That is bollocks because you've all decided
	What I'm supposed to say
	And what I'm supposed to do, so
	Why don't you just spit it out.

MEL: If we were a couple.

JAY: We are a couple. I thought.

MEL: A couple living together.

JAY: Where'd we live? There's no room at / yours

MRS REYNOLDS: / Jay – just listen.

MEL: And then if I took Mikey back we could go on the
	housing list.

JAY: So?

CASSIE: Obviously there can be quite a wait till you get
	somewhere but there are schemes –

JAY: There are always bloody schemes…

CASSIE: – there are places in the north with houses standing
	empty.

MRS REYNOLDS: So you could have somewhere a lot quicker.

MEL: And you, and me, and Mikey would be a family.

CASSIE: And you'd be away from the people and places and
	situations, that might lead you into trouble.

JAY: Right.

CASSIE: I know it's a lot to take in…

JAY: When you say, places in the north –
	– do you mean, shitholes?

	A look between the women.

JAY: It just strikes me that if there are houses standing empty
    It's cos no bastard wants to live in them.

MEL: Jay…

MRS REYNOLDS: What if you and Mel just go and take a look?

CASSIE: In fact the council will pay for you to visit the area for
    a day.

JAY: *(Beat.)* No.

MEL: You won't even do
    This one thing for me?

JAY: It was for you, you silly bitch.

MEL: What was?

JAY: The guy, in the pub.
    Saying I'd taken on
    Some slag and her little bastard.
    He called you a slag,
    I took him outside.

MEL: And he stabbed you.

JAY: Yes.

MEL: You could've died.

JAY: I didn't know
    He had a knife, did I?

MEL: Three inches higher,
    You would've died.

JAY: It was for you.

MEL: No it was not.

JAY: What I'm getting stabbed
    For my own benefit? Brilliant Christmas I had,
    Eating hospital crap and eyeing up the matrons.
    Probably see if I can't
    Can get myself shot for Easter.

MEL: Am I a slag?

JAY: *(Beat.)* Anyone who calls my girl a slag
      Is dead.

MEL: I don't give a toss
     What some wanker down the pub says.

JAY: Well I do.

MEL: Yeah, exactly.

   A beat between them.

JAY: I can't believe you're not
     Even a little bit grateful.
     Or flattered. Or something.

MEL: What do I tell Mikey
     When you come home from the pub dead?

JAY: I come home from the pub dead, then –
     – I must've become a zombie so
     You tell him he has to burn me
     Or shoot me in the head.

MEL: Don't you dare joke about this.

JAY: Don't you dare use that boy
     To blackmail me.
     Cos then I might lose my temper.
     I might do that.

CASSIE: Can I make a suggestion?

MRS REYNOLDS: Perhaps you better had.

CASSIE: My suggestion is –
        – that we just stop.
        Because as the emotional temperature rises
        It gets harder for any of us
        To make rational decisions.

JAY: This is my town.
     This is where I grew up.
     It's not like I'm going out
     Looking for trouble –

   (More specifically to MEL.)

You're asking me to run.
And I don't do that.
I do not run away.
If you thought for one second
I ever could, then
You've got the wrong idea about me.
And you have definitely got
The wrong idea about us.

MEL looks at him. Then gets up – leaves without a word.

CASSIE: I'll – [unsaid: go after her]

MRS REYNOLDS: Yeah.

CASSIE leaves, following MEL.

JAY and MRS REYNOLDS sit for a moment. Then –

JAY: What?

MRS REYNOLDS: Well, that went –
– exactly how it was always going to.

JAY: Why'd you bother then?
Me leave town? As if…

MRS REYNOLDS: That girl loves you. She looks at you, she sees
Only the good. Only what you are now.
Nothing of what went into you.
Nothing of the past.

JAY: Well I'm not –

He stops.

JAY: Come on, Mrs R.

MRS REYNOLDS: What?

JAY: I'm not like I used to be. Am I?

MRS REYNOLDS is suddenly terribly upset. But she controls it.

JAY: What's all this?

He moves towards her.

MRS REYNOLDS: Don't. I'm perfectly fine.
I was a silly old woman.
And I hoped
You had grown up a bit.
But what do we learn in the garden?
Bad seed doesn't grow at all.

(Beat.)

You can't help the way they made you, Jay.

He stands back.

JAY: Fuck you, Anna.

8.

The flowerbed. Night. KIERAN and JAY are graffiti-ing the wall, passing spray cans between them.

JAY: I'm sitting there,
My life being carved up
In front of me.
And suddenly I'm like –
– what? What is this?
How did this happen?
Kieran You got pussy whipped, mate.
Happens to the best of us.
Not me, obviously.

JAY: And I'm thinking –
– I took a knife?
For this crap?

KIERAN: So that's it then? You and Smell, done with?

JAY: Yeah.

KIERAN: I might have a crack at that, then. Yeah she's a slag
but still – you would.

JAY looks at him.

JAY: Whatever.

KIERAN: I'm shitting you, you twat.

(Beat.)

Wouldn't touch Steve Olson's sloppy seconds with yours.

JAY snatches a spray can from KIERAN.

JAY: Oh, that is funny, mate.

KIERAN: watches Jay paint.

KIERAN: Tell you what is funny.

JAY: What?

KIERAN: That splashback Nathan Mitchell.

JAY stops what he's doing.

KIERAN: I saw him,
    Coming out of Valentino's night before last.
    He was wrecked. Staggering.
    He turns down some alley for a piss
    And while he was there, acorn-dick in hand,
    I came up behind him
    And slammed his head into the wall.
    Then stamped on him a bit,
    Gave him a one-two-three-four to the nuts.

JAY: You didn't have to do that.

KIERAN: I know mate.

JAY: No, I mean it.

KIERAN: Course I'm gonna – *(Stops, genuinely confused at JAY's response.)* Aren't you still on probation?

JAY: Yes…

KIERAN: Then you need to stay out of trouble for a bit.

JAY: He's my problem.

KIERAN: So what, he stabs you, and he gets away with it?

JAY: I was waiting for my moment.

KIERAN: Yeah yeah yeah except how it looks is –
    – he stabs you, and he gets away with it.
    Then every other little shit thinks he can have a pop.
    Now – a message has been sent.

JAY: I owe you, mate.

KIERAN shrugs.

KIERAN: You'd do it for me.

They shake. JAY pulls it into a hug. When they break –

KIERAN: You filthy poof.

9.

MRS REYNOLDS' living room. JAY is waiting.

On the table, a bottle of Scotch and a couple of tumblers.

MRS REYNOLDS comes in, and hands over a carrier bag.

JAY: *(Indicating the bottle.)* Started early, did we?

MRS REYNOLDS: There you go.

JAY: What's all this?

MRS REYNOLDS: Possessions. Of yours. Which you abandoned at Mel's.

JAY makes to go.

JAY: Alright, see you then.

MRS REYNOLDS: Stay for a cup of tea?

JAY: Don't drink tea.

MRS REYNOLDS: Or coffee, whatever you want.

JAY: Nah, I'm a bit – on my way somewhere.

MRS REYNOLDS: Mel says you just stopped coming round. Stopped phoning. She hasn't seen you in weeks.

JAY: Been busy.

MRS REYNOLDS: Too busy to phone?

JAY: Seems that way, yeah.

MRS REYNOLDS: You could've finished it with her face to face. Shown a bit of backbone.

JAY: Anything else you wanna lecture me about? Didn't brush my teeth this morning, if you're interested…

MRS REYNOLDS: I didn't mean to hector.

JAY: Apology accepted.

(Looking into the bag.)

Half this stuff isn't even mine – who else has she had round there? Christ, once those legs are spread they don't snap shut in a hurry…

MRS REYNOLDS: Just – I expected better. From you.

JAY: And why the hell would you do that?

MRS REYNOLDS looks at him: then turns away, defeated. Pours herself a drink, offers the bottle to JAY – he indicates no.

MRS REYNOLDS: Well then fine.

JAY: *(Of the carrier bag.)* This stuff is all crap, you can bin it.

He puts the carrier bag down on the table.

JAY: So I'll be off.

MRS REYNOLDS says nothing.

JAY: See you then. But probably not.

He starts to move off.

MRS REYNOLDS: Hold it a sec.

JAY: I knew there was something going on. What, Mel's on her way over is she?

MRS REYNOLDS: No, nothing like that.

JAY: You're gonna try and talk me into taking her back?

MRS REYNOLDS: I don't know that she'd have you.

JAY: What, then?

MRS REYNOLDS gets up. Moves to some drawers.

MRS REYNOLDS: I was having trouble,
With my hand, and then my leg.

JAY: Trouble how?

MRS REYNOLDS: The strength going in my hand.
My leg giving way underneath.

JAY: Don't mean to be rude but
   You are getting on a bit.

MRS REYNOLDS: That's what I thought –

   (Beat.)

   In fact no I didn't.

   She opens the a drawer, gets out a big envelope.

MRS REYNOLDS: I was at the doctor,
   I had a bit of a throat infection.
   It was Dr Kabeer and you know
   She's such a sweetheart, she said,
   Is there anything else I can help you with?

   From the envelope she pulls loose printed sheets and pamphlets.

   Hands them to JAY.

MRS REYNOLDS: This is going to be horrible for you.
   I'm sorry.

   MRS REYNOLDS sits back down.

   JAY scans quickly through the sheets, looking at MRS REYNOLDS every now and again as he reads. She sips at her drink.

JAY: So – obviously this is what you've got.
   Motor neurone disease.

   MRS REYNOLDS nods.

JAY: It says there's no cure. You die.

MRS REYNOLDS: Yes.

   He sees that she is watching his reaction.

   And the tosses the papers down onto the table.

JAY: Tough break.

MRS REYNOLDS: That's all you've got to say?

JAY: People die on the streets all the time.
   And a lot younger than you, Mrs R.

MRS REYNOLDS: We're back to 'the streets' are we?

JAY: The streets is where I live.

MRS REYNOLDS: You live with your nan!

JAY: I sleep there: I don't live there.

MRS REYNOLDS: Jay.
    I've got months left.

JAY: Okay.

MRS REYNOLDS: What will happen
    What could happen now quite quickly
    Is that my muscles will waste away.
    I won't be able to do things for myself.
    Soon I'll take my last step.
    I'll be hoisted
    Onto the toilet.
    The spit will be sucked from my mouth
    So I don't drown.
    A machine will breathe on my behalf.
    And through all that
    My mind
    Will be untouched.
    I will know
    Everything that happens to me.

JAY: Sounds bad, yeah.

MRS REYNOLDS: I'm not brave enough, Jay.
    I need help.
    I need a way out.

JAY: *(Beat.)* What?

MRS REYNOLDS: I've tried a few times.
    But I don't get it right.

    She looks at him.

MRS REYNOLDS: I want you to help me die.

JAY: Me?

MRS REYNOLDS: Please.

JAY: And – why me?

MRS REYNOLDS: Who else would I ask?

JAY: Your kids?

MRS REYNOLDS: Too far away.

JAY: They couldn't get on a plane?

MRS REYNOLDS: It'd break their hearts.
    Because they care about me.
    They love me.

JAY: But if I help you die –

MRS REYNOLDS: You would just leave. Afterwards.
    No-one would know you were here.

JAY: Hold on hold on hold on.
    You've known for ages.

MRS REYNOLDS: Yes.

JAY: And you kept it secret?
    And you're telling me tonight
    What, to punish me?

MRS REYNOLDS: Should I have not told you at all?

JAY: You should've said sooner.
    I could've got used to it.
    That is so selfish.

MRS REYNOLDS: Probably it was selfish.
    Probably you're right but
    I'm dying, Jay.
    Perhaps I need to be selfish now.
    Just to get through it.

JAY: You can't – announce it out of nowhere.
    You can't just say, oh by the way,
    I'm dying, and I want you to help me
    Kill myself, and thanks very much
    For popping over. That's not –

    (Beat.)

    Is it a trick?

MRS REYNOLDS: No.

JAY: Some sort of lesson?
     You're gonna scare me shitless and then
     I'll say I'll be nice and be good and
     At the last minute it's all pretend –

MRS REYNOLDS: I kept it to myself because
     I wanted to be free of it.
     Some conversations, a few moments
     When I could just think about
     Getting on with life.

JAY: This isn't the world.
     Little old ladies don't sit
     In their little old houses
     Thinking about how to top themselves.

MRS REYNOLDS: I went to a consultant
     There were examinations to see
     How quickly the disease was taking hold.
     The news was – not good.
     On the bus, I was starting to panic,
     About to cry, thinking,
     Get home, get into the garden,
     Get to work and you'll be fine and then –
     From the end of the street I could see
     Something not right.
     Desi came out of the shop
     He'd spotted some thug on his CCTV
     He'd caught the little shit
     Sat on him till the police arrived.

     (Beat.)

     And you had destroyed everything.
     Every plant stamped on, kicked to pieces.
     The roses were too tough so you just
     Tore every flower off.

     (Beat.)

     I went in.
     I curled up and
     I howled

For my dead mum, my dead dad,
My dead husband.
They are all gone.
You –
You owe me.

JAY: No no no.
What we'll do is –
– I'll look after you.

MRS REYNOLDS: You will?

JAY: This is it.
This is what I'll do.

MRS REYNOLDS: No.

JAY: I'm offering.
I'll look after you.
Not a stranger. Someone you know.
Someone you can trust.
I'll do everything – how you want it.
I'll move in. It'd be great. It'd suit me.
My nan's gonna chuck me out any minute –

MRS REYNOLDS: You'll feed me,
Wash me,
Take me to the toilet.
Wipe my backside.
You will?
You?

(Beat.)

Alright.
Tell me you can do that.
Look me in the eye.

JAY: I will.
I mean,
I'll try.
I'll do my best.

She looks at him.

MRS REYNOLDS: Your best isn't good enough, I'm afraid.

JAY: If it was someone else.
    Someone better.
    Would you say yes then?

MRS REYNOLDS: But you can help me.
    Stay with me, and
    After I pass out – make sure.

JAY: What d'you mean, make sure?

MRS REYNOLDS: You know.

JAY: Not a chance.

MRS REYNOLDS: It would be a kindness.

JAY: This is wrong. You know it is.

MRS REYNOLDS: I've tried already. Got the pills. Stacks of
    them.
    Drop of Scotch to wash them down.
    Couldn't do it. I just sat there, crying.

JAY: Doesn't that show
    You don't really want to die?

MRS REYNOLDS: I don't want to die, at all!

JAY: I thought – maybe you were thinking
    Of heaven, or seeing your husband?

MRS REYNOLDS: I don't believe in any of that nonsense!

JAY: Well I don't know, do I…

MRS REYNOLDS: I could live
    For another thirty years, by rights.
    I should have decades in me.
    Want to die? Are you mad?

    (Beat.)

    But I am dying.
    Whether I like it or not.

JAY: Look. Look. Look.
    Can you say you are
    A hundred per cent sure
    This is the right thing to do?

MRS REYNOLDS: Of course I'm not.

JAY: So – you admit you might be wrong?
　　Doesn't it make sense
　　To wait until you're sure you're right?

MRS REYNOLDS: I'm afraid, Jay, this is how it is,
　　Being an adult. You make decisions,
　　Half the time you haven't got a clue
　　If what you're doing is right or not.

JAY: So you're taking
　　The easy way out.
　　You're not going to fight?

MRS REYNOLDS: I'm going to kill
　　Rather than die. So I think
　　I must be fighting. Mustn't I.

JAY: When are you going to do it?

MRS REYNOLDS says nothing.

JAY: Tell me.

MRS REYNOLDS: The second you leave.

JAY: Tonight?

MRS REYNOLDS: I'm getting weaker every day
　　And I can't risk it, I can't risk
　　Getting caught.

JAY: This is insane.
　　You could have months yet, you said…

MRS REYNOLDS: What I have hated most
　　In all the years since my husband passed.
　　Is falling asleep on my own.
　　I'm lost.
　　I'm absolutely bloody terrified.
　　And I'm alone.
　　I wish I had someone.
　　But I don't.

JAY: Is that really how you feel?

MRS REYNOLDS nods.

JAY: I'll stay.

MRS REYNOLDS: What?

JAY: If you're going to do it, tonight.
　　If you've made up your mind.
　　I'll sit with you
　　Till you fall asleep.

MRS REYNOLDS: And then?
　　Will you make sure I've gotten away?

JAY: Mrs R…

She collects herself.

MRS REYNOLDS: Right. Right then.
　　I'll go and –

JAY: You want me to come with you?

MRS REYNOLDS: I can't have you watch me taking the pills.
　　If you watch me, I won't be able to do it.
　　So will you stay here?

JAY: Yes okay.

MRS REYNOLDS: And you'll still be here when I come back?

JAY: Of course. Are you alright?

MRS REYNOLDS: You keep bloody asking me that, and / of
　　course [unsaid: I'm not]

JAY: / I don't know what else to say!

MRS REYNOLDS: Just, think before you speak. It's a good
　　general rule.

(Beat.)

I'll go and do it then.

MRS REYNOLDS goes.

JAY is left on his own.

Gets quite upset for a bit.

Collects himself.

He stops: listens.

JAY: Are you alright?

(Beat.)

Mrs R?

Footsteps approach.

JAY: Are you, alright? *(For having asked, again.)* Sorry.

MRS REYNOLDS: I'm fine, thank you.

She hesitates for a moment, steadies herself. She is wearing the pearl necklace she planted in JAY's jacket.

JAY: Nice necklace.

MRS REYNOLDS: Only decent bit of jewellery I've got.

Mrs Reynolds reaches for the bottle.

MRS REYNOLDS: I know you don't like whisky, but –

JAY: No, I'll have some.

MRS REYNOLDS pours.

Sits down.

Lifts her glass.

MRS REYNOLDS: Cheers.

They clink glasses, drink.

JAY: How long will it take?

MRS REYNOLDS: Don't know.
Probably depends how quick
I polish off this Scotch.

She knocks back her glass. Refills.

JAY: Will you tell me things?

MRS REYNOLDS: What sorts of things?

JAY: I don't know the first thing about you.

MRS REYNOLDS: You know my name.

JAY: And that's pretty much it.

MRS REYNOLDS: We've always had other things to talk about.

JAY: Me? And my stupid life?

MRS REYNOLDS: You, for one thing.
　　The right way to plant a bulb, for another.

JAY: I don't know – where you grew up.

MRS REYNOLDS: A farm.

JAY: In the country?

MRS REYNOLDS: In Wales.

JAY: You're Welsh? You haven't got an accent.

MRS REYNOLDS: I left thirty years ago…

JAY: What was it like?

MRS REYNOLDS: It was like –
　　– time was different then.

JAY: How?

MRS REYNOLDS: In spring you'd be sowing for that year's
　　crops.
　　And there'd be lambing, and calving.
　　In summer there were shows,
　　And sales, and marts.

JAY: What's a mart?

MRS REYNOLDS: A market. Where you buy and sell animals.

JAY: You had animals? What kinds?

MRS REYNOLDS: Cows and sheep. Cows for beef, not dairy.
　　Geese. Hens for eggs.
　　Dogs, you know, collies, working dogs mostly but
　　I had a pet, a terrier cross called Susie. Used to
　　Sleep on my bed, mum hated that. Then cats in the barn,
　　Dozens of them, more or less wild, to keep
　　The rats down. We had
　　A few pigs one year but
　　Dad didn't much like them.

JAY: What was wrong with pigs?

MRS REYNOLDS: Ever tried slaughtering one?

JAY: I can honestly say I have not.

MRS REYNOLDS: They scream.
   It's not something you want to hear.

JAY: I'll take your word for it.

MRS REYNOLDS: Didn't put me off the sausages, though.
   Then there'd be harvest, baling the hay,
   Getting the bales stacked in the barn.
   Everyone would come and help,
   Aunties, uncles, cousins, neighbours.
   So many people in the fields, and these huge meals,
   Everybody loading up their plates in the kitchen,
   Going out into the garden to eat
   Cause there wasn't room in the house.
   Then in the autumn – ploughing, preserving.
   Blackberrying, fingers stained from juice
   And if you weren't careful of the thorns, blood.
   Blackberry and apple tart, with loads of sugar
   The warm smell from the shed
   Of Dad cooking up his homebrew.
   Then winter. Sharp air, smoke drifting from chimneys.
   Wringing the geese's necks, then feathering them.
   Splitting logs, drying socks on the Rayburn.
   Christmas: asking the tree's permission
   Before you cut down the holly. Climbing up a rowan for
   mistletoe.
   New Year, and tinkers coming up from Devon,
   Mostly in vans but some still with horses and carts,
   Swapping our goosefeathers for sacks of apples.
   And then – this time, the worst time,
   The dead months when Christmas is gone
   But winter's still dragging on.
   But you get through because you know
   In the end, spring will come.

   (Beat.)

   It was like the year had a story to it.
   You always knew where you were.

JAY: It sounds amazing.

She indicates the Scotch.

MRS REYNOLDS: Pour us a bit more.

JAY does as he's asked. MRS REYNOLDS takes a drink.

MRS REYNOLDS: My Dad. Now there was a man.
　　Firm, you know, took no nonsense but
　　Men in those days could get away
　　With a lot and
　　Well he never did.

JAY: They get away with a lot these days too.

MRS REYNOLDS: Yes I know.

Beat.

MRS REYNOLDS: The one thing you could do
　　Would really make him angry was to say,
　　You didn't care. If I was having an argument
　　With my brother and Dad heard me saying,
　　'I don't care,'
　　He'd be in there like a shot.
　　He'd say, you must always care. You must.

She stops.

MRS REYNOLDS: I might
　　Prefer to lie down, I think.

She moves onto the couch. JAY helps her arrange cushions behind her head.

JAY: That okay?

MRS REYNOLDS: Fine.

She drinks. Coughs slightly. Recovers herself.

MRS REYNOLDS: I remember when I was about ten
　　I started getting these terrible headaches.
　　Migraines I suppose. I'd be seeing colours,
　　Throwing up, I'd have to lie in a dark room,
　　Crying from the pain.
　　And the worst thing was I could feel it begin.
　　I could feel the aching start, and
　　As it got going I knew nothing could be done

144

I would just have to suffer it.
Then once Dad was home in the day,
I felt one of these headaches come on.
I started crying straight away, not
Because of the pain but because of
The pain that was on its way.
Dad sat me down, on the floor,
He sat in a chair behind me,
And he stroked my hair,
Tugged at it, gently, ran it
Through his fingers, pressed down
On my forehead and my –
– so gentle. And whispering something, I think.
And kept on. Might've been ten minutes
Might've been an hour. And eventually
I fell asleep. When I woke up,
The headache was gone.
I swear it was a miracle.
And those two days when I should've been in bed
Crying and being sick –
– it seemed like everything was perfect.

(Beat.)

He never did it again though.

JAY: Why not?

MRS REYNOLDS: No reason, it just
    Never happened that way.
    He was in the fields when the headaches came.
    Or he'd be busy and he'd have to stop
    After a minute. My brothers would be around,
    Clamouring for attention.

Beat.

JAY: I could stroke your hair for you.

MRS REYNOLDS: Would you?

JAY: I won't be as good as your dad.

MRS REYNOLDS: Oh I'd love that.

JAY: Right. Well.

MRS REYNOLDS sits up slightly on the couch, so her head is resting on the couch's arm.

JAY: Okay.

He fetches a chair, sits down behind her.

And very gently, begins to stroke her hair.

MRS REYNOLDS: Sorry if it's a bit greasy.

JAY: It's fine.

He tries rubbing her scalp.

MRS REYNOLDS: Oh that's lovely…

JAY: Good.

MRS REYNOLDS: I could just float off.

JAY stops stroking her hair.

MRS REYNOLDS: Oh…

JAY: There's just
A couple of things more
I want to ask you –

MRS REYNOLDS: But it's so nice…

Beat.

JAY begins stroking her hair again.

MRS REYNOLDS: Don't feel you have to carry on.

JAY: I don't.

MRS REYNOLDS: I mean if your hands get tired.

JAY: They won't.

MRS REYNOLDS: They will in the end.

JAY: I don't think so.
You just –
– you go to sleep now.
If that's what you want.

JAY keeps on stroking her hair.

He stops.

Stands.

Looks at her.

JAY: See this is stupid.
Cos I could do this.
I could.
I could look after you.

MRS REYNOLDS is still.

JAY: I could though.

Something changes in him.

JAY: I could.

He stands for a second. Then he rushes to her.

JAY: No no no, Mrs R!
Mrs R, wake up!

He gets out his phone, dials.

JAY: *(On his phone.)* Yeah, hello?

Yeah I need an ambulance.

10.

The planter.

A crisp day in early spring. Beautiful golden sunlight.

JAY arrives with a bag, and a few tools.

Hanging around his neck is what looks like a mobile, but is actually a cheap, short-range walkie talkie.

Gets out a bin bag and starts picking up litter from the planter.

MEL enters from the other side.

MEL: Alright.

JAY: I'm great. Yourself?

MEL: Fine. *(Beat.)* Are you? Really?
You look a bit tired.

JAY: I am a bit.

MEL: It's nice – that you're still doing all this *(Looking after the planter.)*

JAY: What was I, just gonna stop?
Any time you feel like lending a hand, though…

MEL: Yeah, maybe I will.

But JAY isn't paying attention – he's distracted by something from off

JAY: Oh, will you ever learn…

MRS REYNOLDS arrives. She's in an electric wheelchair, which she controls with a joystick. She has a walkie-talkie round her neck, just like Jay.

JAY: I told you to buzz me if you wanted to come down.

MRS REYNOLDS looks at him.

JAY: And don't give me that look – one wrong move and you'll be off that thing and in the gutter.

MEL shifts to be a bit more in MRS REYNOLDS' field of vision.

MEL: Hiya, Mrs R.

MRS REYNOLDS looks at her.

MEL doesn't know what to do. Waves, a bit limply.

JAY: *(To MEL.)* She's not big on conversation without her computer. But you can fill in her side just by imagining the grumpiest possible thing a human being could say. *(To MRS REYNOLDS.)* Isn't that right?

MRS REYNOLDS looks at him.

JAY: Mrs R, I'm shocked!
(To MEL.) You don't often hear that sort of language from an old lady.

MEL: Anyway – I best be off.

JAY: Oh – okay.

MEL: Nice to see you, Mrs R.

MEL leaves.

JAY and MRS REYNOLDS watch her go.

Then JAY looks to MRS REYNOLDS.

JAY: I know, I know.
  The thing with Mel is – this time I'm playing the long
  game.
  I'm just gonna reel her in, you know, step by step.
  She won't even know it's happening.
  She'll just wake up one day and realise
  She can't live without me.

MRS REYNOLDS shifts her chair slightly.

JAY: Do you want me to – yeah?

JAY manoeuvres the wheel chair so it's next to the bench.

JAY: Look, you've got a bit of –

*He gets out a tissue and gently, gently, wipes saliva from the side
of her mouth.*

He sits on the bench next to her.

JAY: Those cuttings I had off your roses?
  All taken. Every last one.
  And when me and Mel are back together,
  And we get ourselves a little house
  In some dump up north,
  They will be the first things I plant.

She lifts her hand from the joystick.

He takes it.

JAY: I know we're getting close to the end now.
  I know it's getting really hard.
  Just the sweet peas from the autumn are budding.
  They're going to flower tomorrow, the day after.
  Be great if you could stick around for those.

  (Beat.)

  But if you've had enough.
  If today's the day you want it to end –
  He can't say any more, just looks for her response.
  The tiniest shake of her head.

JAY: No?

No.

You can manage another day?

He watches her again. No motion this time – he sees the answer in her eyes.

JAY: Yeah. Me too.

He sits back, a huge weight lifted.

JAY: Look at it.

Will you look at it.

What a morning.

The End.

LOVE STEALS US FROM LONELINESS

for Steffan

Acknowledgements

My thanks to – John and Lucy and all at National Theatre Wales, for making me part of their inaugural season, despite my resistance. To Chris, Amy, Arwel, Elen and Sian and all at Sherman Cymru, for showing such faith in me over the last few years. To Paul Stockton, former Samaritans Regional Representative in Wales, for some conversations that shaped my thinking about this project. To Elin Phillips, Lynn Hunter and Rob Wilfort, for brilliantly showing me where I had gone wrong at the workshops. To Roger Burnell of Bridgend Youth Theatre and Guy O'Donnell of Bridgend Council's Culture Department, for letting me see how different today's teenagers are to my generation, and how similar. To Sarah Bland, Harley Smith, Rebecca John and Charles Smith, for contributing their stories. And thanks to Matw, Ben, Mathew, Andy W., Andrew P, Luke, Ruth, Grace, Lara, Anita, Andrea, Louise, Carolyn, Steph, Rhi, Rachel L., Rachel D., Welly, MacArthur, Bartle - thanks to all the Bridgend boys and girls. Even the rugby lads.

Love Steals Us From Loneliness was commissioned by National Theatre Wales and co-produced by National Theatre Wales and Sherman Cymru. It was first performed at Hobo's Rock Club, Bridgend on October 7th 2010 with the following cast:

BECKY, Remy Beasley
CATRIN, Katie Elin-Salt
MAGS, Nia Roberts
SCOTT, Mark Sumner
MIKEY, Matthew Trevannion

Creative Team

Writer, Gary Owen
Director, John E McGrath
Co-designer, Neil Davies
Co-designer, Anna-Marie Hainsworth
Lighting Designer, Nigel Edwards
Sound Designer, Mike Beer
Emerging Director, Elise Davison
Casting Director, Sam Jones C.D.G
Production Manager, Nick Allsop
Stage Manager, Brenda Knight
Deputy Stage Manager, Sarah Thomas
Assistant Stage Manager, Charlotte Neville
Assistant Producer, Hannah Bevan
Set Construction, Mathew Thomas and Gareth Gordon

Author Notes

Dialogue

A forward slash ('/') indicates an interruption point. A slash at the very start of a line is simply a reminder to the actor that they need to interrupt the preceding speaker.

A long dash ('–') indicates a speaker diverting into a new thought, or a new choice of words to express that thought, or a struggle (real or feigned) to find words.

A clause within two dashes is a parenthetical remark within the main thrust of the sentence.

Words in [square brackets] are unspoken, and included only to clarify the meaning of spoken text.

Music

In the musical sections, actors stay in character, but can acknowledge and respond directly to the audience. The characters are under no illusions about their musical skill or lack of same, but are utterly committed to their performance, no matter how embarrassing they may find it.

Characters

CATRIN

SCOTT

MIKEY

MAGS

BECKY

BEFORE

We're in a pub.

SCOTT enters. His dialogue here is a guide – the performer should feel free to improvise in this section.

SCOTT: Alright?

We're gonna kick things off with a little musical number.

From me.

I know. Gulp.

Anyway I hope you enjoy. And - if you know the chorus, why not sing along?

Scott sings 'Please Don't Let Me Be Misunderstood', by the Animals.

And then we are –

– outside. Outside a church.

CATRIN is wearing a witch's costume – long black wig, green nose.

She is centre stage, squatted down, knickers round her ankles.

SCOTT: *(From off.)* Cat?

CATRIN swears under her breath, and SCOTT enters before she can get up.

He looks at her.

SCOTT: Are those your knickers?

CATRIN looks back at him.

CATRIN: These? No, I'm keeping them warm for a mate.

SCOTT: Having a piss, are you?

CATRIN: What else would I be doing in a graveyard?

SCOTT: Dunno. Might've popped in for a chat with your nan.

CATRIN: I'm not gonna piss in a graveyard where my nan is, am I?

How fucking disrespectful would that be?

SCOTT: You should've had a piss in the pub.

CATRIN offers her hand – SCOTT helps her up.

CATRIN: No, I couldn't, Scott. Because when you're stropping off, the whole point is, you strop off. And then you're gone.

SCOTT: Okay.

CATRIN: If you're gonna strop off, it's all - or it's nothing. You get me?

SCOTT: I do, definitely, get you.

CATRIN: So –

SCOTT: So that's a valuable lesson, thanks.

CATRIN: So I still need a waz.

SCOTT: Right, I'll –

He's moving off.

CATRIN: No, now you're here, do some good. Stand guard.

CATRIN retreats to find a likely spot. SCOTT stands guard. After a second -

CATRIN: Could you like... chat or something?

He turns round.

SCOTT: What?

CATRIN: Don't fuckin' look at me you perv...

He turns back, sharpish.

SCOTT: Sorry.

CATRIN: I'm just having trouble, cos you're gonna hear me?

SCOTT: When you... urinate?

CATRIN: You're gonna hear the little tinkle. So just... chat. You know how to chat, don't you Scott? You just open your mouth, and shit comes out?

SCOTT: Chat about what?

CATRIN: Anything. I'm not actually gonna be listening.

SCOTT: Okay. Well. *(Giving it a go.)* Nice night.

CATRIN: *(Focussed on other matters.)* Is it.

SCOTT: If you're into zombies. Which I am. Probably my favourite supernatural monster. I like the zombies played for comic effect in films like 'Zombieland' or 'Shaun of the Dead'.

CATRIN: Oh thank Christ for that...

CATRIN is urinating. SCOTT a bit unnerved by this.

SCOTT: Also I enjoy the old school killer zombies of the original George Romero movies and more recent work like '28 Days Later'. Course in '28 Days Later' the most terrifying monster of all was the army major as played by Christopher Eccleston, which is like saying, who is the real monster? The zombies or – society ?

CATRIN: Alright, enough.

SCOTT: Okay good –

CATRIN's shaking her tail, and then looking round for something to wipe herself with.

– cos I was running on fumes there. Not even fumes. I was running on the homeopathic / memory of fumes

CATRIN: / Have you got a tissue or something?

SCOTT: Got a hanky.

Under his lab coat, he's wearing a suit jacket, and in the pocket, a white handkerchief.

CATRIN: Like a proper one? Material?

SCOTT: Are you wanting it to wipe your... regions?

CATRIN: That or go pissy.

SCOTT: It's my dad's? Got his initials sewed in.

CATRIN: Right.

D'you like your dad?

SCOTT: Not really.

CATRIN: Well then...

SCOTT: Fair enough, yeah.

CATRIN's still squatting down on the ground, knickers round her ankles.

CATRIN: Are you gonna bring it me, or shall I use the Force?

SCOTT brings the hanky to her, taking care not to look down at CATRIN, then retreats.

CATRIN wipes herself down, then pulls up her knickers.

CATRIN: *(Of the hanky.)* I could wash it and give it back to you?

SCOTT: Nah, you're alright.

CATRIN: Tell your dad I said he's a ledge.

SCOTT: So you coming back in?

CATRIN: On a mission from Lee, are you?

SCOTT shrugs.

CATRIN: Didn't think to come himself?

SCOTT: He's respecting your space.

CATRIN: He is not respecting my space...

SCOTT: He is respecting your fucking space, actually. He can see by you stropping off you don't want to be around him, so he's not coming after you – but at the same time, obviously yeah he is concerned about your fuckin' happiness and well-being. So Lee says to me, Scotty, pop along and mind she's alright.

CATRIN: And along you pop, Scotty dog.

SCOTT: Seems that way.

CATRIN: Abandoning your pint –

SCOTT: Was down to beige spit anyway.

CATRIN: Striding off into the night –

SCOTT: Bit of fresh air's nice.

CATRIN: What are you, his bitch?

SCOTT: No: his mate.

(Thinking of it too late.) And I thought you were.

CATRIN looks at him, not getting it.

SCOTT: His bitch.

CATRIN: [If] You'd've got that five seconds faster, it might actually've been funny.

SCOTT: So Lee says, are you coming back in or what. So are you, cos if you're not I can just fuck off.

CATRIN: *(Of his costume.)* What are you even supposed to be?

SCOTT: Frankenstein.

CATRIN: Frankenstein all stitched together body parts and the bolt through his neck? I'm not really seeing it.

SCOTT: What you've got in mind there is Frankenstein's monster. I am Professor Frankenstein, the doctor who created Frankenstein's monster.

CATRIN: And that's it - that's your dressing up? A white coat?

SCOTT: Well, what are you?

CATRIN: A sexy witch.

SCOTT: I know you're a sexy bitch, but what are you dressed as?

CATRIN: That's the second time in five minutes you've called me a bitch. Calm it down.

SCOTT: I did say sexy.

CATRIN: You just plonk a white coat on – and you think that's enough?

For Halloween?

In the Big End?

You fuckin' disgust me...

SCOTT: It's not just a white coat, I've got a suit underneath – jacket, pressed shirt, waistcoat, the lot.

CATRIN: What sort of doctor wears a suit? My doctor wears a fleece. Can see his nasty little chest hairs poking through the zip...

SCOTT: An olden days mad professor sort of doctor wears a suit. Watch any film.

CATRIN: When I first started going out, Halloween in town used to be mental. Now it's people like you –

SCOTT: People like me what?

CATRIN: Ruining it. Just not making the effort. You call that a costume? That's a disgrace.

SCOTT: If it wasn't for my disgrace you'd still have a pissy minge, so –

The second he says this, CATRIN is open-mouthed. He tries to carry on.

So just, so just be grateful...

He can't go on.

CATRIN: I can't believe you just talked about my minge.

SCOTT: Nor can I really.

CATRIN: My 'pissy minge'.

SCOTT: It was just words, I wasn't thinking about what they meant -

CATRIN: Yes you were, you sick bastard.

SCOTT: - I wasn't, like, visualising yellow drips / hanging off little hairs...

CATRIN: / Fuckin stop it right there!

SCOTT stops it.

What do you think Lee would say, if he heard you talking like that?

SCOTT: I think he'd do the serious voice, where it goes all low and quiet? And he'd give me the serious look, where it's like he doesn't blink, but obviously he must. And then he'd say, Scott, you're my pal, I love you like a fucking brother – but up with that, I will not put.

And I'd have to apologise to you and creep round the place like a buggered dog.

CATRIN: Yeah. I would bloody well think so.

SCOTT: And then after you'd gone we'd all have a fucking great laugh about it.

They look at each other.

SCOTT: Are you coming, back in the pub?

CATRIN: Yeah, alright.

SCOTT: Okay good.

SCOTT turns back toward the pub.

SCOTT: Actually though – look.

CATRIN: What?

SCOTT: The queue's fuckin' insane now. That's a forty-five minute maybe a full hour queue there.

CATRIN: Who the fuck would queue for the Roof?

Obviously, we do, but – seriously who the fuck would?

SCOTT: We could just... hang here.

CATRIN: Hang here?

SCOTT: Hang here for a bit the queue might go down and we can just... stroll in.

CATRIN: Hang here - in this graveyard?

SCOTT: Or queue for an hour with a bunch of townies and valley commandoes?

CATRIN: I do actually fuckin' hate townies and valley commandoes and cannot bear to be near them.

SCOTT: Who doesn't?

CATRIN: Okay. Hang in a graveyard. Happy Halloween.

CATRIN finds a place to settle. SCOTT does likewise.

CATRIN: I'd be fuckin' freezing, if I wasn't hammered out my skull.

SCOTT: Thank Christ you are.

CATRIN: Just what if I sober up?

SCOTT reaches into his briefcase, and pulls out a number of test tubes filled with brightly coloured liquid.

SCOTT: Which d'you want?

CATRIN: All of them?

SCOTT: But imagine that I wanted some too?

CATRIN: Red and green.

SCOTT: Strawberry and lime, excellent choice madam.

CATRIN: Hold on – these are like, test tubes: to go with your mad professor thing. You actually put some fuckin' effort in.

SCOTT: Nice that you noticed.

CATRIN: Just not so anyone can see. All anyone can see is a shit white coat.

SCOTT: Shit white? Is that a new shade they're doing in Dulux? Paint your walls the sensuous colour of a dried out dog turd...

CATRIN: Yeah, keep your effort tucked away secret and just be a smug cunt about it, why not.

They down the shots.

SCOTT: You know they're gonna ban these? Cos they're all curved there's no way to put them down –

CATRIN: You can totally put them down.

She puts down an empty tube on its side.

CATRIN: Ta-da!

SCOTT: But not without spilling the booze, you can't. You have to knock them back in one go.

CATRIN: And?

SCOTT: Encourages binge drinking.

CATRIN: It is not the curves of some test tube drives me to binge drink.

SCOTT: What does, then?

CATRIN: Your face. Plus what sort of twat sits nursing a shot of fruit-flavoured vodka? You chuck 'em down and get back to your pint. Or white wine spritzer.

She necks a shot.

CATRIN: Shit. I think there was actual fruit in that. I'm having a reaction. Oh God. Oh God...

SCOTT: Are you alright?

CATRIN: *(A few big breaths.)* I'm fine. And don't do that.

SCOTT looks at her – do what?

CATRIN: Don't ask me if I'm alright. Makes you look like a cock.

CATRIN sits, discontented.

CATRIN: D'you know what I hate? I hate how we can't even go out in our own town Friday Saturday cos of all the valley commandoes coming down and smashing the place up.

Like, last Saturday I saw this total fuckin' roider, tattooed head to foot, muscles like fuckin' boulders, moustache out of the Village People – doing a shit in the middle of Nolton Street.

And I said to her, D'you act like that where you come from love?

SCOTT: What she say?

CATRIN: She just made a series of grunts and animal noises, cos that's how they talk. And you know they only come here cos we got poles and they haven't.

SCOTT: Apparently they're all going home. Cos of the recession.

CATRIN: Not fuckin' – Poles as in plumbers. Poles as in dancing. Say you're getting a bit frisky at the end of the night, with us you hop up on the pole and bust your moves. But they got none of that up the valleys. They want to pole dance, they've gotta go out into the street and do it round a street lamp. And that always causes ructions cos half of them still worship electricity as a god so it's like desecrating a holy shrine. *(Off Scott's look.)*

What?

SCOTT: My mum's from the valleys.

CATRIN: And it's amazing, all the words she knows now.

SCOTT: Also – it's Friday tonight.

CATRIN: What d'you want, a prize?

SCOTT: You said, we can't go out Friday Saturday. But it is a Friday. And here we are – out.

CATRIN: And don't fuckin' do that.

SCOTT: Do what?

CATRIN: Don't – take things I've said, and then think about them, and then say things about the things I've said, and try and make me look a twat. Because if you do – that is the actions of a cunt.

Alright?

SCOTT: Alright.

CATRIN: Obviously we go out Friday Saturday. You got to go out Friday Saturday. It's gotta be done. But it's better Thursday Sunday, cos Thursday Sunday the trogs are all back in their holes. I'm not saying Thursday Sunday's any good – it's still shit cos of the townies.

But it's not quite as shit, is all.

SCOTT: What's the difference between a townie, and us?

CATRIN: I dunno, what is the difference between a townie and us?

SCOTT stares at her for a second.

SCOTT: Sorry no that wasn't a joke – I'm actually asking.

CATRIN: A townie is someone you see in town. Cos they're always out. In town.

SCOTT: We're always out in town.

CATRIN: But a townie lives in town. Like, closer to town than we do.

SCOTT: So the rule is, if you live closer to town than us, you're a townie...

CATRIN: Correct.

SCOTT: ...but if you live further away from town than us, you're a valley commando.

CATRIN: *(Like Aleksander the Meerkat.)* Simples.

SCOTT: Bit random, isn't it?

CATRIN: Random is where you pick something, like, at random. This is not that. This is a rule. A rule is the opposite of random.

SCOTT: So what if you moved, into town? Would you be a townie then?

CATRIN: You're doing it again.

SCOTT: What now?

CATRIN: Taking things I say, and then thinking about them, and then saying things about them.

SCOTT: I'm not allowed to think anything, or say anything, about anything you say?

CATRIN: It is the actions of a cunt, and no good can come of it.

SCOTT: Alright, so what if –

CATRIN sings over him, to shut him up.

CATRIN: *(To the tune of 'Twenty-Four Hours From Tulsa'.)* I was only twenty-four hours from Brackla, only one day away from your arms...

She stops singing.

You shut up now?

SCOTT: Looks like it.

She finishes her last shot, then raises the empty tube to SCOTT –

CATRIN: Cheers!

- and chucks it away.

SCOTT: I think you're supposed to say cheers before you drink?

CATRIN: And that's just me: a fuckin' rebel. Got anything else to drink? I bet you have.

SCOTT produces from his briefcase a silver coloured metal hipflask, and hands it to her.

As CATRIN swigs at the hip flask, SCOTT collects the tubes CATRIN has discarded, and puts them away in his briefcase.

CATRIN watches him do this without comment.

Then once SCOTT is settled again, she says

I was thinking about you, the other day. I was thinking – why doesn't Scott get himself a nice boyfriend?

SCOTT looks at her.

I mean properly nice. Because it's gonna be your first time, you don't want some townie cunt leaving you all traumatised. Like me and Lee, my first time I got like really panicky and my head was spinning and I was gonna chuck, and I thought if I try to stop him now, he's gonna go wild, he's just gonna you know hit me and it'll be like a rape thing and I can't hack that so I'm just gonna have to go through with it - and he stops.

He says, you alright?

I don't say nothing cos I'm like – on a knife edge.

He climbs off me, goes what's wrong?

Right then I gag. I clamp my hands over my mouth, not quite quick enough to stop the first wave of cider-vom spraying all over him.

And does he go wild? Does he fuck. He holds my hair, strokes my back while I'm chucking up into his mum's u-bend, and dabs the little strands of sick away from my mouth with pink quilted toilet paper. All this still with a huge hard-on poking out his boxers.

And I'm riding the spasms of puke, thinking - please God, please God, please don't let me wee myself in front of him - because that might be a step too far on a first date.

But then in between retches, I turn, and I look into his eyes - still watering red from the acid in my sick - and I realise, it's alright.

Lee's a really really decent bloke.

He'll accept me for who I am.

And I just – relax.

SCOTT: You let the golden shower flow?

CATRIN: And he's fine with it. Puts my knickers and the bathroom mat in the wash, lends me a pair of his pants.

Even says I look cute in them.

He's that lovely.

And that's what you want, for your first time. A nice boy.

Don't go to Cardiff, cos all the Cardiff gays are hard-faced body fascist bitches, my uncle Teddy says.

And don't go with a rugby lad cos they're awful rough and they do get a bit self-hatey afterwards. Even with girls.

Find yourself a nice, floppy haired boy from say, St Brides, or Wick: someone you actually like, and not just sexually. And you can have a kiss and a cuddle and he'll get the lube and warm it up in his hand so it isn't cold going on and then he'll, very gently, very lovingly, penetrate your bumhole with his throbbing bell end.

Sound appetising?

SCOTT: I'm not freaked out by the thought, if that's what you're trying to do.

CATRIN: I'm not trying to freak you out, lovely. I'm trying to help.

SCOTT: Just I happen not to be a poof.

CATRIN: This is the twenty-first century, Scott. It's actually a bit embarrassing to be that repressed. Fair enough in like the nineteen seventies when it was actually illegal, but every other cunt's a homo these days. Just fucking get over yourself.

SCOTT: Are you serious? Are you not fucking around? D'you seriously think I'm gay?

CATRIN: You know the rugby player Gareth Thomas, Scott?

SCOTT: We've never met, but I'm aware of his work.

CATRIN: You know he used to play a game, then go out, drink till he was full to burst, then run so hard and so long that he chucked up every last drop, and then he would start drinking again on a painfully emptied stomach?

SCOTT: I have heard anecdotage along those lines.

CATRIN: If a fighting 'n' fucking, gap-toothed, balding, ex-ginger like him can turn round and go, fair play lads, I'm a massive muscle-bound queen and have been the whole time, and all that happens is everyone goes, Alfie, we just love you all the more, you great big try-scoring gay bastard – then just maybe, an obvious nancy boy like yourself could man up long enough to stagger out of the closet and into the world of cock which eagerly awaits you.

SCOTT: But I'm not gay.

CATRIN: Scott: you're not a stomach-turner to look at, you're not a complete prick to be with – but you've never been with a girl, ever.

SCOTT: Went out with Becky last year.

CATRIN: As camouflage for your obvious gaysexuality.

SCOTT: I don't go out with anyone, so I'm gay. I go out with Becky - and I'm still gay?

CATRIN: You went out with her for six weeks. You did nothing. And I love her to bits but the girl's a fuckin whore.

SCOTT: We did... a lot.

CATRIN: Yeah you'd snog. Plenty of fumbling in the breastal area – but loads of poofs love tits, Christ knows I've clocked you gawping at my golden globes often enough – but beyond that, not a shag, not a suckoff, not a titwank, not a thighjob, not a footfrig – not even a swift five-finger fuck off the wrist.

(Off SCOTT's look.) We're girls, Scott. We talk.

SCOTT stops. And when he starts again, he's ready to make a confession.

SCOTT: Alright...

CATRIN: Thank God.

SCOTT: What it is,

CATRIN senses it's not the confession she's hoping for.

CATRIN: Please stop hiding from the truth.

SCOTT: When I was twelve, I found out I had a sexually-transmitted disease.

CATRIN: You're a virgin.

SCOTT: Except to my pillow, yes.

CATRIN: How does a person who's never had sex, get a sexually- / transmitted

SCOTT: / When you're a boy, in terms of cocks, you basically just see your own. You don't spend too much time looking at other boys' cocks -

CATRIN: Because, as a gay man, doing so would make you sexually excited.

SCOTT: So you don't know what's normal, and what's not. And looking at my cock, I became convinced there was something wrong.

CATRIN: Is it bendy?

SCOTT: *(Beat.)* Yeah, a bit, but that's not it.

CATRIN: What then?

SCOTT: It doesn't matter.

CATRIN: Is it just microscopically small, but you thought it had actually died and rotted and shrivelled up to nothing?

SCOTT looks at her.

SCOTT: This is serious, alright? This was a serious fuckin'... trauma in my life. And I absolutely believed there was something wrong with me. I knew, if ever a girl did... fish little Scott out into the light, she would take one look, scream, vomit – probably onto little Scott – then scarper.

So I just decided I would never go out with anyone, and would have to die, alone and a virgin.

CATRIN: That's so sad.

SCOTT: Thank you.

CATRIN: Sad as in pathetic, because then you did actually go out with Becky, so what's the story with that – didn't mind if she caught your cock rot?

SCOTT: Well that was... she came round to mine with a bottle of wine and she was looking – like not too much on show but everything quite tight, so you got a good idea what was on offer, and she said, I know you're married to your music,

CATRIN: - but have you got time for a mistress?

SCOTT: Sorry?

CATRIN: I was really proud of her coming up with that. Cos it was actually Rachel's dress she was wearing, the body con one, and we wondered should it be cans cos you're more of a lager drinker, but in the end we thought, no, bottle of wine – bit of class, like.

SCOTT looks at her.

CATRIN: We're girls, Scott. We talk, a lot.

SCOTT: Are you saying, every interaction I've ever had with a girl, her and her mates have planned it out before in exhausting detail?

CATRIN: No.

SCOTT: Are you lying?

CATRIN: ...Possibly.

SCOTT: And you're going to talk about this, aren't you? About me thinking I had VD?

CATRIN: Not necessarily –

SCOTT: Which I haven't, by the way.

CATRIN: - and that's good to hear. But no, actually; a confidence like this should be respected.

SCOTT: Thank Christ for that.

CATRIN: But then – there will no doubt come a time, some point in the future: an evening when drink has been taken, and – I might not be able to resist. So let's say – I'll do my best but yeah, probably three to six weeks and every fucker in town will know.

SCOTT: Brilliant, cheers.

CATRIN: So how come you haven't got VD now then?

SCOTT: Becky's round mine, she's brought this magazine and I'm taking a crafty look, cos it's a magazine for the modern woman, and most of it is telling modern woman she needs to work hard at being a really filthy shag or modern man will piss off and find himself someone that bit sluttier, and obviously I find that material all quite... educational. And there's this article about cocks. Cock do's and don'ts, cock varieties and uses, cock features, cock foibles. And reading it, I realise – the thing I thought was weird and wrong is actually perfectly normal. There is nothing at all wrong with little Scott.

CATRIN: And what did Becky say?

SCOTT: Nothing. I didn't tell her about my imaginary VD.

CATRIN: No, course not. *(Off SCOTT's look.)* Cos if you had, she'd've told me.

SCOTT: Well, of course…

CATRIN: So how come you didn't do it with her, once you knew you weren't foul in the crotch?

SCOTT shrugs.

CATRIN: Christ, I would, just to try it out.

SCOTT: The thing with Becky was

I went out with her because

I knew I could tell her no.

Like if she wanted to do it

I could tell her no, and it wouldn't be a problem.

175

If she liked me, that was nice,

If she was pissed off with me, that was alright too.

And I had to go out with someone like that: someone I could say no to.

Because I was contaminated.

But then I realised I was alright, and I could go out with anyone.

Like someone I properly liked.

So I dumped her.

CATRIN: When you say, 'then', you mean…

SCOTT: That day.

CATRIN: Oh my God.

SCOTT: It's like pulling off a plaster. Do it quick, before you think about it.

CATRIN: All men are fucking psychopaths, I swear to Christ.

SCOTT: *(Beat.)* How's that, sorry?

CATRIN: You're on about dumping Becky –

SCOTT: Dumping. Not killing and dismembering.

CATRIN: You're talking about dumping my friend, like it was nothing.

SCOTT: Not nothing, but – you know.

CATRIN: Was she upset?

SCOTT: Yeah, course.

CATRIN: Did you give a toss?

SCOTT: Yeah, but – you go out with people, some point you're gonna get dumped.

CATRIN: Oh my God – have you ever thought of becoming a relationship counsellor? Or maybe like a religious leader? Cos that is so much fuckin' insight you've changed the way I'm gonna look at the world forever.

SCOTT: I'm saying, it's gonna happen. Relationships end. Which means someone's got to end them.

CATRIN: Alright one time, me and Lee were having an argument –

SCOTT: 'Bout what?

CATRIN: And I said it was over and

SCOTT: You finished with him?

CATRIN: I said I was finishing with him, cos I was pissed off – and he folded up. Like all the bones had come out of him. He was rolling on his back. Grabbing at his guts like it actually, physically hurt. And I thought – that is what love is.

SCOTT: Is it?

CATRIN: I thought this guy properly loves me.

And I had no idea,

Till I saw him choking too much to even cry.

SCOTT: Fucking hell.

CATRIN: Breathe a word and I will slice you up, swear to God.

SCOTT doesn't say anything.

CATRIN: Lee loves me so much, he literally can't go on without me.

And that's why he sent you after me. He gets scared when I get angry, cos –

SCOTT: - cos you might finish it.

CATRIN: Just in my anger, like. Not for real. So when I lose it, he runs off. Or I do. And he never comes after me, he doesn't dare. But he sends his poofpal to look after me, cos he's that much of a sweetheart.

Pause.

SCOTT: Didn't know you two'd ever broken up.

CATRIN: We didn't.

SCOTT: But for a bit

CATRIN: For like ten seconds

SCOTT: I never thought you two argued even, you always seem so / just happy

CATRIN: / Which shows what a twat you are. Everyone argues.

SCOTT: I wouldn't know.

CATRIN: It's part of a healthy relationship.

SCOTT: Never seemed healthy when my mum and dad rowed.

CATRIN: There's healthy ways and unhealthy ways.

SCOTT: And you and Lee argue in healthy ways.

CATRIN: Yup.

SCOTT: How d'you know the difference?

CATRIN: Well like your dad used to smack your mum about?

SCOTT: *(Beat.)* Yes he did.

CATRIN: That's pretty fucking unhealthy.

Pause.

SCOTT: So… you and Lee argue a lot then?

CATRIN: No.

SCOTT: But every now and again.

CATRIN: Yeah.

SCOTT: Like how much?

CATRIN: Like a normal amount.

SCOTT: Every week, every day, every hour…

CATRIN: It doesn't even matter how much. They've done research, and there's a ratio. For every act of anger, five acts of kindness. And they have proved, it doesn't matter how many actual fights you have; so long as you make up with five times as many acts of kindness, you're alright.

SCOTT: Where'd you read that, on the web?

CATRIN: On the web and in an actual book by an actual psychologist, actually. It's like a known issue.

SCOTT: So these psychologists say, you could be fighting ten times a day, but so long as you're nice to each other fifty times a day, it doesn't matter.

CATRIN: It actually makes the relationship stronger, if anything.

SCOTT: And was that quite reassuring, to find that out?

CATRIN: Well yeah.

SCOTT: You and Lee argue a lot then, do you?

She doesn't answer immediately.

CATRIN: It's a very passionate relationship. We fight. And then we're nice to each other. Very, very nice, if you get me.

SCOTT: Yeah, I get you.

CATRIN: I wouldn't think you do. Virgin.

SCOTT: So, literally, the two of you fight and then you make sure you do five nice things to make up for it?

CATRIN: Yeah.

SCOTT: How does that work? Say you take him upstairs for a bit of bedroom action, and he gets a bit of hand shandy, a blowie and then a shag – is that three nice things, or one?

She looks at him.

SCOTT: I'm serious. In the relationship stakes I'm a total newb and this seems like a really valuable opportunity to learn from your experience.

CATRIN: Alright. In that situation, I suppose it depends on, does he come? From the handjob, and from the blowjob and from the shag?

SCOTT: No I'm thinking it's all part of one...

CATRIN: Session?

SCOTT: Yeah.

CATRIN: Well then it's one. I'd count that as one nice thing.

SCOTT: So the orgasm is the key.

CATRIN: Lee seems to think so.

SCOTT: And then what, to get you up to five?

CATRIN: Maybe go out get him chips and curry sauce, that'd be one thing.

Then clean it up so he doesn't have to, that'd be another.

Then whatever. Like if he wants to watch a film, watch what he wants not what I want.

And then -

SCOTT: Maybe another shag?

CATRIN: If he's up for it.

SCOTT: And it's like a rule? And you're there, following the rule the whole time, counting up and thinking of new nice things to do?

CATRIN: Yeah.

SCOTT: And what if you fight again, before you've finished your five nice things?

CATRIN: Then you add the next five on.

SCOTT: What – you keep a running total?

CATRIN: You have to.

SCOTT: And what's the total now?

CATRIN: Well, we had a rough patch last week, so – I owe him seventeen. Plus another five cos of this tonight.

SCOTT: Fucking hell...

CATRIN: You gotta work at things, Scott, when it's a proper relationship. 'Course you have.

SCOTT: And then - how will that work when Lee's gone away to uni? Like if you have a fight and then you're not seeing him. Send him some dirty texts? That's gonna get old.

CATRIN: Obviously that'll be different. Cos you don't know what's gonna happen. You go off to uni, you're doing different things, meeting different people. You're gonna change.

SCOTT: Are you?

CATRIN: I mean he is. He's the one who's going.

SCOTT: And then -

CATRIN: And then what?

SCOTT: And then - he might meet someone else.

CATRIN: It could happen.

SCOTT: And you -

CATRIN: I'd be gutted obviously.

SCOTT: Do you think it will happen?

CATRIN: You don't know, do you.

SCOTT: You do a bit. Like if you look at other people. When they go off to uni, usually -

CATRIN: Yeah, I know, they split up.

SCOTT: Yeah.

CATRIN: And I'm ready for that. If it happens.

SCOTT: Well it will happen. Happens to everybody. I can't think of anyone who's stayed together. Think of like, everyone's brothers and sisters of everyone you know... *(He stops.)* Never mind, maybe you'll be the first.

CATRIN: Maybe.

SCOTT: I think you might, actually.

CATRIN: So do I.

SCOTT: Tell you what, it is weird, though –

He leaves it hanging till he has CATRIN's full attention.

CATRIN: What?

SCOTT: You just now, talking about when you finished with Lee – and he had basically a fucking mental breakdown right in front of you. And then you talking about Lee going off to uni and finding someone else –

CATRIN: And I said I'd be gutted.

SCOTT: Yeah you did. You said that. You said it – very calm, very cool. The thought didn't seem to bother you too much.

CATRIN: News just fuckin' in Scott: there's a difference between things actually happening in real life, and thoughts. Obviously if it really happened I'd be in bits.

SCOTT: Obviously. *(Beat.)* Be a bit of a relief, though. Not having to keep a running total of all the nice things you owe him...

CATRIN: All I care about, is Lee being happy, and you know if that turned out to be with someone else then – I'd have to deal with it.

SCOTT: You are saying some very complicated things about your feelings for my best friend.

CATRIN: Feelings are complicated.

SCOTT: I think Lee's feelings about you are very simple.

Stand off.

And then SCOTT makes to leave.

CATRIN: Where you off?

SCOTT: Lee loves you.

He thinks you love him. In a very uncomplicated way.

And if you don't, then – he should know that. So I'm gonna tell him.

CATRIN: What fucking business of it is yours?

SCOTT: His mate. And it's mates before muff, Catrin, every time.

He's still going.

CATRIN: Alright alright alright.

Let's cool it down, shall we?

SCOTT: I'm about as cool as I need to be, thanks.

CATRIN: Will you just listen to me for one second?

SCOTT: I'm listening.

182

CATRIN: Alright.

    Alright.

    Most of the time I feel like I love him, like

    If something bad happened to him I'd die.

    And then sometimes –

SCOTT: Sometimes you hate the fucker?

CATRIN: Cos who even knows?

    How d'you actually tell, if you love someone or not –

SCOTT: Well, that's what they say, in all the films:

    When it's true love, you'll – just not be sure either way.

CATRIN: That is not what they say in all the films.

SCOTT: What d'they say then?

CATRIN: They say

    When it's love,

    You'll know.

SCOTT: Yeah they do. Yeah.

CATRIN: Well, fuck them. Fuck films.

    Lee is so lovely. He's been so lovely to me. And I'm gonna
    stay with him and give him everything I can and then
    when he goes off and he meets someone so much better
    than me, then –

SCOTT: Then –

CATRIN: Then alright. Then fine. Then I'll cry – and I will cry,
    cos it'll fuckin' hurt – but I'll let him go.

SCOTT: And you'll be glad. A little bit.

CATRIN: I'll be glad he's happy, yeah.

    They look at each other.

CATRIN: And he could have a year with me, being happy
    enough, and then find someone better.

    Or you can go tell him all this now, and break his heart.

And for what? For nothing. Just to be a cunt.

SCOTT: Alright.

CATRIN: Alright?

SCOTT: That makes sense.

I'll keep it shut.

CATRIN: Promise?

SCOTT: Oh yeah for definite.

A moment; they're looking at each other.

CATRIN: What?

SCOTT: I love how everyone thinks Lee's this fucking angel.

CATRIN: He's not an angel. He's just nicer than... you, for instance.

SCOTT: You remember the first weekend you got off with him? That beach party, down Rest Bay. We were – fourteen?

CATRIN: That was so not the first time I got off with him...

SCOTT: Well it was the first time I'd been to a beach party.

First time I'd been to the beach since I was little, with my mum.

I turned up in like my jeans, and then just my trunks.

Everyone else had shorts and t-shirts, me there in my itsy-bitsy Speedos, feeling a teeny-weeny bit...

CATRIN: Exposed. Cos someone might see your rotten little willy?

SCOTT: We all got pissed, and you got off with Lee, and everyone ran off to play frisbee. But I couldn't get up cos I was sitting there, with like my t-shirt on my lap, to cover up... my embarrassment.

CATRIN: I don't remember that.

SCOTT: You were pissed.

CATRIN: Or your 'embarrassment' wasn't worth remembering...

SCOTT: You'd come in cut off jeans and a shirt over your swimsuit, and Lee'd worked you out of your shirt and every now and again he'd risk just skimming his hand over your tit, never really touching down on it – and then he slid one of the straps down your shoulder.

Your right shoulder, as I was looking at you.

CATRIN: Fourteen, and my tit hanging out on Rest Bay. That is so shaming.

SCOTT: No. It was just – your bare shoulder. With girls, just how they dress you're gonna see a bit of leg, you're gonna see a good few inches of cleavage, you're gonna see some belly now and again. You can see all that any fuckin' street any night of the week. But a bare shoulder. You only see that when you've slipped a girl's strap down. Or you've pulled her top off over her head. You only see bare shoulder when you're undressing her. And she's letting you.

CATRIN: Bollocks you do. Halter top, boob tube, any kind of strapless dress, you see a bare shoulder...

SCOTT: And all the time I'd been trying not to look at the two of you but I just could not stop staring at your shoulder and – you looked up. And looked at me. And you said -

CATRIN: Don't remember any of this.

SCOTT: You said, "I think Scott wants some. Well tough luck, Scotty dog, cos you're never gonna get it."

And then Lee hauled you up. You were staggering a bit but he led you to this little cranny in the rocks where the two of you could lie down and no-one could see you.

You were in there for about ten minutes. And then you came out. You and the girls decided you wanted to go to the water for a swim. And once you were all just dots in the sea splashing about, Lee leaned over, and he stuck his finger under Damian's nose, and he said, smell that.

And he went round all the boys, making them smell his finger.

CATRIN: Did you? Smell it.

SCOTT: No.

    CATRIN looks at him.

CATRIN: Yeah you did.

SCOTT: Alright then. Yeah I did.

CATRIN: What did it smell of?

SCOTT: *(Not immediately.)* Nothing.

CATRIN: Yeah, cos I never let him finger me on the beach.
    There were fuckin' little kids everywhere.

SCOTT: Thought you didn't remember.

CATRIN: I was just as bad, boasting to the girls about pulling
    a boy from the year above – so what's the difference? No,
    I wouldn't've gone round shoving my hand up the girls'
    noses going 'Way-hey, get a load of the precum on that!'
    – but that's cos women are innately much more fucking
    dignified.

SCOTT: And you go on how you finished with him but then he
    was bawling...

CATRIN: Yeah...

SCOTT: You know they discovered something called feminism
    like fifty years ago and it meant girls could do like bloke
    stuff? And you're so fucking smug cos you think you rule
    now, it never occurs to you boys might've learned a trick
    or two.

CATRIN: The fuck you on about?

SCOTT: You try to dump him – he turns on the waterworks.
    Oldest trick in the book.

CATRIN: No way.

SCOTT: When he starts to go, does he like – turn away?

    Cos he's so ashamed at how vulnerable you make him?

    And does he cover his face with his hands, and you pull his
    hands away – you find you can, even those he's stronger

than you at that moment he is so heart-breakingly weak
that you can overpower him and expose -

Yes!

The tears.

The tears glistening in his never-more-beautiful eyes.

(A beat: and he switches into Star Trek voices.)

Captain! Imminent dumping on the starboard bow!

Deploy the sob shield, Ensign!

Sob shield deployed, sir. Dumping neutralised.

(Back to his voice.)

We're 21st century boys, Catrin. We talk.

And I didn't come out here like Lee's fucking bitch.

CATRIN: What then?

SCOTT: I saw you strop off in a right state and I thought,
someone best go see she's alright, and I looked at Lee
expecting him to shift... he just fucking sat there.

CATRIN: You came after me off your own back?

SCOTT nods.

CATRIN: That is really sweet. That is so sweet, / Scott.

SCOTT: / But it's fine.

He'll go off to uni, you'll just… drift, and it'll all wrap itself
up without any nastiness.

Except

Lee's going to ask you

To marry him.

CATRIN: What?

SCOTT: Not yet. Second his student loan comes in though
– he'll be down Elizabeth Duke for some tasteful yet
affordable sparkle.

The boy you love, wants to marry you.

This must be the happiest day of your life.

She doesn't answer.

SCOTT: Because it's not fair, what you're doing.

It's not fair on Lee you're stringing him along.

It's not fair on you, you're with someone you don't love.

And it's not fair on me.

CATRIN: You?

SCOTT holds out his arm, his palm flat, parallel to the ground.

SCOTT: See that?

CATRIN: Your hand.

SCOTT: And what's it doing?

CATRIN: Just sort of – hovering there.

SCOTT: It's shaking.

CATRIN: I can't see it.

SCOTT: Well it is. A bit. And it is shaking because

Every muscle in my body wants to come over there

Grab you, pull you to the ground

And just fucking devour you, right here, right now.

CATRIN: Oh.

SCOTT: Because I love you, Catrin.

CATRIN: Oh again.

SCOTT: And that's enough, actually.

That's enough to have said those words out loud, looking into your fucking amazing eyes, cos Christ knows I've said them in my head enough times.

Actually I'm lying. It's not enough.

I want you. I want all of you. I want you now and I want you forever.

Actually – that sounded shit – 'I want you now, I want you forever'. That's because it's a line I came up with God knows how many years ago and imagined saying it to you, one day, but now I do it's fucking lame.

What I'm saying is – the reason why I've never been out with anyone, it's not cos I'm diseased, it's not cos I'm a poof. It's cos I've always wanted you. No-one else is worth the effort.

And I would never let you run off into the night because I was scared you were gonna dump me. I would always be there, making sure you're alright.

And I don't care about getting my heart broken because I would take a day an hour one fucking second with you even if it meant being heart-broken the rest of my life.

And I know I'm not good enough for you because you're so / amazing

CATRIN: / I'm not amazing...

SCOTT: You are, you are amazing.

CATRIN: How am I amazing?

SCOTT: *(Struggles for a bit, then.)* I don't know where to start.

I mean look at you.

CATRIN: What about me?

SCOTT: *(Again, struggles: and then.)* You're a sexy witch.

You're magic. And gorgeous. And amazing. And maybe people in this fucking stupid town don't get it but I do, I see how amazing you are and I just hope whatever happens we stay friends always, because I wanna be around to see what fantastic things you're gonna do with your life. And like I say I know I'm not good enough for you but being with you would make me be better, I'd be a better man, for you, every fucking day.

I love you.

I love you Catrin.

And it is so – amazing, to finally say it.

AFTER

Karaoke music starts.

MIKEY: Oi Cat.

Cat you're on.

CATRIN: Now?

MIKEY: Or never. Come on, get over here.

CATRIN sings a couple of verses of 'You Always Hurt the One You Love'.

She gets a little way into it, and then MAGS starts to talk to the audience.

MAGS: Look at you.

Look at you all.

BECKY: Mum.

MAGS: Look at your faces.

BECKY: She gets like this sometimes.

After a drink.

Not a lot you can do. Just have to ride it out.

MAGS: You're waiting for things to go back to normal.

MIKEY: Who's next? Mags? D'you wanna go?

BECKY: Mum, calm it down.

MIKEY: Mags, you'll do a song, everyone else has...

MAGS: Normal's gone now. Wave it goodbye.

Come on, wave with me. Let's all wave good-bye to normal.

Bye-bye! Bye-bye!

Why aren't you joining in?

BECKY: Did it bring us closer?

No. Then yes for a bit.

Then no no no, for a long time.

Then yes. Eventually.

MAGS: The first thing they do when something like this happens –

They look at the family.

What were the... circumstances.

Alright then.

SCOTT: I know it's gonna be horrible. I hope it's gonna be worth it. Love, Scott kiss kiss.

MAGS: People would say to me sometimes – Mags, how come you stuck that husband of yours so long's you did?

I'll say, well, he was funny. Always telling jokes. Always raising a smile.

People say, what kind of jokes, Mags?

Well... he'd say, I call my wife treasure – cos she looks like something you dug up.

He'd say, I call my wife the queen – cos she looks like a bloke in drag.

He'd say I call my wife pumpkin – cos I'd like to take the top of her head off, scoop out the inside for soup, then stab her in the face where her eyes should be.

And I would fall for a silver tongue, when I was younger.

BECKY: Message one of forty five. Home in twenty. Can you put the oven on? Maybe chuck some burgers in?

MAGS: People say, do they know, Mags? Your kids.

Do they know what a bastard he was?

Why don't you tell 'em? You should tell them. They got a right to know.

Not a chance.

Those kids don't get much from me but what I can, I give them.

BECKY: We've got nothing in.

MAGS: And what I give them is nothing,

Compared to what they give me.

BECKY: We got nothing in, mum. For tea.

MAGS: That was his favourite thing, after he passed his test.

He could bomb down the beach in the dead of night

Walk in the waves, looking up at the deep dark sky

And the cold light of all those stars.

Absolutely loved it.

SCOTT: Just call if you need me.

MAGS: He'd always go on about how much blacker the sky was

How much brighter the stars,

Just those couple of miles out of town.

BECKY: We're at Tuskers till two, the Roof till four,

Then we hold out at the York till six.

Those last couple of hours I can't say too much about, except

I spent them parked on the lap of a tearful fortysomething,

Who kept the drink coming while his ring and middle and index

Went about the old up and under: under the skirt,

Up the thigh, till his nail scratched knicker and I leaned in and said

What was your daughter's name again?

Cos maybe I know her?

Like from school?

MAGS: It's happening again.

It's happening, now.

SCOTT: Let me know how it went.

CATRIN: Lee ran, jumped in his mini,

And he was gone.

And I am never gonna be free of this.

BECKY: I was walking home.

I these flip-flops on, cos

The heel'd come off my shoe.

I remember the step I took wrong, off the kerb outside the Roof

And this crack, and my foot twisting and giving way

And for a second I thought fuck, I've broken my fucking ankle or something

But then I saw my ankle was alright, it was my shoes that were fucked

And even though the shoes were basically my favourites

I didn't really mind, cos I was just super-relieved I hadn't broken my ankle.

I even chucked the shoes in a bin –

Like just to show how totally alright I was about it?

SCOTT: I love you.

I can't believe I get to write that.

BECKY: Later I thought, that was fuckin' stupid cos you can get a heel fixed.

And later again someone said to me aw Bex look your fuckin' foot's bleedin'.

And it was, from like glass or something somewhere.

And I looked and there was this trail of little red blotches on the floor, following me around,

Showing me where I'd been.

MAGS: Here's what really kills me.

Here's – one of the things that kills me.

All that night I'd just been fannying about worrying the electric was gonna go off.

I'd had twenty on a token and put it through but

The bastard didn't work. The bloke in the garage said

Can't help you love, you've put it through, I can see the mark.

All I could do was buy another token and hope that one worked.

All I needed for that... was money.

BECKY: Message six of forty-five. Yes, course I will, you've only told me like a million times.

MAGS: I'd been through the house like a robber and turned up maybe eighty pence in change

But then I found a scratchcard Lee'd given me Mother's Day

And it only went and turned out to be a winner.

But then there's nowhere open I can collect on a scratchcard,

Then get back to the garage to buy another electric token before it shuts at ten.

So I'm into the Bells and asking Huw not for a lend but

A swap, cos a winning scratchcard is basically money in the hand

But Huw-

BECKY: Mum?

SCOTT: Cat will you just give me a call?

BECKY: Mum.

There's nothing in the house, shall I go for chips?

MAGS: Yeah, alright, go on.

BECKY: So do you want a piece of fish, with yours?

MAGS: I'm telling you, now, about him.

And then it all comes over me: the memory of him.

How can it be, I remember him

Even when I'm remembering him?

BECKY: Or will just chips be enough?

MAGS: I hear the couple over the road,

    Ken and Jan. Lovely, both of them.

    Ken's a bit older. Got cancer in the throat and

    They're just letting it go, so he can have

    What time he's got, you know.

    I hear Jan helping him into the car, and then

    She's saying – are you sure you feel like going?

    It's everywhere. It's too much.

BECKY: Mum?

MAGS: Bex. Love. Get chips, don't get chips,

    But what the fuck you asking me for?

BECKY: Cos you know the street pastors?

    If you've been out here, you know 'em.

    I'd always thought the street pastors were

    Just a bunch of cunts really. Cos

    They're there, in their little street pastor gang

    With their little street pastor anoraks

    With 'STREET PASTOR' written on them.

    Like they're so fuckin' pleased with themselves

    And they just make you feel – you know

    They're looking at you and they just think

    You're a stupid drunk slag, but then

    I went up to them, gave it some chat, I said

    I broke my shoes and then I chucked 'em in the bin and now my foot's bleedin.

    And they gave me these flip-flops?

    For nothing like, just handed them over.

And I was walking home with

The flip-flips all squishy under my feet and thinking

They're alright, really, the street pastors.

I mean, it's fuckin' sad that people have got nothing better to do

Than tramp round town on a Saturday, not even getting drunk but

I thought they were cunts, and they're not.

Fair play, I was wrong about that.

And then a police car went by me.

And then a ambulance.

And I thought –

Not a thing.

Cos when d'you ever have a night out here,

And not see police, or ambulance?

Fuckin' never, is when.

SCOTT: Cat will you just give me a call cos

Someone said something a bit... weird.

BECKY: I saw the police,

And the ambulance,

That were going to him.

And I didn't think a thing:

I was pissed.

MAGS: I'm in the Bells with a winner in my hand and this baldy fucker at the bar says,

I'll have the scratchcard off you.

And he holds out a fiver.

I say, three the same on a scratchcard's a tenner.

He says, I know. But a fiver's all I'm offering love,

Take it or get to fuck.

And I take it.

And I run,

So my son can bring his girl home to a house with the lights still on

I get to the garage at nine fifty seven:

The bastard place is closed anyway.

And this is it, starting to happen now –

I come awake somewhere round half four

When I hear Lee start his mini and the headlights flick full on

And everything in the lounge is white light or deep shadow

Then Lee pulls away, and dark takes the room again,

And out the window I see Catrin, standing on the pavement,

Crying.

And I think, good for you, son.

I know.

BECKY: I put a couple of painkillers to fizz in a pint of water

Took them down in six or seven burpy gulps,

Sat still and propped upright to try and keep them all down and

And I must've fell asleep like that.

When I woke I got my phone hoping for a message

From this boy I snogged between Tuskers and the Roof and -

And there was.

A message.

But from my mum.

It said

Lee's dead.

I thought

Fuckin' brilliant.

Cos I thought like it meant

He'd done something and mum

Was gonna finally, totally kill him this time.

SCOTT: Okay, panic over. He's alright.

MAGS: He came off in a lane, on the way to Monknash.

Wasn't wearing a seatbelt.

Was thrown clear of the vehicle.

Apparently, a taxi came past only minutes after. But

Apparently, the driver didn't see Lee and reported

A car, crashed and abandoned.

The despatcher assigned it a low priority.

And it being a Saturday, and the emergency services

Tied up dealing with twenty thousand drunk bastards in town.

It took the police two hours to get round to checking it out.

Once they were actually in attendance at the scene

Apparently it took them thirty or so seconds

To find my son.

One officer began to administer emergency first aid

While her partner radioed for an ambulance.

They say he was probably unconscious, those two hours.

They say it like that should be a comfort.

Better he be unconscious, than be lying there,

Hurt and alone.

SCOTT: He's at casualty in the Princess of Wales, he's gonna be alright. But please call.

I don't want anything I just wanna look after you.

MAGS: And that night.

> That last night.

> Those last hours and minutes while my son was here –

> All that fuss. About the fucking electric.

BECKY: Half asleep I was thinking –

> Say something really happened,

> No way'd you just text, Lee's dead.

> You'd never just – say the words, and say nothing else.

> You'd say something more:

> To try and make it better?

MAGS: And that bloody taxi driver.

> If he'd just got out his car.

> If he'd just looked.

SCOTT: Oh God.

BECKY: But what?

MAGS: I hope he feels like shit.

> Not being funny but, I mean that.

BECKY: What words could you say?

SCOTT: Cat I just heard.

MAGS: And if I can run about like a nutter cos of the electric,

> Why couldn't I run out, throw myself in front of the car?

> Grab a knife from the kitchen and slash his tyres?

> Loads of mad things I could've done

> That would've saved him.

BECKY: Message nineteen of forty-five. If you're in Boots, can you get me some deodorant? Ran out today and my pits are hanging.

CATRIN: I went to my room like a naughty child.

> My mum brought me cream of tomato soup, scrambled eggs and toast

– food for when you're sick –

She didn't come in.

Just knocked on my door, left the plates on the landing.

After three days I turned on my phone and

It was full.

More messages than it could take.

All of them saying –

SCOTT: I wanna be here.

I am here. I'm here for you.

Just call. Just text. Just –

I'm here.

CATRIN: – just saying sweet, and useless things.

BECKY: I remember staring at my ankle once –

About ten years of age, this was.

The veins there are really close,

Just below the ankle bone.

And sometimes, you can see your pulse.

Have a look. Come on, have a look now.

See it?

That bump, bump, bumping, in the skin.

It's barely anything.

It's you.

Because if that stops.

Then you will too.

And I couldn't get my head around it.

Everything I think and everything I say

And everything I do and everything I'll wish I'd done

All gets wiped out

If that flicker under the skin ever stops.

It's fuckin' ridiculous.

I remember the first time I did it the bloke saying

It feels soooo fucking good being inside you.

And first I was thinking – alright mate, you got what you want

So give the cheesy chat a rest, why not?

But then thinking –

Hold on, you're not.

You're not inside me.

You're just in my body.

MAGS: The pinging stops,

They switch off the machines

You're waiting

For him to cough

For his eyes to open

For the nurses to call the doctors and

The doctors to start bang bang banging on his chest.

You're looking ahead to the time

When you can cast your mind back and say

That was a close one.

Son, you had me bloody worried then.

These things you're waiting for, don't happen.

A nurse brings you tea and they get on

With tidying up, tidying round you,

Tidying away.

And you wonder what it is that's wrong

What it is that's bothering you and

It's the clock. Ticking on the wall,

When it should have stopped.

And every tick is taking you further away

From the time when your son was alive.

BECKY: Message twenty-two of forty-five. I know. I'm sorry.

CATRIN: He didn't tell.

I saw his mum and

MAGS: He said, you and him'd had a fight.

And it was all his fault,

And he wanted to see you, so the two of you could make it up.

SCOTT: He was gonna use it.

Drips in his arm and machines pinging away his heart's beat –

He was planning how he'd guilt you into going back out with him.

And I would never say that. If things were normal, if this was a normal conversation.

But it's true. I'm sorry.

I'm not sorry, actually.

MAGS: He softened me. For definite.

Because I would never say words like poo, or do-doos.

Thought that was pathetic: a grown-up saying 'poo'.

I would call a shit a shit, never a 'number two'.

But then he was born and I could never say

Look, he's still got shit in the little fat folds of his thighs,

Best give him another wipe.

Couldn't do it.

BECKY: Mum, shall I go and get chips?

CATRIN: He was forgiving me. Was he?

He was letting me off. Was he?

That's why he didn't tell everyone

What a fucking bitch I'd been.

Wasn't it?

SCOTT: Or – and I'm just putting this forward as another way
of thinking about things

Say he'd ploughed into a gang of kids walking home from
town?

Say he killed one of them – we'd've been thinking, selfish
cunt.

Well – I'm thinking it now.

Letting you off? Like fuck.

MAGS: Has he still got poo-poo on his little legs? Aw, poor
little sweetheart...

SCOTT: It wasn't up to him to let you off. Selfish cunt.

MAGS: Mummy clean it up for you. There we are...

CATRIN: And on the third day I got up

And found Scott.

And we got drunk.

Obviously.

SCOTT: Shall we then?

CATRIN: D'you wanna?

SCOTT: I'm just – you know. Is this the... moment?

CATRIN: What else is it the moment for, Scott?

SCOTT: I don't – what d'you mean? We could do anything.
Drink more, watch a film...

CATRIN: Watch a fucking film? Will I – sit and watch a film?
D'you fucking think?

SCOTT: I mean, we can do whatever you want.

CATRIN: I can't do what I want.

SCOTT: What do you want, that you can't do?

CATRIN: I want to make it not have happened.

MAGS: In the olden days they used to have loads of kids.

BECKY: She just went to pieces.

I mean: of course.

MAGS: I always thought they had loads of kids cos in the olden days

Loads of kids died, and you wanted to have a few left

To look after you when you were getting on.

But that's not it.

They had loads of kids in the olden days cos, when one dies

It's only the others keep you going.

BECKY: Shall I get you some chips, if I'm going?

CATRIN: I might need... a bit of space, for / a bit

SCOTT: / Is that... the best thing?

CATRIN: Yes it is.

SCOTT: Is that the best thing, to be / on your own

CATRIN: / Yeah it is though.

SCOTT: I could just, be with you, be there, not saying / anything –

CATRIN: / Yes it fucking is the best thing, for me to be on my own.

Alright?

BECKY: Shall I get you some chips and a piece of fish or a sausage or a Peters Pie or what?

MAGS: And it's happening now.

It's happening, again.

SCOTT: We used to go for chips every dinner time.

We'd cross Merthyr Mawr Road, then cut in the back of the tennis club,

Then by the side of the river, into town.

There was a chip shop with a pool hall above.

It's a rock club now.

You may know it.

We'd bomb down there and wander back

Stopping on the bridge, sitting on the stones in Newbridge Fields for a bit

With chip cones steaming off vinegar in our hands.

One day you said

D'you think you go on after you die?

Or is that just it, once you're gone you're gone?

You said, it'd be handy to know either way.

But so far no-one in history had figured it out.

And you said

Well then boys.

Looks like it's down to us.

We decided that whoever ghosted first should return and

Using our poltergeist powers turn off a light

On October the tenth, at ten o'clock precisely.

The tenth of the tenth at ten.

All the tens, you said.

Never gonna forget that, are we?

We spat in our hands and shook: I should Welly's hand,

Welly shook Rob's hand, Rob shook Huw McArthur's,

Huw McArthur shook yours, and then you shook mine.

And shaking spit round the gang

Sealed our oath –

That for the rest of our lives, on the tenth of the tenth, at ten

We would all be looking out

For a message from the dead, in the dying of an electric light.

And then we all had to finish our chips eating with the wrong hands

Cos our right hands were covered in spit.

BECKY: Message twenty-nine of forty-five. No. Thanks.

MAGS: I would pray for disasters and every night

The news answered my prayers.

Have you seen this, love?

BECKY: What's that, mum?

MAGS: 'Glacier breaks off from Antarctic

Raising global warming fears'.

BECKY: You're not going to eat anything, then?

MAGS: Terrorism, floods, the collapse

Of the international financial system,

I lapped it all up. Because if my son lived

Seventeen good years and then died,

Just in time to miss the end of the world,

That would make sense.

SCOTT: And yeah

That first year

On the tenth of the tenth, at ten

I was on the look-out.

Course I told myself I was

Honouring him

Remembering him

I sat with every light in the house blazing and

Waited for my spit-brother to show.

None of us had said but I talked to Huw and Welly and Rob after and

They'd all done the same.

My sister said

You'll get a message from him, in the end.

Course you will.

She said, if you wait enough years one of you

Will have a bulb go or a fuse blow

And maybe it won't happen at ten o'clock but at ten to,

But of that'll still count cos it was all about the tens.

You'll get your sign

If you want it enough to sit tight till it comes.

But I sort of think

I sort of thought

If a bulb went or a fuse blew

And it happened at exactly the right time

You were waiting for a sign –

- then that would be a sign. Wouldn't it?

Like if now, we say it's ten o'clock,

On the tenth of tenth –

I know it's not but if we pretend

- and if the lights go off right now,

At the very second we're pretending then

That would be a message. Right?

Like even if they go off cos

Someone trips on a wire or

Someone presses a wrong button.

That'd still be something.

Like even if they go off now

Cos someone listening switches them off deliberately

That would still be something, wouldn't it?

Like this light here.

If someone switched that light off now,

That would tell us something,

For definite.

BECKY: Message thirty-six of forty five. Sunday.

MAGS: The funeral... well at the funeral, you know what to do.

But then after...

You hear of people, when they lose someone

Keeping their rooms like they were?

So at first I do that.

But it just looks like a room no-one lives in:

Dust in drifts, dirty socks sitting on the floor,

A mug with an inch of coffee in the bottom, that dries up

And then furs up with mould and

Everytime I look at it

I can't help but think

What must be happening

To his beautiful body

Down there, in the ground...

BECKY: I'm gonna go put some flowers.

D'you wanna...

You feel like coming?

MAGS: I decide to just be normal.

Like things were still normal.

I charge in, pull back the curtains, push open the window

Gather up the socks and boxers and t-shirts and

I'm two steps from the washing machine and –

BECKY: You can't tell. Like mostly those first few months she was just

Very quiet, didn't get out of bed, didn't wash, didn't want to eat

But then one time I come home and found her

On the phone ordering these like... bags she'd seen on the telly,

Like JML vacuum bags and she was really hyper –

MAGS: They've got an airtight seal!

BECKY: Okay. I understand. What d'you need a bag

With an airtight seal for, mum?

MAGS: For this!

BECKY: She had this bin bag. Tied at the top.

With all Lee's dirty clothes in.

MAGS: Now of course the bin bag's just

A temporary measure, when we get these

JML vacuum bags we'll be able to look at the clothes

And keep them sealed so they won't lose –

BECKY: - the smell of him.

MAGS: And I was that close to washing them!

BECKY: So yeah some progress and then sometimes

Right back to step zero.

SCOTT: It was the third year after he died, a message finally came through.

There was a lamp on the table next to me and

At ten o'clock precisely on the tenth of the tenth I realised

The bulb was flickering. And it occurred to me if you could slow down time

What looked like a flicker would actually be the light going off and on

Just really quickly, like two thousand times a minute.

And then I realised I didn't need to slow down time.

Because I realised I could see quickly enough to count the flickers.

I realised the flickers were a form of Morse code.

I stared at the bulb for maybe two and a quarter hours

Till I was sure I had the pattern of flickers right,

Then I spent the rest of the night on the net, deciphering the message

And what that flickering light bulb said was

Mate: when you're gone

You are fucking gone.

And that was me told.

BECKY: Message forty. Okay, you're forgiven, but I am gonna do some nasty stuff to you later

to make up for it, you sexy bitch. Kiss kiss kiss Lee.

Message forty-one. Mum. I think I just sent you a text for Cat. Really really really sorry.

CATRIN: I didn't leave town.

It's wasn't like a big thing, 'Catrin Leaves Town'.

I went to stay with my dad, and that

Was easier.

Cos here you had everybody putting on their sad faces

And watching what they say

And it's easier,

To not deal with that.

And of course I come home to see mum just

I don't go into town.

Don't really call anyone.

And that's easier. For me.

And soon enough people stop calling me, so

Seems like it's easier for them as well.

SCOTT: It is a bit embarrassing – you leave town

For the bright lights and big city,

And you get as far as... Cardiff.

But it's got a stadium, a castle,

A rift in the space-time continuum –

What more d'you want?

BECKY: I talked to one of these counsellors, CRUSE, for bereavement?

I told them what she was like and they said,

Yeah that's all normal. Which didn't fuckin' help.

And I said, so when's it gonna get better then, and

What they said was, you can't expect any improvement

For at least the first year.

I said, are you fucking kidding me?

They said, the first year, it's just reminders.

Like, the first Christmas without him. The first birthday. The first summer...

MAGS: The first breath.

BECKY: All these really big markers.

MAGS: The first night. The first morning.

BECKY: And each one of them, you can't help but think, this is the first time we've done this,

Without the person who isn't there.

Which makes sense if you think about it.

MAGS: The first time you fill a kettle

For the first cup of tea.

The first time you put the rubbish out

And there's no volcano of crap spilling from his bin.

The first time a light bulb goes, and he's not there

To fetch down a spare from on top the cupboard.

The first time you get an official letter for him and have to phone them up.

The time you realise the letters for him

Have stopped.

The first time someone goes, how many kids've you got

And without thinking, you get the answer wrong.

The first time snow falls, and you think

How he still loves snow now, just like he did when he was a kid

And you hope he'll never lose that no matter how old he gets.

The first time you see the stars.

The first time you see the stars, on any particular night.

BECKY: Message forty-five of forty-five. Yeah will do see you later.

MAGS: The first time someone goes, how many kids've you got

And you get the answer right.

BECKY: So I didn't expect her to get better, that first year.

And she didn't.

MAGS: The first time... you get a new phone.

BECKY: You could just copy them out.

212

MAGS: It's not the same.

BECKY: How's it not the same?

MAGS: I can't carry bits of paper round with me.

BECKY: Um... but obviously you can.

MAGS: I want them on my phone. So I can read them, on my phone. I'm not sitting on the bus getting out bits of paper like some / mad woman...

BECKY: / Alright, so... what do we do?

MAGS: I forward the messages to you. And then, when I've got the new / phone...

BECKY: / Aren't they all on your sim anyway?

MAGS: Are you trying to finish me off?

   Are you?

   (Beat.)

   When I've got the new phone, you send them back to me.

BECKY: I spend a night sending my mum

   Forty-five text messages from my dead brother,

   Her dead son.

   There's a lot of that sort of thing.

MAGS: Thank you. Thank you, for being a help.

BECKY: Like afterwards they gave us his stuff back.

   Stuff from the car?

   He'd got it for two hundred quid from a bloke in Wildmill

   And it broke down loads, so he always had like blankets,

   A bottle of water, some of those little snack bars made out

   Of seeds and nuts.

   And tapes. Cos there was only a tape player, and a bust radio.

   And we didn't have any tapes but

   Dad had left thousands of tapes behind

And in all those, a few alright ones.

We would pack loads of us in Lee's mini

He'd drive us to Southerndown, Monknash,

And we'd sing all these old songs, of dad's.

BECKY sings 'Regret' by New Order – possibly with SCOTT and CATRIN backing her up.

Mikey, alone, echoes a line.

MIKEY: You used to be a stranger

Now you are mine…

SCOTT: And once I was in Cardiff I started going out.

I'd get so pissed I'd lose my friends, usually my phone, very often my wallet,

Then pick my way home at dawn, navigating

By the spires of the stadium,

And it was fine.

But then this one time

I got jumped.

And the guy had a knife.

So I handed over my phone, my wallet.

Carried on walking along the embankment.

Then

Ran back after him,

Caught the fucker under the railway bridge and

He was maybe – fifteen? And he could not fucking believe it

When I came charging at him and then

Back at my flat

Chucking my shirt in the bin, I thought –

BECKY: No. No you're right.

I talk a lot about my mum.

Not much about Lee.

Funny that.

MIKEY: The conversation's tailing off, and I let it.

I let it die and she's still standing there, getting

A bit nervous, looking round, glancing at the bar

Glancing back to me then to the pub's wall-mounted plasma screen,

Suddenly transfixed by the subtitling on Sky Sports News.

I leave it oh till it hurts and then

I say to her

CATRIN: I start seeing this guy and

With most people, you'll wind round to a conversation

About history: who was your first, how did it go... how did it end?

There's none of that with this guy.

MIKEY: I say

What the fuck you doing still talking to me for?

CATRIN: He's a bit of a prick, to be honest.

MIKEY: Ninety-nine girls out a hundred

You hit them with a line like that,

And they're gonna run.

But you know what?

I've had ninety-nine girls out of a hundred,

Including your sister, your girlfriend and your mum,

And I am bored with them.

I'm well past it.

I want that one girl

Who you can look right in the eye, and say

What the fuck you doing still talking to me?

And she'll stand there, and take it.

Because that girl – will take anything.

CATRIN: Actually, he's a total prick.

And a prick is all I can handle, so – fair enough.

MIKEY: I am going to ruin you.

I am going to ruin you for all other men,

Because after you've had a night

Like we're gonna have tonight

You are never gonna be satisfied with

Any other fucker's limp-dicked effort again.

CATRIN: We get back to mine – and he's so pissed

He collapses. Spark out.

MIKEY: You might think talking the big talk

And delivering nothing makes me look a twat:

But actually, you're the twat.

You're the kind of bloke whose girlfriend I brutally shag

While you're off on some fucking stag do.

Because falling asleep on her toilet floor -

It's an assertion of dominance.

I am laying the groundwork for

Some pretty fucking avant-garde sexual experimentation.

CATRIN: I sort of change my mind and tell him I've got my period,

And he says, but we could just cuddle, couldn't we?

MIKEY: One second you're all – I'm gonna put whatever I want

In whatever hole I want, and you're gonna love it.

Next second it's – can we have a little cuddle?

They never know what they're gonna get.

Keeps 'em on edge.

CATRIN: I lean in, kiss him, hard,

Bang my teeth on his lips and push my tongue

Right to the back of his mouth.

He staggers back, looks a little bewildered.

MIKEY: I wake up on the settee and there's a torn out page of Cosmopolitan

A biro scrawl says 'Where we are', and gives an address, a little map

Showing the nearest bus stop. And a phone number.

The phone number is crossed out. Next to it, the message,

"Don't call."

Which means, do call.

So I don't.

So she calls me.

'Course she fuckin' does.

CATRIN: And one of those days things are rattling round my head

I call him and at the end of the night, the bouncers are circling, we

Shuffle off for the next place or maybe home and I realise

I've left my scarf behind, and the pub is locked up.

MIKEY: Now – *(Picks someone.)* you, in that situation,

You would probably say, oh I'll buy a new scarf for you,

And you'd think you were being a smooth fucker.

But you know what you are, actually?

You're a domestic contents insurance policy.

Boor-ring!

CATRIN: I hear him touch down in the beer garden, then

Run inside the pub, bouncers shouting then –

MIKEY: Got it!

CATRIN: He scrambles back up the beer garden wall,

My scarf streaming from his hand, and

He jumps

MIKEY: A stunt like this, it's all about showing a girl

You're not like anyone she's ever met before. You're spontaneous,

Wild, uncontrollable. Time spent with you will always be an adventure.

CATRIN: He flips mid-air, and comes down – sideways.

And screams.

I'd never heard a man scream like that before.

But apparently it really really hurts, when you break your pelvis.

MIKEY: I can tell you, it definitely, definitely does hurt, yeah.

MAGS: D'you know what the kids do to remember him?

BECKY: Halloween, we said we'd go out,

In Lee's memory.

MAGS: They go on the piss.

Obviously.

BECKY: We'd do it every year, we'd all come back

On Halloween or the weekend after and meet in Jaggers,

Which was Lee's favourite club,

And it'd be like – a positive thing, you know?

Celebrating his life, and

Keeping his memory bright because

If people still remember you, then

In a way, you're still alive.

SCOTT: And we do that, the first year,

And yeah it's great seeing everyone.

BECKY: Not everyone.

SCOTT: Catrin doesn't come.

BECKY: But other people do.

And it's not depressing or sad, we're all making it really positive.

Cos that's what Lee would've wanted.

SCOTT: But then Jaggers burns down.

So we get the message round, for the next year

Move the party up the hill to Bowlers but then

That closes down, and they knock it down,

BECKY: So then it's meet in the Roof cos even though Lee said

He hated the Roof he was there like three four times

A week from the time he was sixteen on and

SCOTT: It's the fifth year

When people start making excuses.

BECKY: Not excuses then. But like

Rhi's in Australia, Sarah's in Nottingham,

Steph's in Derby, Welly's in Aberdeen

– Geoff's in Los Angeles, for Christ's sake.

Louise is still there but she works in casualty at the Princess of Wales

And she's on shift that Saturday.

And then it seems like everyone else has got kids, and they

Might come out, but it depends on mums or sisters or babysitters.

SCOTT: Five years.

And every fucker forgets.

BECKY: They don't forget.

SCOTT: They don't forget

But the memory isn't enough

To move them, any more.

CATRIN: And first there are the paramedics, and the ambulance,

Then the hospital, the doctors and nurses

And then – they send the prick home.

MIKEY: Jesus Christ, talk about disco damage.

CATRIN: So... give me a ring, you need anything?

MIKEY: What, are you –

CATRIN: What?

MIKEY: Are you going?

CATRIN shrugs.

MIKEY: Did you just – shrug?

CATRIN shrugs again.

MIKEY: I can't walk, I can't do anything and

You're just shrugging at me?

CATRIN: Did you want me to do something?

MIKEY: Yes!

CATRIN: Alright.

Say what it is, then.

MIKEY: I thought you were gonna

You know.

CATRIN: No I don't.

MIKEY: Look after me?

Beat.

CATRIN: Did you?

MIKEY: Well, duh.

CATRIN: And... why?

MIKEY: Because we're –

You and me, we're –

CATRIN: It gets so that sometimes

I go into the toilet and just pretend

To be having a dump so I can take

A few minutes away from him, and then

I hear his voice

I get to know the way he says my name

MIKEY: 'Cat-rin?'

CATRIN: With the 'rin' bit rising at the end.

I know it and I hate it because

It means another fucking thing

He wants doing.

And when I was little I remember thinking

Love was this fluffy... cloud.

This feeling

Just being really happy all the time.

But lying on that cold, damp, slimy bathroom floor

Wanting nothing but to just be allowed to stop -

There was this space inside me

Something empty where all the lovely fluffy feelings

Should be.

And as the weeks went by I realised

This empty place was filling up.

There was something hard and heavy, in my guts.

And that hard and heavy thing

Would not let me walk away.

MIKEY: I lay on that settee

Felt all those hours in the gym working up

My biceps, my triceps, my quads

Going to nothing as my body turned pale and soft.

Nothing existed outside that lounge.

On telly I watched any live event I could find

- footy, show jumping, curling, even

The Pembrokeshire County Show and the Llangollen

International Eisteddfod, just to reassure myself

There was still a world out there.

And Catrin –

CATRIN: Oh, fuck...

MIKEY: - Cat?

CATRIN: Alright, alright...

MIKEY: Cat-rin?

CATRIN: Yes, what?

MIKEY: I was calling and calling.

CATRIN: Sorry, needed a dump.

MIKEY: Right.

Okay then.

CATRIN: It seemed like forever. Apparently it was only a
couple of months -

MIKEY: Okay. Let's do this.

CATRIN: And then he had to learn to walk again.

MIKEY: Fuck. Fuck. Fuckity fuck.

CATRIN: And obviously that hurt.

MIKEY: Bollocksy bollocking shit.

CATRIN: And I would watch him.

MIKEY: Bum balls willies tits poo!

CATRIN: In agony.

MIKEY: Can I stop?

CATRIN: Just do one more set.

MIKEY: The physio said, do them twice a day.

CATRIN: And?

MIKEY: That'll be ten times today, I do them again?

CATRIN: Don't you want to get better?

MIKEY: Course!

CATRIN: Well then...

MIKEY: Once I got my legs back, I wanted to use them.

    I went down the gym once or twice but it was just

    Lifting these blocks of metal up and down,

    I wanted to be out, looking around at everything

    Looking down at my legs, pushing me through the world

    Down streets, through parks –

    (To Catrin.)

    Made it to the barrage today.

CATRIN: Is it?

MIKEY: Am I babbling? I'm babbling a bit, aren't I?

    It's these fuckin' endorphins.

    He's just smiling at her.

CATRIN: What?

MIKEY: This is you.

This is all you've done this.

I don't just mean just my bones

CATRIN: Could you... give me a sec, yeah?

MIKEY: Cat?

CATRIN: Yeah just popping to the shop for milk...

MIKEY: And I thought that was a bit weird.

And I then I heard her car door opening and I thought –

She's obviously not going to the shop.

I heard her car start.

MAGS: It's happening now.

MIKEY: I sat down.

I thought well fair enough I see your point.

MAGS: It's happening again.

MIKEY: And then I was up, out the door

And she was already at the end of the road

Indicating left - I tear down there, bang on the window

People coming out the shop looking at me like I'm fucking nuts

She turns, her eyes are just

(To CATRIN.)

What? What?

CATRIN looks at him; doesn't answer. MIKEY picks up his story.

MIKEY: Come back, please,

Let's just talk about it. Can we? Cat?

She looks away and pulls away and

She's going. She's just gone.

The road is a long and unwinding one and I can watch her

For maybe half a mile, trundling away.

Not even going fast. Not even rushing. Just

Getting away from me.

BECKY: So you don't want nothing?

MAGS: No I'm fine thank you.

BECKY: Just not gonna eat nothing.

Mum.

MAGS: Love, what?

BECKY: Look how thin you've gone.

Look at the veins in your hands.

MAGS: What about them?

BECKY: They're all standing out.

Look at me, look at my hands.

You can't see veins.

Look at yours.

MAGS: I've got to worry about my hands now as well, have I?

BECKY: I'm saying, it's cos of how thin you've gone.

You're basically starving yourself.

No wonder you feel like shit, when you're starving yourself.

MAGS: That's why, is it?

That's why I feel shit.

Because I'm not eating.

I wish.

BECKY: Aw, / mum...

MAGS: / I wish it was that.

BECKY: And you do eat actually.

I see the wrappers.

Dairy Milk, Wagon Wheels, blocks

Of that nasty cheese from the paper shop.

You do eat.

You must, or otherwise you'd be dead.

So why pretend like you don't?

MAGS: My son.

BECKY: Yes.

MAGS: My son.

BECKY: I know.

MAGS: He doesn't eat.

BECKY: No.

MAGS: So how can I?

BECKY: Cos you must.

MAGS: How can I?

BECKY: Because you must.

MAGS: How can I?

BECKY: Because

You want to.

Because he died.

But you want to live.

MAGS: No I bloody don't.

BECKY: But you must.

You must do.

I've seen the wrappers.

SCOTT: Some guy in a club tells me that people

Are only really dead once they're forgotten.

I think he was a Dr Who fan.

But all the same I sort of know what he means and

I try and keep Lee in my head. I try and have
conversations with him

And the thing is – it gets boring.

I've got mates who've been twenty-five since before 9/11

But Lee – is forever seventeen.

He's got no opinion on any of the major world events

Of the last few years. He thinks there will never be a black president

Except in all films. Has fuck all to say about the recession.

Doesn't even know what Facebook is.

And trickier still, he doesn't know me.

He still make lots of cock jokes.

And they would still make me laugh

Just I've fuckin' heard them all, so many times.

MIKEY sings 'Back When I Was 4', by Jeffrey Lewis.

BECKY: After A-levels I went on to art college, then a degree in fashion and knitwear design.

I was the first in my family of miners, steelworkers and barmaids

To sit A-levels, let alone go on to university.

Far as I know, I'm the last.

Mum cried when I graduated.

I hope it was cos she was proud.

Might well've been cos of Lee.

Cos he didn't graduate.

I got a job, assistant clothes designer, worked my way up and

After 5 years, I was head of design for... a company you'll've heard of.

Actually you'll've worn my stuff.

Actually... some of you still are.

I did that, and then –

I became mum to a lush, curly haired girl.

We called her Grace

I had to go back to work when Grace was 6 months for financial reasons and

I hated it.

I hated leaving Grace at nursery every day and the thought of having to leave her in clubs in the school holidays as well was the final straw.

The job I'd worked for and studied for and loved all those years – and now I hated it.

So after a lot of sums and a year of saving every penny I went back to university to retrain as a teacher.

Like I say, no-one in our family'd been so I thought might as well have a couple of goes.

That was 2 years ago and I am now in my first full year teaching technology and design.

Already it's like I've been doing it for years. School holidays doing fun stuff with Grace are great, and I haven't missed my old life as a clothes designer one single bit.

I found one career I loved so much – I can't believe I found two.

MAGS: I carry on.

I carry on cos I can't find how to stop.

CATRIN: *(To MAGS.)*

Mrs Davies I don't know if –

Of course you remember me.

MAGS: I'm hardly likely to forget.

MIKEY: Come on, Mags, your turn...

BECKY: So if you're eating, why not eat with me, Mum?

MAGS: But then it's Becky.

BECKY: Just a couple of fucking chips...

MAGS: Becky,

Typically bloody inconsiderate

Goes and has a little girl. Grace.

And she's –

She hugs trees.

Throws her arms round them, and kisses the bark.

She loves animals. We take her to the petting zoo or if

She sees a cat on the street, she'll stroke it and

Some kids are rough, but she is so gentle.

She comes round here and

She doesn't like the door closed

When she's on the toilet.

She likes it open so she can talk to me in the kitchen.

And I've got all these paintings and pictures of hers

Up on the side of the fridge.

And she was sitting there last week

Looking at them all, and she said to me,

Isn't it nice, Nan,

Seeing all those paintings I did

When I was just a little girl.

She's five.

She's five and so

The world can't end:

Not until she's finished with it.

SCOTT: I start volunteering for a charity

That's there to listen when people are in

Despair or distress. That's all we do,

Let people get things off their chest

When everything feels like too much.

This kid comes in one day.

He's pissed off about a lot of stuff.

And what often happens when someone's angry is

They take it out on the nearest person, and the nearest person is me

And he says, what the fuck's wrong with you?

Who the fuck would be here, listening to a twat like me?

Why the fuck would you do that?

And I wonder, what it is, makes me do it.

What makes me get up, quarter to five in the morning,

Bike through the rain and wind

Put in three hours listening to sobbing strangers and the occasional pervert,

And all before a full day at work.

What is it? What is it makes you do that?

BECKY: I was a bit impatient with her.

I think I had to be.

There are years when we don't speak much.

Cos I'm pissed off with her.

Then when Grace comes –

What the fuck are you doing?

MAGS: Nothing. Watching telly.

BECKY: You can't let her sleep like that!

MAGS: She was grizzling on her back, I put her on her front

And not a peep for hours.

BECKY: The risks of cot death

Are significantly raised when babies

Sleep on their front. Look on any website.

MAGS: You slept on your front. You were alright.

Actually they used to say, babies had to sleep on their front.

BECKY: They say different now.

MAGS: Because if they were sick in their sleep,

On their backs they could choke.

BECKY looks at her.

MAGS: I remember now the health visitor telling me.

Snidey little bitch...

BECKY: But Gracie sicks up loads...

MAGS: I know.

BECKY: So - she could choke.

MAGS: Put her on her front.

BECKY: But then it's cot death!

MAGS: Split the difference, pop her on her side?

BECKY: I'm just gonna have to watch her.

MAGS: All night?

BECKY: I'm just gonna have to sit up

And watch her

And make sure she keeps breathing

And make sure she doesn't choke.

That's obviously the answer.

MAGS: *(Beat.)*

I'll get you some coffee.

SCOTT: We get a house in the valleys, Alex and me.

We become valley commandos.

It's falling to bits, electric's buggered, chimney's caving.

But apparently Alex likes mending old neglected things.

I say, what – like me?

MAGS: Been nice seeing you.

CATRIN: And you.

MAGS: Don't leave it so long next time.

CATRIN: No.

MAGS: I mean I know why you did.

But don't.

CATRIN: I might be back

A bit more / now.

MAGS: / That'd be nice.

Because it helps, sometimes,

To remember the good things.

CATRIN: Yeah, of course.

MAGS: And you were the love of his life.

CATRIN: Mrs Davies,

I don't think I was.

MAGS: Of course you were.

Who else?

No, you wouldn't have been.

But as things stood: you were.

You were what he got.

Cos of you, he knew what it was like

To be held, and hugged, and loved.

CATRIN: I wasn't –

MAGS: You weren't what, lovely?

CATRIN: You know it was my fault.

MAGS: It was an accident...

CATRIN: I did something horrible.

I said horrible things.

It was cos of me –

MAGS: No. Now – shut it.

Just shut up.

I know what happened that night.

My son did something stupid and selfish and reckless

He did the sort of stupid, selfish, reckless thing

Teenagers do every day, and ninety-nine times out of a hundred,

They get away with it.

He didn't get away with it.

He was that one time when it all goes to fuck.

And that's not fair, it's not nice, but

There's no reason why.

It's just – the worst possible luck.

And I can say all that.

I can believe it, more or less.

But if you tell me.

If you say to me what happened.

If you put me there, in his head,

If you make me feel how bad he felt

And ask me to, what, forgive you for it?

SCOTT: I go into it quite realistic, thinking

There'll be good times and bad but

The truth is me and Alex never argue.

Just never do. He won't allow it.

Except this one time, when I tell the whole story

About Lee, and what a selfish twat he was.

And Alex says – right. And you're so hard on him

Because you think it's your fault?

I say sorry what the fuck?

Alex says of course you blame yourself. I know I would.

We argued that night.

For basically all of the night, in fact.

MIKEY: Back then.

CATRIN: Looks like.

MIKEY: Didn't have milk at the end of the road?

CATRIN: Just fancied a drive.

MIKEY: Right.

CATRIN: And then a trip home.

MIKEY: For a week.

CATRIN: Had a few people to catch up with.

MIKEY: Might've rung.

CATRIN: Left my charger behind.

MIKEY: Might've borrowed someone else's phone or used a landline.

CATRIN: Don't know your number.

MIKEY: Might've emailed.

Might've skyped.

Might've poked me on Facebook to let me know you were alright.

Ninety-seven per cent of first class mail reaches its destination by the

following day so you could've sent me a postcard, if you liked.

But you didn't.

CATRIN: That's just me. A free spirit.

MIKEY: Because once you take something like that,

You let somebody drive off without a word

And stay away as long as they like, well

They've won.

Cos they know, you'll take anything then.

You just have to hope they came back

Because of something good.

And not because they're going to use you and torment you

To try and work off some past unresolved hurt.

MAGS: Anyway I know what you did.

You did the sort of stupid, selfish, reckless thing teenagers do every day.

And ninety-nine times out of a hundred, they get away with it.

Didn't you?

CATRIN: I suppose.

MAGS: So then

Let yourself

Get away with it.

SCOTT: I used to make up stories.

What Lee would have done.

Who he would have loved.

And I spent ages

They were so detailed, intricate,

Like an actual biography, pages and pages of typing.

Alex found them once and he

Cried. And he's not the type.

He said you should do something with these.

So I did.

I put them through the shredder with our bank statements.

CATRIN: Just another night of carnage in the Big End.

Good for a few hundred blurry photos on Facebook,

And hungover gossip in the morning.

SCOTT: He wasn't an angel, but he was an alright bloke.

But all anyone remembers now is that he died.

And

And I wish you could have met him.

MAGS: No, it never gets better.

That moment, when you realise he's gone,

It never goes. And it never gets easier.

CATRIN: And I'm alright.

I'm not amazing.

But I'm alright. I can say that.

BECKY: With Grace,

I start to see

What mum went through. Because

When you're young, all you know is, you're here.

You don't know what it means that someone carried you,

Felt you start to move inside them.

Maybe felt your foot poking into their belly,

Pushed gently at it, and felt you push back.

You don't know that when you came out

You couldn't even hold up your head.

Didn't even know how to suck.

So much goes into a kid –

But when you are a kid, you can't see it.

You don't remember the care it took to make you.

And so you're careless, with yourself.

And there are gonna be times when

You feel like you're worth nothing.

But the very fact you're here, feeling so bad

Means you're worth the world, to somebody.

And you've just got to fucking hold on to that.

MAGS: After the car crashed, and he lay there for two hours,

They say he was most likely unconscious.

I think he was awake.

I think he was looking at the stars.

I think he knew what he was losing.

The doctor said, he is a fighter,

He's not going anywhere, he's holding on,

But then he was saying to me

I'm so tired, mum.

And I said, well have forty winks then.

He said I can't, I'm scared.

What if I never wake up?

And I said

You sleep now, lovely.

You sleep now, if you want to.

He says you promise me?

He says you promise me I'll wake up again mum?

And I say

To my own son

Close them eyes, baby boy.

Mammy'll be here when you wake up.

And I still am.

I still am.

BECKY: She got better, in the end.

You wouldn't see it day to day. You had to think back

Remember how she was – a year ago, or six months.

I'm going for chips – shall I get you some fish, as well?

Mum?

MAGS: Ask them if it's haddock or cod;

If it's haddock, alright, if it's cod – don't bother.

BECKY's looking at her, hugely relieved.

MAGS: What?

BECKY: Just... you're so fuckin' fussy.

MAGS: They say time is a healer,

But they lie. Because time doesn't work after something like that.

Time gets all jumbled up.

Because that moment is never gone.

It's happening now.

It's happening – now.

And it never gets easier,

In my head, and my heart, it's still going on.

What times does is

It brings you other stuff.

It brings you your daughter back.

It brings you a grandchild.

It brings you Grace.

It brings you more love, that comes surging up inside

Whether you can bear it or not.

And sometimes you'd rather / lay down and

MIKEY: / Mags? It's your turn.

MAGS: Me?

BECKY: Go on...

MIKEY: Go on, sing for us.

CATRIN: Everyone else has had a go...

ALL: *(Chanting.)* Mags, Mags, Mags, Mags...

BECKY: *(As the chant continues.)*

It's your birthday, and you are singing

And that's the end of it.

MAGS: Alright, alright...

MAGS takes up the mike.

MIKEY: You ready?

MAGS: No.

MAGS sings 'A Fire In My Heart' by the Super Furry Animals.

BEFORE

Back to the very first scene: CATRIN and SCOTT, where we left them, outside the church.

SCOTT: And?

CATRIN: I dunno.

SCOTT: I just told you I love you and – you don't know?

CATRIN: Can I have like one second to think about it?

SCOTT: Course.

Just leave me hanging...

CATRIN: How d'you know you love me?

SCOTT: I think about you all the time, and I think you're amazing, and in case you hadn't noticed, I'm the one who chases after you when you strop off out the pub, so...

CATRIN: You are really easy to talk to.

Lot easier than Lee.

SCOTT: You know what we have to do?

We have to kiss.

And then how we feel in our bodies will tell us.

CATRIN: I can't, I can't, I can't, I'm with Lee, I can't –

(She stops.)

Oh, what the fuck...

She grabs SCOTT, and they kiss.

When they break –

SCOTT: Well?

CATRIN: I felt... a little bit giddy. A little bit out of breath. A little bit... like I couldn't believe I was actually kissing you.

SCOTT: Like you couldn't believe it was happening?

CATRIN: Yeah.

SCOTT: You couldn't believe it was happening to you?

CATRIN: But it is. Oh my God.

They look at each other.

CATRIN: I'm gonna have to tell Lee.

SCOTT: I know.

CATRIN: I can't believe it's really happening.

After all this time –

– love.

A snatch of the chorus of 'Regret' by New Order, sung by LEE and BECKY and CATRIN and SCOTT, in LEE's car on the way to Southerndown, years earlier.

And just as abruptly as it came in, the sound is gone.

Ends.

IPHIGENIA IN SPLOTT

i Gruff, a'i fam

Acknowledgements

Thanks to Chris Haydon for giving me the idea. To Róisín McBrinn and Chris Ricketts for running with it.

And to Rachel O'Riordan for making it actually happen.

Iphigenia in Splott was first performed at the Sherman Theatre, Cardiff on 8 May, 2015 with the following cast:

EFFIE, Sophie Melville

Creative Team

Author, Gary Owen
Director, Rachel O'Riordan
Designer, Hayley Grindle
Lighting Designer, Rachel Mortimer
Sound Designer, Sam Jones

The play had its Scottish premiere on 24 August 2015 at Pleasance Dome, Edinburgh, and its English premiere on 27 January 2016 in the Temporary Theatre at the National Theatre, London.

1

You lot.

Sitting back, taking it easy, waiting for me

To – what? Impress you? Amaze you? Show you what
I've got?

Well boys and girls, ladies and gents – I'm afraid not.

You have got it back to front, arse about tit, and your up
side

Is definitely down. See I know what you think

When you see me pissed first thing wandering around.
You think –

Stupid slag. Nasty skank.

But guess what? Tonight

You all are here to give thanks

To me.

Yeah I know it's a shock.

But you lot, every single one

You're in my debt.

And tonight – boys and girls, ladies and gents –

I've come to collect.

You all know me.

I strut down the street, and your eyes dive for the ground

Face on I'm too much for you to handle

The second I'm past your head snaps up

To catch an eyeful of this firm yet juicy arse –

– and it is, so don't even bitch.

That's my flat, on the corner.

My nan remembers when it used to be a shop – like almost
every house on the block,

Oooh, she says, it's not like how it was. I say Nan: wake up love.

Everything changes, everything moves on.

Nan loves to have a moan about the world, the way it's gone,

Course when she moans about how the world has gone,

What she's really moaning about – is me. My life.

Cos I live my life a million miles an hour, do what I like, when I like, and

Oh look, I've got – this[1] – for you, if you can't deal with it

Nan says, this place used to have everything you need

Shops are gone, bingo hall burned, pubs closed, doctors shut,

STAR centre getting pulled down and more flats thrown up.

She says we used to live. You could live here and live well.

Now they're stacking us up, and we're supposed to just exist.

I say Nan you're such a moaning old trout I swear

Nan scowls at me she is up and out

Says – I'll tell you what young miss –

It is eleven thirty-five in the morning and you have taken drink!

Nothing good can come from living like this.

I say to Nan: if you don't like the way I live

Maybe you shouldn't come round no more. How'd you like that?

Nan grumps off,

Slaps down a couple of tens on the table as she waddles by

And I should

I should

Pick them up go after her stuff them down her throat

But

I let the money sit.

I let her shuffle down the stairs

I let the front door slam because

I need those notes.

See the only way I get through the week is a cycle of hangovers.

And I'm not talking, bit of a baddy head here.

I'm talking proper, brain-shredding three day bastards.

I'm talking hangovers that start, you're under a table at Chicken Cottage,

You've already chucked so much you're just heaving big empty sick-flavoured burps, till

Some secret trapdoor springs open in your guts

And this thick green gloop shoots out your gob

This sour liquorice juice, pints and pints of it,

Where the hell was that tucked away? And you wake

In a stranger's bed, or a bathroom floor, or police cell.

But you wake,

Your muscles ache, your throat's sore, teeth fizzing from all that acid

In your puke the night before. You wake and you know

– that's half the week sorted!

Because you'll be day one in bed, crying and wishing you were dead,

Onto the settee for day two, sweating into your duvet, eating twenty pee noodles, watching whatever shit comes on Dave ja vu.

And on the third day you rise, and put yourself back together; start with a scalding hot bath mid morning to lift the shit from your pores then a ten hour programme of sanding down surfaces, picking, plucking, painting before you're ready to go again.

But last night I didn't get there. Last night, don't know why, don't know what,

I just didn't have the commitment to getting absolutely totally fucked and now

Disaster. It's Monday morning, and I've got a brain functioning on full power.

That is not natural, it is not normal

And it is definitely not safe.

I am going to need those notes from Nan,

So tonight I can put right last night's wrong, get totally fucked

And wipe myself out for the rest of the week.

So I let the woman walk.

I don't stuff those grimy tenners back in her face.

Sometimes you've just got to take it.

But still,

Even if I've got an escape from real life tonight

That leaves me with a day to get through

My body buzzing, all this energy and fuck all to do with it.

This means one thing.

Trouble. In the end for me

But before that, for… losers like you, basically.

I wander down to the pavement, scan the street for targets

Who's gonna volunteer? Who will step up, be victim of my fury?

And –

Yes.

This prick. This prick coming now.

One of these pricks you see snarling on the weights at the STAR

Glugging down protein shakes, gazing at himself in the mirror.

Session after session pumping up his arms and chest,

But leg day: leg day, the prick pisses off down the pub,

So he's got arms like thighs, but thighs like cheese straws.

He totters down our street every day, little legs barely bearing the weight

Of his steroid-boosted bi's and tri's and pecs

Walking his nasty little dog, some kind of mongrel, maybe not a pug

But fucking pug ugly for sure, and this prick

Lets his nasty little dog shit all over our street. And that really pisses me off

Not just cos I have to walk through it but – *so does he!*

How fucking stupid do you have to be

To let your dog shit on the street *you* walk down

Every single day of the week?

There's so much crap, he has to do this little dance

Just to dodge the turds he's left lying in wait for himself.

I watch him, pirouetting down the pavement like he's having a fit

And sometimes, I wonder

Why exactly I even go out with the prick.

He sees me sat on the kerb lifts his hand says

Alright slag?

I say –

What did you call me, Kev?

Smile fades, he says

Whassat now?

I say, did you just call me a slag?

He says, I calls you that all the time, you loves it you do.

I go I have had a fuckin gutsful of you –

He goes chill the fuck out I was joking like

You *prick* I shout and I'm off down the street,

He skips after me, snapping at my heels, I'm screaming

You twat, you bastard, you fucking shit

It's like a whole routine we got worked out,

We usually pull it – three in the morning?

Screaming at each other, staggering up and down the street.

You might've heard us. Or you might've been trying to sleep?

So we're raging across the road, and

Some fat mum with a massive buggy full of fat kids says

Would you mind watching your language

Or lowering your volume, please?

I say the fuck you say to me?

One of the fat kids starts to sob.

She goes, your language is upsetting my little girl, alright?

She's belly rolls bulging her leggings from black to sheer grey

And blinking at me, breathing through her mouth like the dog she is.

I say the fuck d'you think you are bitch?

Christ look at that hair. Rat black then three inches of grey roots.

I mean I can see the bitch is busy popping out sprogs

But five minutes with a pack of Nice n Easy would sort that,

It's so fuckin sad when a woman loses her self-respect.

Kev limps up. Fuck's this 'en?

Bitch fucking started on me, trying to tell me what to do.

Kev's like who the fuck's she think she is? I'm like that's what I said.

Pug ugly dog's snapping around her buggy, bitch backs away

That dog comes near me I'll have the police out –

I step closer, fast, and she's not expecting it, and –

Ewwww, the greasy sludged up pores in that T-zone,

Bitch hasn't deep cleansed since a million years BCC – before CC cream.

I say, you fucking call the police love.

You just try it.

You just try.

And she's gonna say something.

But then I look down at her buggy.

A wriggly red newborn, chubbed up toddler, sobbing,

And a cheeky girl, riding the rail at the back.

And fat mum sees me look. And she thinks.

She thinks about her soft little babies.

Who have to walk this street,

Play on this street,

Live on this street,

With me.

And she thinks better.

I go that's right love, you walk away, you cunt.

I go to Kev, you see that, you see how she was having a go?

He goes what a fucking bitch aye

I go that's got me all riled up that has

He goes yeah no I'm not surprised.

But if you're all riled, maybe I can help you relax?

He brings out this massive bag of weed.

I go where'd you get that?

Blagged my way into some student party Crwys Road

Found it under a mattress next to a foot long dildo?

I mean who needs a foot long of anything?

And I… don't crush his innocence.

We slink back to the flat,

We light up, kick back, haze through the hours

Smoking and shagging, even better for killing time than a hangover

Cos there's none of the shivering, and not so much of the self-hate

And then the sun goes down – and I'm up, off the bed.

Kev's like – whassis now?

I'm – we're off out, I need to get hammered.

He goes, I'll hammer you right here right now love

And even though I've shagged him four times in the last five hours

When he says it like that it makes me wanna fucking kill the prick.

But

For tonight, I let him live.

I work out my anger banging on Leanne's door.

Leanne's my flatmate, I love her, she's a fucking warrior.

She screams, what the fuck? I scream, we are fucking off!

Chuck Dove 72 on the pits, rummage with a baby wipe between the legs, and

Leanne, we are fuckin leaving you behind!

Leanne bursts out of her room, smoothing down a new halter neck

Says, Eff, be honest now – d'my tits look big in this?

I say – fucking massive love. And we are off.

First bar's Las Iguanas, cos

Leanne's got a voucher. All pitchers two for one.

Which means you pay fifteen quid to get two pitchers of basically ice water

Quelle fucking bargain. But then Leanne whips

A quarter bottle of vodka from her clutch bag

I grab it, cheeky slug, then dump the rest in the pitcher.

Straight off, a git with a badge saying bar manager teleports in next to us,

He goes, guys guys guys hope you're having a great night just need to check – is there vodka in this?

I say, well it's supposed to be a vodka martini

So I would fucking hope so. He goes

You know what I mean, miss. Can I see in your bag please?

I'm breezy, cos the bottle's not in my bag,

It is behind my back, tucked into the band of my skirt. I say

Go ahead love, if that's how you get your kicks

He has a little poke around, I tell him

Those would be tampons? Just in case you've never seen them.

He chucks the bag back to me, defeated but then

As I grab the bag,

I sort of lean forward, and the bottle sort of pops free,

Falls out my skirt, clatters on the floor, between my feet.

Leanne says Effie, love: did you just shit a vodka bottle?

Manager git goes, out, now! – and security's closing in,

I pick up the pitcher

Git says – you throw that at me…

I bring the two pint jug, brim-full, to my lips

I see, in the git's eyes, the thought: you can't.

He has no fucking idea.

I start to drink and people nearby fall quiet

I get halfway down the jug there's clapping and cheers

I hit the bottom – the whole room goes up, people whooping, whistling

Even the git is giving me this grudging smile, like he's in on it?

I shove the empty jug at him, he grabs it, both mits

So he's got nothing left to fend me off when I clamp my hands to his cheeks,

Pull him in like to give him a great big smacker of a kiss and then –

Burp right in his fucking face.

I grab Kev, I get Leanne by the other hand

March them off towards St Mary's Street,

And the first place we can get into is

The Great Western.

I know. It's shite.

From the outside seems empty but once you're in packed four deep to get a drink.

I dive into the crush – buttoned-up undercut at the front is handing Jaeger shots back

Over the heads and shoulders, I grab one – boom, that's gone

I push in further, scuse me, scuse me, I slink in, right to the front

Get my elbows to the bar, prop myself up, cast my gaze round and

There.

Oh God.

There.

At the back.

Little gang of guys.

All of them pretty fit – not gym fit, not primped and preened

Not muscles like boulders, just, you can see

Their arms and legs and bodies are solid.

And not one of them with – that desperation

The eagerness to please, that screams off every guy

Trying his luck on every rainy Cardiff night.

And in the heart of them,

There he is.

Looking at me.

And he's –

Kev finds my side snakes his arm round my waist and

I'm expecting the guy to look away but

He doesn't.

And he's nice looking, yeah, that's a face

I'd grind myself all over but still:

Staring straight at me,

When he can see I'm with another man?

So fucking arrogant.

Now if Kev sees that, it's gonna fuckin kick off

Course Kev doesn't see that, cos he's a dull twat

So I say,

Kev.

Kev.

He's angling for the barmaid's eye, jussasec love.

I say no, Kev

I've gotta tell you right now.

He goes 'ssup bitch?

I say, Kev, look over b'there yeah.

And I point.

And he looks where I'm pointing I say

What can you see?

And he says

Uhhhh…

I can see…

Sign says toilets?

I go, yeah. That's right. I want you to go down,

Find the cubicle furthest from the door.

And wait.

Because I am up for it. Right here right now.

Fuck yeah! he says. Ladies or gents?

And I go – well am I a fucking lady or am I fucking not.

And off the prick trots

And what?

You think I should put up with whatever wanders down
my street

Dodging the dog shits, and be grateful? Fuck that.

I turn round, to face this guy

No shy little look, no flirty glance

The full on stare,

Lips parted to show some tooth,

But a snarl not a smile.

Nine out of ten guys, can't take it. Will look away.

This guy – stares me right back.

And so I walk. Straight at him.

The crush parts before me – course it fucking does.

I cut a path right through the dance floor

And no one touches me. None of them could.

I close on him like a fucking cruise missile and he's staring
back

Trying to hold his nerve but then –

There it is.

Just a split second.

Little flicker of fear in his eyes.

He packs it away quick as he can, but I've got him now.

I stop.

Turn my back and –

 – up till then music has been shit

But the second I start to move to it,

It becomes fucking sick because I am like

A multi-million dollar video that distracts from the shitness
of the track

Except I'm in real life.

I've come half way to this guy, now I'll make him come

The rest of the way to me. And he'll think he's doing it

Of his own free will but, not really: I'm drawing him from
over there

To over here, where I want him to be.

I shut my eyes,

And still the lights pulsing through my lids

Or maybe it's the blood in the tiny little veins

And every time I breathe in, I feel like I'm floating up

Off the floor, I kick off my shoes

I dance like I don't know how,

I spin, and I don't know what my body's doing

I'm just watching it, except

I'm not me

I am me

But I'm someone else as well and then

And then

And then

The song ends.

And I look

To where this guy should be –

Right next to me.

But next to me there's no one.

Fucker hasn't moved.

He's propped up, just where he was

Have I lost my powers? What is going on?

No man resists me: literally no one.

And I'm looking at him now,

Not seductive, or hopeful, just actually

Actually quite angry at

Who the fuck this idiot thinks he is

And that second

The crowd shifts,

And the gang he's got surrounding him move

And I can see the guy

Head to foot.

And what I see is –

– the fucker's on crutches.

And he sees me see.

He sees me, laugh.

At him, and, at me,

Trying to lure him to the dance floor,

When the poor fucker can't walk.

So I walk, for him.

All the posturing and posing gone.

I put my arms round his neck.

I say,

Hello, you.

And I snog his fucking face off.

2

I'm Effie, I say, and he nods like, yeah, he already knew.

He says, I'm Lee. And I feel like I knew that too.

I say Lee we might wanna make a swift exit. There's a boy,

Gonna be coming up those stairs any sec not pleased

To see me with you.

Worried what he'll do to me, are you? says Lee.

And I say, no. Other way round, I think.

We grab a couple of taxis from the road-blocked top of St Mary's

And I realise what it is, Lee and his mates.

Why they look like a gang. I say, you're soldiers, aren't you.

Lee's chucking his crutches in the boot. He swings round the side of the car,

Leaning on it the whole time, little frown like not pain but

Really concentrating when his weight's on his right foot.

He opens the door, holds it open, for me. Says,

They, are soldiers. I was.

Till this.

And he means –

Whatever hideous event put him on those crutches.

We're in the car, heading to his mate Tom's. Tom's got a flat,

Far side of Tremorfa. We kiss, me and Lee, I

Press my hand down his belly, not going *there* yet,

Sliding past to his thigh,

I knead the heavy muscle, and –

– he snatches my hand. Holds it tight.

I say, what?

He says – wait, alright?

I can wait. That's fine.

We get to the flat. New estate creeping out from the
railway line.

And you'd think – me on my own, and these five strange
guys

You'd think I'd be a bit fist clenched round my keys,

Ready to kick off, but no. Nothing like.

They're all polite, without being creepy.

Funny, without being pricks.

It feels – never like I'm in danger, more like

I'm this maid of honour and

They're my personal body guard.

We sit in the lounge, few drinks, chat.

I slip my hand into Lee's. Give it a squeeze.

And he looks at me…

And when we head off, there's no

Fuss and nonsense from the boys, like you'd expect when
their mate

Takes the girl he's pulled upstairs.

They're just all – g'night, nice to meet you.

Like me coming home with Lee is… fate.

He dawdles a little while following me up,

I head into a bathroom, quick swipe of Colgate

Over the teeth, scrape the moss off my tongue, and then –

He's leaning against a futon, uncurled into a bed

That takes up most of the floor of the spare room.

And for a second I'm scared. Not scared of him, fuck no,

Scared of –

And to fight it, I grab his belt, like, fuck it,

Let's get stuck in but

He stops me. Holds me back. Says

I've got something to show you.

He pulls off his top, and – it's nice, lots of muscle but

A little bit of slack around the belly and to be honest

I like that more, there's something weird about boys who are

That obsessive they're not carrying an ounce of fat.

He goes for his belt, says

Okay. Don't freak out.

I say, mate

Anything up to a foot, I can take,

But more than that, and certain positions are gonna be no go, okay?

And he smiles at me.

A smile that's a bit sad.

And though I just meant to lighten the mood his smile makes me wish

I hadn't said anything like that.

And he pulls his jeans down. And his legs

Are lovely

But one of them

Stops.

At the knee.

And there's straps and plastic.

He sits back kicks off his jeans and

His right leg. It's plastic from the knee down.

He gets to work on the buckles.

Pulls the plastic free

And something comes out.

A stump of flesh, that just ends.

The skin folds over

265

To a red, angry ridge,

Black stitch marks where they stuck

The flaps of skin together.

How'd it happen?

He says, d'you know what an improvised explosive device
is?

I say not really. He says well I do.

He tells me

He's not been able to show,

Himself, to anyone

Since.

So I kiss him. I kiss him and kiss him

And kiss him, and kiss him, and kiss him, and kiss him

And then I'm on him. And he's in me.

And the first time it's so fast. Like almost instantly.

And he's embarrassed, he's sorry, and I'm

It's alright. We've got that over with. And now

We can do it properly.

And I kiss him again. I kiss him and kiss him and kiss him

I slide my lips down his side, down his thigh, he says

Please don't,

But I won't stop, I kiss everywhere, I kiss

And he's pulling away, says please don't, but

I kiss the cut, I kiss the stitches, and it feels

Like nothing I've ever kissed,

And I say, there. You see?

He says, it's so fucking ugly.

And I say well actually

I think it's beautiful.

And something goes wrong then.

He turns away from me.

But I can see, from the shivers of his shoulders –

I say –

Look I'm sorry. That was just fucking bullshit. I don't know why I said that. I wanted to say something to make it better. You're right, it's fucking ugly, actually. It's ugly and it's scary and looking at it puts the shits up me cos I think, look at us, we are these little soft creatures and it's so easy to hurt us, anything could happen any time and ruin us. So it's not beautiful. It's as far from beautiful as anything can be. But it's part of you. And if it's part of you, I can take it.

And Lee turns back.

He grabs my face. And he kisses me, and kisses me, and kisses me.

And we make love again and it's hours.

Hours pressing our skin, pushing into each other,

Flipping and rolling over the bed cos the bits of us that aren't touching are jealous of the bits that are: tangling our limbs,

Licking and sucking and breathing each other in,

Getting as much as we can of him into me and me into him, just being, being together and alive.

And after, he tells me.

It went off right under the guy next to him.

This guy caught the worst of it.

Both his legs gone, one of his hands.

On the helicopter, medics trying to keep the guy going

Talking him up

But he knew.

And he was sobbing and shaking

But not cos of the pain.

Cos of his kids. All the years they'd have to live

Without a dad.

All the nights they'd cry themselves to sleep

For the want of him.

Knowing he was breaking the hearts

Of the ones he loved most.

And that was his life.

His last seconds

Terror and pain and guilt and defeat

And Lee flips round to me

Sinks his face in my neck, howls like a hurt child.

I wrap my arms around him, squeeze him all I can, and –

– and I take it.

I take it, and –

And that was the end of my life.

3

Lying there wrapped up in Lee I'm feeling something new.

That something new is – not alone.

I'm not alone.

And it feels like I'm gonna feel not alone, always.

But I want to see.

I want to see if that's how I am now.

So I get up. Lee's mostly sleeping.

I scribble my number, he reaches up, pulls my face down

For a last kiss.

I say, we're not gonna do that, wait three days to call shit, right?

He says course not.

I say no I know. So I'll speak to you later.

He says what you doing tonight.

I say you, if you've got your strength back.

And he smiles at that.

I pad down the stairs.

His mate Tom says, shall I call you a cab.

I say no and I don't know why.

But I just go with it.

I walk down busy roads that have gone quiet for the night.

Not down Tremorfa. On and out.

Past the big Tescos, past David Lloyd

To all the massive factories like

Crashed spaceships, the metal mountains,

Train tracks from nowhere, cranes and pipes and chimney stacks

And it's scary, but a couple of gypsy ponies find me,

Wander up the verge, bump their big heads against mine, telling me,

Keep going, you'll be fine.

A helicopter swoops low

Like it's gonna scoop me up – or crash.

I follow its path, come off a roundabout

Find a landing pad. I see three figures climb out the 'copter's cabin,

All in black, like stormtroopers of death,

Then they pull off masks and helmets,

And they're just these guys, laughing.

And as the whine of the blades fades,

I hear something else.

Something huge.

Something breathing.

Or something roaring.

I carry on down the road.

Find a hole in a fence.

And there, right in front of me,

Is – the sea.

And a beach.

A beach a mile from where I grew up,

When the fuck did that happen?

It is the worst beach in the world, mind.

Strips of metal, car wheels, half a toilet,

Whole walls crumpled onto the sand,

Concrete slabs cracked, smoothed into soft shapes,

Glass glittering back the moon.

I sit there. Can't see anyone. Can't hear anyone.

Ahead of me a broken brick road, leading into the sea.

I'm as on my own as I can be.

And…

It's still there!

That feeling

Of being not alone any more. Even though I am, I'm not.

Because I've found what I am for.

I am – for making Lee better.

That's what I'll do.

That's what I'll be.

His better half.

And being his better half I'll be so much better than I've ever been.

That's it now.

That's me.

4

So next day.

If I was Lee I'd text first thing, but I'm not.

And he doesn't.

Typical fucking bloke playing it cool, but

I've still got that feeling of not alone anymore

And I trust it.

I'm really calm and quiet, and I just

Stay in the flat. Me. In the flat. Sober.

Not exactly waiting but…

Happy and chilled and thinking about

How it'll be when he does call, and where we'll meet and what I'll wear and where we'll go

And how long we'll stay there before we head back home and

Will I move into his or will he move into mine and

What kind of wedding and yes I get it

Those are insane things to be thinking but

This feeling – not alone –

This feeling says, thinking all those insane things

Is fine because

They're not insane, this time.

They're just what's on the way.

So I spend the whole day waiting, for him to call and

He doesn't.

Okay.

So

The next day I text, just saying,

Hey, it's me, hope you're alright.

I get nothing back.

And I know how it looks.

It looks like I've been fucked and dumped.

But looks are deceiving, ask anyone.

Plus that can't be it,

Cos I've got this feeling.

This feeling of not-alone.

And the feeling makes me not panic, not freak out.

It makes me think – rationally.

It makes me think well if I haven't been fucked and dumped then

What else, could it be?

It could be a million things.

He might've written my number wrong.

Or I might've misread his. I *am* basically fucking dyslexic.

So I look at the receipt where he scribbled his number and yeah

That five might be an eight. Actually so might that three.

And is that one a seven or what?

I have just texted some random most likely.

So I

Text again.

Say about… fifty times.

To all the different variations Lee's number might be.

I get a few answers: most confused, lots saying hi back to me, and

Three pictures of erect penises.

But nothing from Lee.

(No, I'd know.)

And so… I leave it. A while.

Just playing it cool, like Lee obviously is.

So I wait.

Like a week.

Or two.

And I know. I know what it looks like.

But I can't bear it because

Even though I know

I don't. Because this feeling, of not-alone

Is still telling me: this is just some fuck up

That he's not been in touch.

He feels same as you do and if you don't find each other again

You will lose the only thing that's gonna to matter in both your lives –

So I walk

Through Tremorfa, out to Pengam, and

Inside me still, this feeling, not-alone,

Saying yes, this is fine, this is *absolutely* a sane way to behave.

I get to the friend's flat, and press the buzzer.

No one there. Course not, it's the middle of the day.

I leave a note. With my number. Written in numbers,

And letters, just in case.

I'm imagining how it will be a story, me and Lee

Tell people, how we had this one night together and then

He lost my number, but thank God instead of stropping off

I dropped a note round – and we were reunited!

And as I turn to leave I hear something.

But I'm not sure what.

I look up, there's – no one, at the window of Tom's flat.

I get home up the stairs flop down on the settee

And there

I cry

Because I do know

I know what that thing was I heard,

Back at Tom's flat. I know now and I knew then.

It was someone, laughing.

Not someone. It was Tom.

Lee's mate. He saw me

And pretended not to be there.

He saw me, come to post my meek little note.

And he laughed.

Because I have been fucked and dumped.

I know it. I know.

And at the same time

In my heart, this feeling, still –

Not alone. Not alone.

And I can't bear that feeling one second more.

Cos that feeling is the most perfect and certain thing

I have ever felt before –

– and it is a lie.

Into Leanne's room, chest of drawers by her bed,

Always loads of change. Scrape it together,

Tip it in a carrier from under the sink, drag it over the road,

Pile it up on the counter, and it piles just short

For a half bottle of vodka. I tell the guy I'll owe him

And he just wants me gone, says, go on,

Back up to the flat, can't find a glass

Why the fuck would I even need one

Bottle to my open mouth, I breathe in and

The first fumes of alcohol hit –

– and my guts explode.

Before I even take a gulp, I'm chucking right across the room,

Again and again, I drop the bottle, I'm sobbing,

I'm puking like I've never puked before

Leanne pokes her head round the door.

Was you in mine just now when I was sleeping? she goes then –

Seeing me

What the fuck is this fucksake?

And I tell her.

I tell her it all.

She says you know what this is. Come on…

But I don't. Or I can't. Or I won't.

Quick trip up Clifton Street, next thing

I'm perched over the porcelain, pissing on a stick.

Well? says Leanne, through the door.

And I'm watching a little strip of white,

Watching little spots go dark, join up

Form themselves into two clear blue lines.

And I realise.

I am not alone.

5

The first thing I feel is

Glad.

Cos no way can Lee shrug me off now.

So I just phone – the number I had down, which I knew was right, all along,

I phone I say

Lee. It's Effie. We've got to meet. It's important. Don't ignore me,

Because I won't stop.

I leave that message on the hour every hour morning noon and night for…

Five days? And finally the penny drops

That I really, really will not stop.

Text pings back.

He'll see me, one o'clock, Fat Cat Café Bar.

I spend three hours before we meet making sure I look

Like the only girl a guy would need to fuck for the rest of his life –

And that's not for him. It's for me. So I can be, confident like, at ease –

And waiting there for me at the Fat Cat Café Bar

Is not Lee. It's Tom.

And Tom says

Hey,

Seems like there's been some sort of

Misunderstanding?

Lee thought you knew what was going on –

It was only ever gonna be a one night thing.

I mean – you had your tongue down his throat

Before you even knew his name.

And to be fair to you sweetheart,

You put the kid back on track.

Cos he's not been able to – deal, with the physical side of things,

Since the injury. And it's been a real issue,

For him, and his wife.

The fucker's fucking married?

Well, you knew that. You saw the ring.

But I saw no such thing. Cos I never thought to look.

And the whole time Tom's saying this, he doesn't even look at me.

Just plays with his phone. Cos he doesn't give a shit?

Or cos he knows he's being a shit, and there's a tiny bit of him ashamed.

And there is a thought forming in my head. And I get out my phone. Call Lee's number.

Tom's phone lights up in his hand.

And for the first time Tom looks at me, says… yeah. Sorry.

Lee didn't dare give you his real number in case

You know.

I keep my mouth shut.

Because I do, know. I do.

Tom says look, Effie, you were

Two people had a great night together.

We all like a fuck, let's be frank –

And I see him seeing me.

Stupid slag. Nasty skank.

And I say –

Yeah, I know. I'm just pissed off cos I thought I was gonna get a fuck

Tonight.

And I look at Tom.

And I do not look away.

And Tom puts down his phone.

Says, shall I get you another glass of pinot grigio?

I say make it a bottle why don't you.

And he basically fucking runs to the bar. I

Pick up his phone.

Swipe through his contacts.

Find 'Lee'. Listed is not the number I've got.

I'm out the door.

I ring – my sister-in-law.

My sister-in-law works at a call centre for a phone company.

She says, Effie, it's more than my job's worth and he probably isn't even with us.

I say,

You fucking do this for me or I'll tell Steve what happened in Bournemouth

And so she says yes.

And I give her Lee's number.

And she gives me his address.

6

Lee's place is in Ely. Other side of the world but

I jump on a number 18, I'm there in ten minutes.

I spend the trip working out what to say, when I meet the wife:

Hi, you don't know me, but your bloke does. Intimately.

Hi, you don't know me, but we are what I like to call, cock sisters.

In the end I settle on –

Hi, you don't know me, but I'm the girl your husband just knocked up.

I hop off on Grand Avenue, though why you need a grand anything

In a shithole like Ely I haven't got a clue.

My phone takes me to his place.

Tiny terrace house. I get there and –

– I don't know what to do.

And it's raining, like always.

The place opposite Lee's is boarded up, like half the houses on the street.

Grass that reaches for my belly in the front yard hides a wrecked car.

I push through the battered back door.

I'm there with the stink and grime who knows how long

And then – a car, losing speed, Lee at the wheel.

I move, back out the back, back round the road,

And I see Lee, swinging his legs to the ground,

Pulling his crutches out the boot, fixing them on the floor,

Hauling himself up –

Just as the front door of his house opens.

And out comes

His wife.

One of these girls

Who's gone thinner than looks good on her.

Too much skull showing through that skin

A face that falls into a frown till she properly pulls it into a smile.

And when she sees Lee she

Doesn't, smile.

She just watches.

And then –

A girl – five, six, who knows with kids –

Darts out the door, past her mum.

Pretty little thing, and in her you can see

How pretty her mum must've been, before.

The little girl holds out her arms, to Lee

And Lee

Stops.

Mum's hand goes to her mouth.

Lee lets the crutches, drop.

And he takes a step

On his own.

And you can see it's hard, you can see it hurts

But he keeps on, he limps, skips, staggers,

Half falls, but

Makes it, to his little girl then

Steadied by his wife, lifts the little girl up, flings her in the air

She shouts,

Daddy!

And I remember

I remember shouting like that

And –

And the wife says to me,

Sorry, can I help you?

Because I am standing on their drive.

I have walked right up.

I am no passer-by

I've come with intent

I have come to tell her –

And Lee looks at me.

This soldier.

This man who has killed.

This man who has seen his friends in bits

He looks at me –

 – and I am scaring the life out of him.

And he deserves what I am going to do

He deserves it,

And she deserves to know what a liar he is

So I say, to his wife,

Hi, you don't know me, but –

And I see Lee look away, bury his face

In the little girl's neck –

I see her eyes close

I see her lips move and though I don't hear

I know what she's saying

She's saying

Daddy

And I remember

I remember

– sorry, you wanted what? the wife goes.

I say

– *fuck* –

I say

Yeah I'm just trying to find my way back to Grand Avenue?

And she says, aw no you're not far at all.

And I turn.

I walk away.

I spare him what he's got coming.

And every step away from him hurts but

I can take it.

So I do take it.

For that little girl.

7

The doctors.

It's rammed, like always.

Three quarters of an hour in the rain before reception even opens

So by the time we get in we're soaked and sweltering, steaming up the place.

A dozen chairs and three dozen bodies, coughing and sneezing and spitting.

I can feel myself getting ill breathing in what these sickos are breathing out.

The door opens – oh look. It's fat mum

Now with four inches of grey roots,

And her massive buggy, and her massive kids.

The whole room sighs as she unloads, taking up most of the floor,

Everyone having to edge their way round her.

We're all waiting and bored and the doctor's not even here yet.

Fat mum's flabby boy starts to whine, her alien baby howls,

She rocks the buggy, tries to sing

In her drippy little voice, but the baby screams harder,

And every fucker in the room sighs, again.

Sweat beading on fat mum's head,

She asks reception how long's the wait.

Reception says only the one doctor on again today so

We're looking two hours, at least?

Fat mum rocks a bit harder, gives up singing,

And fair play I would too, she can't sing for shit

She shouts at her little boy, he shouts back and

She slaps his hand. And then he cries.

And she kisses his head all guilty like and turns,

Rolls her whole load out the door.

The room sighs. Relief this time.

When I get in to the doc I tell her: I can't have a kid.

I've got problems with drink and drugs and, I'm mental –

Ask anyone.

She makes me an appointment up at the Heath

But it's a fortnight to wait:

Two whole weeks.

And feeling sick all the time and I can't drink.

It gets so I'm gagging from just the smell, even when Leanne

Has a drop, which obviously is every fucking night.

And one day Kev's there, not quite sitting on a radiator,

As I shoot for the bog, hands clamped over my mouth

I hear Kev say, how the fuck's she hungover? She han't

Been out for weeks.

Leanne laughs. Oh, Kev love

You thick twat. She's up the fucking duff.

I hear the door go,

Kev's feet bang down the stairs to the street.

I go lie down, drift off, then, Christ knows when

Kev is back.

On his knees by the settee

He says Eff, I know I'm a prick.

But maybe this is what I need.

A kid. Make me sort myself out.

Cos I really think I could do it.

I really think I could be a dad.

See look at this –

– and he gives me a roll of tenners.

Maybe two hundred quid.

I been down Cash Converters.

Sold the Xbox, games, the lot.

For you. For our family.

And the thing with Kev is –

Like, I know he is a person? With feelings?

But I don't think he is really.

He's like some big ugly dog that no one wants

But no one can be arsed to drown.

And next to him I'm basically a goddess

And the idea of us getting together properly –

A goddess – and a dog?

It just makes me wanna laugh but –

But what if that's wrong?

What if it is, him and me.

Or what if it could be.

He can see I'm thinking about it.

I can see him, getting all excited.

I look at Leanne and she's like

Once you got a kid, you're sorted you get

Child allowance, loads of shit.

Kid's basically a fucking meal ticket.

Kev says I swear to you

Everything

All I got

For you

And our baby

If you will please just keep it.

And I say

There's one thing.

And Kev says, you name it love.

Because if I'm gonna take him seriously

If I'm gonna take his life

I can't start with a lie.

I say,

You can be this kid's dad.

And live with him, and love him

And do all that.

But you gotta know

You are not the father.

Kev says

Sorrywhathefuck?

It was some soldier I met, the Great Western, you
remember.

Kev says – hold on hold on hold on

But we shagged that day, when we went out the Great
Western.

So it could be mine, it could be his.

I say it can't. Cos you and me, used a condom.

And I didn't with him.

Kev says but you never. You never let me do it without.

But you did, with some random guy.

Fuck's sake Eff, why?

And I tell the truth:

Cos I wanted him so much.

I keep my eyes tight till I hear the door slam.

And when I open them,

In a mess on the floor

Is all Kev's money.

8

Leanne sticks a drink in my hand.

Come on, get that down you. You need it.

I feel my gut start to quiver,

From the cold of the glass

But I take a sip.

The lovely burn on the lips that smooths out

On the tongue, down the throat

And then hits my belly

And something in my belly isn't pleased with me.

You see, says Leanne.

You want a drink.

It's just the fucking baby that doesn't.

And who's in charge?

And Christ, it's not even like you're keeping the thing –

– are you?

Course I'm fucking not.

I take another sip.

The thing in my belly tries to kick the booze back up my throat but

I hold it down.

Good girl, says Leanne.

That's my Effie

And she pours me another.

I put it away in one go

Cos this is my body, and I'm the fucking boss.

Another glass, a proper drink this time

Three, four fingers

I sink it, and the kick back from my belly

Is getting weaker

Let's finish the fucking bottle, shall we? Leanne says

I say – fucking go for it love.

She fills my glass to the top.

And I raise it up.

And out the window I see this

Mangy old tabby cat.

See her all the time, she wanders up and down our street.

And I remember, when we were kids

Some of the boys found a kitten, wild

The trees by the park. Too small to even have her eyes
open.

They caught her

Shut her in box.

Starved her.

Till in the end she'd take anything.

They gave her antifreeze.

This tiny thing.

I remember her, staggering about

Mewling and puking everywhere

Sick then spit then nothing

Then blood.

I didn't ask for this. I didn't want it.

I want it gone

But still

A tiny thing.

– I say

No.

No.

I'll drink, when it's gone

Alright?

She goes but if you're getting rid what's the point –

I say – I drink, when it's gone,

And that's the way it is.

And if you don't like it you can fuck yourself, bitch.

Leanne goes alright you mardy cow, strops off.

My head's in a mess now

Cos I've not touched anything in weeks so I lie down.

I wake up. And there is music and voices and

Moody boys in tracky bottoms and vests all over the place

I nod round and they nod back.

I stagger into the lounge, Leanne bounces up says

Sorry Eff, got bored, got people round like but look –

I made you flapjacks!

I'm like – you fucking what?

Flapjacks. It's oats, like from porridge,

And syrup. Like from a tin, of syrup.

I have known Leanne all my life, and she has never given any hint

She even knows what an oven is,

So this is massive.

This is like a big sorry for being a bitch about the drink.

I take a bite, and it's

Chewy, sticky, sweet.

You like that, she says?

I have another, and another again

Right, steady on, she goes.

And I sit watch the telly a bit,

Show about trucks lost on the ice then

My mouth's dry so I stand to get a drink

– and my head swims.

Leanne looks at me.

She's sort of… giggling.

I say, Leanne,

What have you done to me?

She says,

Effie you are stressed to fuck.

You have got a stressy baby

And it is stressing you right out love.

Are you gonna be like this the whole time

Till they whip it out?

I say, Leanne, what the fuck have you done?

She goes it was just weed, alright?

It relaxes you.

It relaxes the baby.

I say –

– you have given my baby drugs?

She says it's natural you silly cow

It can't do no harm –

Next thing Leanne's flat on the floor

Her lip dripping blood down her chin.

She says, Effie I love you like a sister but you are pushing it now

I look round the place.

Fuckin bottles, fuckin cans, fuckin ash trays.

Fuckin boys swilling their drinks, bobbing their heads to the music,

Looking sulky as fuck, and shit, shit,

Anywhere there's space to cram something, there is something: and it's shit.

I can't be here.

I stamp down the stairs.

She's saying Eff you silly bitch, come back –

I let the door slam.

– Eff! –

I hit the street.

– Eff! –

All the windows up and down are dark,

Maybe the flicker of flatscreens.

Just our flat is light and loud.

Effie!

And I walk away from it.

I got no job. No boyfriend. Nowhere to live.

I am all alone. And I am going to have

A baby.

9

Cos it's called morning sickness, I thought

It was a sickness that happened, in the morning?

Not a sickness that starts in the morning and then just

Carries its merry way on through midday afternoon
evening and night.

So that's a thing I learn, early on.

Health visitor says walking or swimming might help, so

Every day I walk to the pool. And the swimming does help.

Until they close the pool down. Then every day I just walk
for ages

Through the rain, so I still end up tired and wet

But it's not really the same.

At twenty weeks I learn I'm having a girl

And she's coming along nicely, so far as the nurse can tell

And then the other thing I learn is

That I'm not alone.

Nan helps me get a place, just a room in a house on Ordell
Street?

But mine, and she gets me what she can to make it nice.

She tells me she had a bit saved. But that's a lie.

I go into the Co-op one night there she is,

Back behind the tills like when I was little.

I tell her, you're too old to be working,

She says – call me too old for anything again and I'll tan
your hide, girl.

Kev keeps trying to give me the money from his Xbox.

I won't take it so in the end he just buys a buggy,

From the cancer shop. Course it's too big to get in my
bedroom door,

And it basically falls apart when you tried to fold it, but still

The thought's the thing. They say.

And then

I'm going through piles of clothes, one of the charity shops Clifton Street

And there is pain, in my belly.

No big thing there's pain often enough

With little miss doing her baby boogie on top of my internal bits

But this pain.

Is not a kick.

It's a cramp.

And this is week twenty-nine.

Too early for all of that.

I phone just to hear them tell me don't be so daft but

They say

Come in, just in case.

I haul myself down to Habershon Street.

And then half an hour bumping around the bus, and then

What seems like even longer to limp

From the bus stop to maternity, but –

They say, there's a test.

If it's negative then we're ninety-nine per cent sure

It's not early labour 'kay love?

I say it can't be, she can't come yet

Nurse says, let's not get worked up now okay let's just do the test, yeah?

I piss into a tube, lie back on the bed.

Out the window I can see, snow. It's snowing.

The test comes back.

Comes back negative.

It's not labour.

Nurse says, okay so now we know

You're doing fine, baby's doing fine

But you won't be meeting her tonight.

It's just a matter of finding

The right kind of pain relief, to get you through these cramps.

She moves me off maternity, wheels me, two different lifts to a floor

That looks like it's closed.

Dark. Quiet. No one about.

Nurse switches on a light, says

Doctor'll be round, he'll give you something make you comfy

And then the nurse – goes.

Leaves me there.

On my own.

And not alone.

And me and my little girl wait

For the pain, that comes in waves

Every half an hour the nurse comes back again says

Doctor'll be along, just a sec

And in the end he is.

He gives me something called pethedine.

And five minutes later I feel better.

But five minutes after that the pain comes again.

I try to walk but my legs won't.

I sort of crawl, arse in the air,

Lights flickering on around me,

Make it to the lifts, press the button – nothing

Press the button – nothing

Press the button – *fuck*

Down to maternity, buzz at the door.

No one comes.

No one comes.

No one comes.

Through the window. I see a girl. Tiny blonde girl, belly so big

It looks like someone's glued her to a hot air balloon

She waddles up to the door, lets me through.

Midwife turns up, says what are you doing

Out of your bed, and I

S C R E A M

Midwife says alright let's just do that test again shall we?

Me and little blonde girl waddle back and fore across the waiting room

Little blonde girl's name is Gemma.

She's got two of them in there. She's bricking it. Says she is never doing this again.

Ben even comes near me I'll bloody stitch myself up.

Ben her partner, not husband, floppy hair, tidy suit, his hand

Swooping down to perch on her shoulder.

The pain comes and Gemma grabs my hand

And I squeeze

And squeeze

And squeeze

And the midwife says

Actually it turns out the test is positive now.

I say –

Sorry *what?*

She says the test was negative, it's come back positive now so

Yeah your baby's coming tonight.

I say *what?*

We'll give you a steroid shot now, help baby's lungs get ready

Because

Your baby's coming very early. You understand that,

Don't you Effie?

Gemma grabs my hand,

Says we'll get through this alright?

Now, did you make a birth plan?

And I barely know the girl but her hand clamped on mine it feels like

We're fucking sisters and then

The midwife comes in says,

Okay. So.

We've not got a bed in special care,

So we're going to have to transfer you.

I say – I don't know what the fuck that means.

Ben swans in says, yeah, special care, it's where they look after

Babies that are premature? They do fantastic work, *so* dedicated.

So, says the midwife, we're going to need you to get ready and

An ambulance will take you to Abergavenny –

I'm like, where the fuck's that?

She says, just a little drive from here,

Ben says, more like an hour and a half,

Midwife says, I think you'll find an ambulance can do it in forty.

And I'll be in the ambulance with you, all the way,

To take care of baby –

And Gemma stops her.

Gemma says to the midwife – you're going?

But who's going to look after me?

Ben says to the midwife can I have a word with you in private please?

And Ben and the midwife go out and

I can hear Ben not shouting but speaking very loud about

The risks of twin births and there's a lot of talk about

Getting some boss doctor on the phone but he's not,

On the phone,

And Gemma goes quiet, and

Lets go my hand and

Walks out and

The midwife comes in.

There's very little chance of you delivering

In the next hour, so

You won't be needing a midwife to accompany you

In any case the paramedics

Are fully trained, so –

And I know I should argue.

I know I should.

But then the pain. I can't speak.

And there is no one to speak for me, so…

I'm on a trolley.

Blankets tucked tight over my arms.

They wheel me, down and out,

Flakes of white drift down,

Touch down on the blanket,

Sit with me for just a second, so pretty

Then they're gone, soaking

The grey of the blanket to black.

Snow, little girl.

Snow on the day you are born.

Paramedic in the back with me, says,

Careful love, she'll be busting out to have a look

And we want her staying in there as long as she can.

The ambulance sets off, sirens and lights
See baby girl? Clearing the way for us to get to a place
Where they're gonna take such special care of you –
And we go speeding down the motorway,
Paramedic whistling, winking at me
As we rattle and roll round the back of the ambulance,
Then we turn off, onto a littler road and
Swinging round loads of roundabouts and
There's some chat, between the guy in the back with me
And the driver. I say what's going on?
He says nothing, lovely, just
Snow's a bit heavier
Cos we're getting up into the mountains
Just having to go
A bit more carefully, is all –
– but you can tell
You can tell
There's something he's not –
And we're going slower and slower
And I say Christ mate I could walk faster than this
And he smiles says, yeah we might have to
And then –
The whole fucking ambulance
Slides
Drifts sideways like nothing with wheels should
And we tip, and totter
We've come off the fucking road.
There's chat on the radio and no seriously it's fine cos
They know we're a priority and they know where we are
And the hospital is just the other side of the mountain,
It'll just be a few more minutes and then –

But you have to stay put little girl.

Just a little while longer and then –

But she is *my* daughter, is the thing.

Does what she wants when she wants and doesn't give a toss.

And right now,

She wants to meet her mum.

She wants to see the snow and the stars.

So she comes.

She comes.

And it hurts.

It hurts so much.

Cos as she's trying to get out

I'm trying to hold her in.

And the driver's back with us too she says

You're just gonna have to push

You're just gonna have to let her

And

I hear her cry

I hear my baby girl cry –

– and then I hear her stop

And they take her

The two of them

Bent over this tiny scrap

They've got a mask over her face

They're pounding on her chest

They're pulling needles out of plastic

Trying to stick 'em in her

But she's too small

She's too small

They're shouting at each other.

Shouting numbers and names of drugs

They're doing Christ knows what, I don't know –

I do know.

They're fighting.

They're fighting with everything they got

To keep her with me.

And they fight

And they fight

They fight for so long.

And then

They stop.

10

I go to hell.

I don't know how long I go there for but, in the end

Kev comes and rescues me.

This is how he does it.

I wake up, I'm on the floor, my room

In Ordell Street. Taste of sick stale booze in my throat.

Don't know why I'm awake. Why I'm there. Why I'm breathing. Then

Kev's peering down at me. He pulls me

Up through the floor, says –

You know what we can do?

And I know what we can do.

Nothing.

Kev says:

We can make

The fuckers

Pay.

11

We get outselves a lawyer.

He is no win, no fee and he says that

In our case, a win is very likely indeed.

First thing, before court is a sort of meeting,

Up at the Heath. They talk for hours and basically

Tell me what happened to me, but in a way that makes it seem

Nothing was their fault. And when it's finished the lawyer says

Well that went *fantastically.*

And I say, did it? Cos I can't tell.

He says, oh yes,

It won't even get to court.

You press, they'll settle.

There should have been a midwife in the ambulance with you, you see.

And now they'll have to pay.

How much, I say, are they gonna have to pay?

The lawyer says, the average payout in maternity cases is

Two hundred and seventy-seven thousand pounds.

You should expect to receive rather more.

And I think what all that money would mean.

Get me a house.

Get me a car.

Get me by; for years and years.

And Kev says – we're going to win Eff!

And all these fuckers can fuck themselves!

I wander down through to the shops, buy –

The first thing I see, that I want. A box of juice.

And I sit, and sip it. And –

And across the way I see

The midwife. She's been in the room all morning but kept her mouth shut.

She stares at me a bit then looks away, stares, looks away, stares –

Like she knows she mustn't look at me but she just can't stop herself she says

I just want you to know, I'm so very very sorry for your loss.

But the thing is, Effie,

I couldn't have saved her, even if I'd been with you

What your little girl needed was

To be born in hospital. In a special care unit.

Where we'd've had the facilities, to look after her.

You were only in that ambulance cos

We didn't have a special care bed left.

We don't have as many special care beds as we used to

Cos of all these cuts. And what do you think happens,

If we have to pay you?

I say, you learn a fucking lesson love.

She says if we pay you, we'll have to cut more.

And more old people will die before they should.

More young people will never get a chance to live.

And more mums, just like you, will lose –

I say I don't know what you're crying about, bitch – apart from your job.

Kev says – that is bullshit the hospital will have insurance, that's

Where the money comes from, bound to.

And I know Kev's right

Or I sort of think he must be –

But my room is full of clothes

Sleepsuits and babygrows, that I picked out of piles

At jumble sales and charity shops;

Washed in the bath,

Hung on the radiator to dry,

Then tucked away snug into drawers.

And there's a cot. And toys. And a buggy that doesn't fit through the door.

And Nan says – do you think money will even help you?

I say I know it won't bring her back, I'm not fucking thick

She says no. No. Listen, for once.

I said, Effie: the state you are in, will money help you?

And I know. I know.

But then what will help? Because I need something, I really fuckin do

And she says, you know.

You know that too.

And so.

And so.

I drop the case.

I don't, make anyone pay.

Because there are years and years ahead of me

That were gonna be filled with loving her,

And getting loved back.

And that broken brick road to the sea

Not a mile away.

I could walk it any day.

And what stops me

What gets me through is knowing

I took this pain,

And saved every one of you, from suffering the same.

Your baby gets sick, she gets well
Because of me. Your mum gets ill
She gets healed, because of me and still:
You see me, pissed first thing wandering home
And all you think is, stupid slag. Nasty skank.
When what you should be thinking is,
Christ Effie, thanks. You took the cut, for all of us.

And I wander home, past
The pubs that shut, the library they closed,
The swimming pool got knocked down,
The bingo hall they burned
So they could turn it into flats.
More and more people packed in this little plot of land,
While they cut everything we need to make a life.
And we can take it. The hobbled soldier,
Limping to his little girl. The fat mum,
Wrestling her buggy out the rain. The pensioner,
Working night shifts at seventy again.
We can take it cos we're tough, the lot of us.
But here's the fucking rub.
It seems, it's always places like this
And people like us who have to take it,
When the time for cutting comes.
And I wonder: just how long
Are we gonna have to take it for?
And I wonder –
What is gonna happen
When we can't take it any more?

VIOLENCE AND SON

for Brigid Larmour,
without whom I would have given all this up long ago

Acknowledgments

Thanks to Vicky and the Classic Paines Plough line-up for sticking with me. To Chris Campbell for a lovely pub lunch. And to Helen Raynor Ltd., for keeping me in a manner to which I am gradually becoming accustomed.

Violence and Son was first performed at the Royal Court Jerwood Theatre Upstairs, Sloane Square, on Wednesday 3rd June 2015 with the following cast in alphabetical order:

JEN, Morfydd Clark
RICK, Jason Hughes
LIAM, David Moorst
SUZE, Siwan Morris

Director, Hamish Pirie
Designer, Cai Dyfan
Lighting Designer, Lizzie Powell
Composer & Sound Designer, Mark Melville

Characters

LIAM, seventeen.

JEN, eighteen.

SUZE, thirties.

RICK, forties.

All but LIAM have south Wales accents.

A forward slash in a speech ('/') indicates the point at which the next speech should begin.

SCENE ONE

A living room in a flat above a convenience store. Beyond, a small Valleys town. Beyond that, all of Time and Space.

LIAM enters. He is dressed as Matt Smith's Doctor. Fez, bow tie, the lot.

He stops. Looks round the place, wary.

He gets out a sonic screwdriver. Tries to scan the room. But there's something wrong with the sonic.

JEN: *(From off.)* And?

LIAM: Sonic's being temperamental. Hold on.

> *He fiddles with the sonic screwdriver.*

LIAM: If I can just reverse the polarity of the – yes!

> *And now the sonic lights up, whines and buzzes. LIAM scans the room.*
>
> *Inspects the reading on the sonic screwdriver.*
>
> *Draws a conclusion.*
>
> *And then he stops performing. Turns back to the door he came in through.*

LIAM: Yeah we're alright. Pissed bastard'll be down the York by now.

> *JEN enters, dressed as Amy Pond, dressed as a WPC strippogram, as in 'The Eleventh Hour'. Wig of long red hair, white shirt, chequered tie, stab proof vest, and a very short skirt. She looks round at the room. Liam watches her for a bit, then –*

LIAM: So it's not exactly Buckingham Palace.

JEN: Well I wouldn't know.

LIAM: I'll take you one day. Queen does a lovely tea, actually. Nice scones. Not stingy with the cream.

JEN: I wouldn't be seen dead with that entitled bitch.

LIAM: Nah, fair enough…

> *He goes to pick up a DVD box.*

LIAM: …she is a bit of a cunt.

He's getting a disc out, giving it a bit of a wipe clean.

He stops.

LIAM: I feel bad now, calling the Queen a cunt.

JEN: Showing off a bit.

LIAM: D'you think?

JEN: Slightly.

LIAM: As an old lady – fine. I got no problem with her. I'm not calling *her* a – she's someone's mum.

JEN: I get it.

LIAM: I'm not the kind of person, would call an old lady a cunt.

JEN: It's the institution –

LIAM: Yes!

JEN: – which is completely cunty.

LIAM: With you, sister.

He offers her a fist to bump.

She looks at it.

Looks at him. He's very serious. Though obviously messing.

She bumps his fist.

He turns away. She's smiling about him a bit as he talks.

LIAM: So we'll start with *Rose*, where we meet the Ninth Doctor. And of course Rose. And obviously… first ep of a reboot, lot to get done, lots of characters and concepts to introduce, and to be fair, Davies doesn't do a bad job of it.

JEN: In your humble opinion…

LIAM: I just can't believe you call youself a fan, and you've never seen Christopher Eccleston's Doctor.

JEN: I don't call myself a fan.

LIAM: She says, got up like Amy Pond.

JEN: I like the outfit.

314

LIAM: *I* like the outfit. And the skirt's…

JEN: What's up with my skirt, Liam?

LIAM: *(Can almost not say it.)* …apart from the hem?

JEN: Is it causing you problems?

LIAM crumbles, turns away.

LIAM: …besides, you know Russell T Davies is actually on record as saying, he's aiming at the 8-year-old kids in the audience?

JEN: It is a kids' show…

LIAM: Family show. Different thing.

JEN: Families include kids.

LIAM: I'm just saying, with RTD, he's writing for the 8 year olds… and you can tell. Whereas with Moffat…

JEN: Yeah but I liked David Tennant.

LIAM: Hey hey hey I am not slagging off David Tennant, David Tennant's easily the third best Doctor ever, don't get me wrong.

JEN: Just with the Matt Smith stuff…it's really good but half the time I'm trying to remember, where in River Song's timeline are we –

LIAM: So it's shit cos you don't understand it?

JEN: Did I say it was shit?

LIAM: About five seconds ago.

JEN: I said it's really good but.

LIAM: Which equals shit.

JEN: It equals really good. But.

LIAM: Why don't we, after we've done the Ninth Doctor, we could always watch the Matt Smith years again, together, and I'll explain it as we're going along, and I really think once you see how Moffat's vision all comes together –

JEN: Yeah alright.

LIAM: Yeah?

JEN: Yeah, give it another chance. I might get it this time.

LIAM: Okay. So… good.

JEN: With you to explain it to me.

He looks at her: she's deadpan.

LIAM: So let's start with Rose.

JEN: I like Rose.

LIAM: Okay good –

JEN: Cos she's a girl, like me, she's into mascara and boys so there's stuff I can like relate to, unlike the other stuff about time paradoxes, cos how do I relate to time paradoxes when I spend all my empty life hanging round the make-up counter at Superdrug?

LIAM: I was just saying –

JEN: D'you have dreams where you bump into Steven Moffat on a train and you and him become mates cos you're the only one who really gets what he's trying to do? And he emails you ideas at three in the morning when / he's just not sure...

LIAM: Yeah, alright.

JEN: Is it? Is it alright for me to like some things but then not like others so much?

LIAM: *(Beat.)* As long as you keep your massively faulty opinions to yourself, yes that's acceptable.

LIAM reaches for the remote.

Stabs at it, with a bit of flourish and ceremony.

The remote doesn't work.

LIAM: Jesus...

He takes off the battery cover, rolls the batteries around.

Tries again.

LIAM: I told him to get new batteries last week.

JEN: Just shift your arse press the buttons on the machine.

He's still trying. No good.

LIAM: Give it a sec.

He picks up the sonic. Sonics the remote.

LIAM: *(Off JEN's look.)* On my life, one time it worked.

He tries the remote again. Nothing.

JEN: But not this time...

He gets up. Goes to the DVD player.

LIAM: It'll take a while thinking about it.

JEN: Liam.

LIAM: Yeah?

JEN: I didn't, really...

She dries up.

LIAM: What?

JEN: Come *on*, mun.

LIAM: *What?*

JEN: D'you think I really came here with you to watch *Dr Who*?

Brings LIAM to a halt.

LIAM: Right. Okay.

He closes his eyes, breathes deep, in a very controlled way.

JEN: You alright?

LIAM: *(Eyes still shut.)* Fine.

JEN: I do want to watch *Dr Who*, even the really old stuff from the Nineties –

LIAM's eyes snap open.

LIAM: You should, McCoy is *massively* underrated.

JEN: But I came here today for another reason.

LIAM: I was sort of... hoping it might be, for another reason.

JEN: D'you know what that reason was?

LIAM: I could sort of guess? But then if I got it wrong, it'd be horribly embarrassing so I think I'd just as well / you told me.

JEN: The reason was you.

LIAM: Well that's sort, yeah, what I – okay. Good.

JEN: Cos – there's you. By here.

She points to a spot in front of her.

JEN: There's all the other boys. B'there.

She points to a spot far from the first.

So I'm saying you're very very different.

LIAM: Do you think I'm secretly a vampire?

JEN: I haven't ruled it out.

LIAM: I'm different… in some ways. Not all ways.

JEN: In good ways.

LIAM: I'll take that.

JEN: Compared to lads round here, it *is* like you landed in a blue box from another planet.

LIAM: It feels like I did, a lot of the time.

JEN: I mean I can really talk to you. The boys round here – they basically just grunt.

LIAM: Yeah isn't that Welsh?

JEN: Quite a cheap joke...

LIAM: Cheap jokes are best, you get so much more for your money.

JEN: And almost racist.

LIAM: That'll be why it's so cheap, no one's doing racism these days, it's really – no one's into it now.

JEN: I am genuinely trying to be serious, so you might wanna – just see if you can respond to me on that sort of level, at all?

LIAM: Yes, alright, okay? I felt it too. First time we talked. It was like we were really –

JEN: Talking.

LIAM: As shit as that sounds.

JEN: I'm actually a bit nervous now.

LIAM: *You* are?

JEN: It's quite a big deal, what I want to ask you.

LIAM: It's a yes.

JEN: You don't know what I'm gonna ask.

LIAM: I don't need to. Oh Jesus. Jesus *Christ…*

He shakes himself out.

LIAM: Whatever you ask, it's a yes. Yes. Definitely yes.

JEN: Well that's – that's… you *sweetheart.*

They look at each other.

JEN: So.

LIAM: So…

JEN: D'you think Jordan really likes me or does he not?

LIAM: Sorry?

JEN: Does Jordan like me, or is he not that bothered?

LIAM: Oh okay.

JEN: Because like – typical Saturday night, right? We go to the pub: he talks to his mates, I talk to my mates. We go to a party: he talks to his mates, I talk to my mates. We get pissed: he wanders over, sticks his tongue down my throat and his hand down my jeans. And that's great as far as it goes. But it's not what I dreamed of, as a little girl.

LIAM: No I can imagine.

JEN: And my friends say – basically they're saying, he's out of my league and I'm… Tina actually at one point said it might be mistaken identity, that he thinks I'm someone else? Someone… better.

LIAM: How could that be?

JEN: Well cos everyone thinks Jordan's brilliant, like, really great body and not a twat and he's getting this development contract with the Ospreys next year?

LIAM: I have no idea what that means.

JEN: It means they'll pay him, to play rugby. That'll be his job.

LIAM: You can get paid to play rugby?

JEN: I don't think anyone would play it for fun.

LIAM: No, fair point.

She thinks. She gets hopeful… and then sad. LIAM watches, rap.

JEN: Like one time I said, Jord, I've watched you play loads, let's do something I like. He said yeah great no problem. So he came round, and we were gonna watch *The Girl Who Waited* –

LIAM: Did he keep asking you who everyone was?

JEN: No we were cwtched, for like five minutes – and then he peels me off starts doing one-handed press-ups. And I'm like, sorry what? And he goes oh I'm still watching your programme. And he was. But like the whole of the episode, he's doing upper body work. And it's –

LIAM: It's not is it…

JEN: – is that romance, seriously?

She stops.

JEN: So he doesn't express an interest in me, as a person, cos… he hasn't got one.

LIAM shrugs.

JEN: I should just finish it then probably.

LIAM: If you've not got anything in common, then…

JEN: So that's what you think? I should finish with Jordan?

LIAM: Well I can't really say can I.

JEN: Why, what broke your mouth?

LIAM: It's not fair, for me to say.

JEN: Oh God, what'm I gonna do? Just even the idea of doing it is making me all tense. I can feel it now my back and shoulders tensing up.

LIAM: Well just… calm down then.

JEN: How can I calm down?

LIAM: Stop thinking about it?

JEN: I'm gonna get a migraine, I swear to God. That's two days in a dark room puking my guts out, and I haven't even done it yet.

LIAM: Is there anything I can do?

JEN: Like what?

LIAM: I was sort of asking you?

JEN: Got any pharmaceutical grade morphine?

LIAM: Just out, sorry.

JEN: I can feel it. I'm gonna puke. Any kind of emotional overload, you know, I'm chucking everywhere.

LIAM: I could give you a rub?

JEN: Beg your pardon?

LIAM: Like, your shoulders. I could rub your shoulders for you. Might help.

JEN: I think we're a bit beyond that.

LIAM: It's just you said it's your shoulders tensing up starts it off.

JEN: Yeah, but unless you've got magic fingers –

LIAM: Just… my mum. When she'd get stressed out. I'd rub her shoulders, and she said it helped. Even right at the end.

It takes JEN a moment to respond.

JEN: That'd be really nice yeah.

LIAM: Okay. Do you wanna –

JEN: What shall I sit on the floor?

LIAM: Yeah okay. Or if I sit first?

LIAM sits down on the settee. JEN sits on the floor, in front of him. She leans her head forward.

LIAM: Okay. Right.

JEN: What?

LIAM: You might have to um – take off the stab-proof vest.

JEN: Sure you're not gonna stab me?

LIAM: I think you're safe.

She considers. Looks at him.

JEN: I reckon I am.

Takes off the stab-proof vest. Sits again.

LIAM begins to knead her shoulders. Gently at first, nervous of touching her. But then more confident.

LIAM: Say if it's too hard.

JEN: It's nice.

He puts a bit more into it.

JEN leans her head forward.

LIAM: That alright?

JEN: Mmm.

He begins to elaborate his technique – kneading with his thumbs just each side of her backbone.

JEN: That is amazing…

LIAM carries on.

Suddenly JEN looks up.

JEN: It's not making you think of your mum is it?

LIAM: How?

JEN: You said you used to do this for your mum. It's not upsetting you is it? Making you think of her.

LIAM: *(Beat.)* This is not making me think about my mum, I promise you that.

JEN: I just didn't wanna, you know. Upset you.

LIAM: You're not.

LIAM goes on working.

And then there's something a little bit fierce, or intense, about his kneading.

JEN looks up. LIAM calms it down, but carries on working.

JEN: Lee.

LIAM: Yeah.

JEN: When I asked, should I finish with Jordan, you said, you couldn't say, because it wouldn't be fair. What did you mean?

LIAM: Just, you're a free individual, you make your own decisions, who the hell do I think I am telling you how to live your life?

JEN: I asked for your advice.

LIAM: Advice, oppression…where d'you draw the line?

She moves away from him.

JEN: You said, it wouldn't be fair. How's it not fair, for you to tell me what you think?

LIAM: Oh come off it.

JEN: Come off what?

LIAM: You know.

JEN: I bloody don't.

LIAM: It wouldn't be fair for me to say, cos…

He steels himself. Big confession.

LIAM: Cos obviously I want you to finish with him.

JEN makes a show of putting it together. There are about three stages. Then –

JEN: D'you fancy me?

LIAM: …do we have to give it a label?

JEN: You bloody do, you fancy me!

LIAM: You know what the Buddhists say, about feelings?

JEN: Why the fuck would I / know that –

LIAM: *(Cutting in.)* Feelings are like weather. They float in. They float away. That's all they are. Nothing to get worked up about.

JEN stares at him.

JEN: Do you think about what it'd be like to shag me?

LIAM can't answer immediately. Then –

LIAM: No…

JEN: You're thinking about it now!

LIAM: Cos you put it in my head!

JEN: I thought we were mates.

LIAM: We are, really good mates.

JEN: I came back here, to your place, the two of us – cos I thought we were mates and *nothing more.* I've got a boyfriend!

LIAM: …who you've been telling me you want to dump?

JEN: And you were hardly going all out telling me not to.

LIAM: Well I'm not an idiot…

JEN: Hold on – so, when you were –

She breaks off.

JEN: When you were touching me, just now. Was there… a sexual element?

LIAM: Absolutely none at all.

JEN: I definitely felt a sexual element.

LIAM: In what sort of a way?

JEN: A sexual element – in your touch.

LIAM: Obviously, it was not a horrible thing for me, touching you. But I would never, never – d'you think that's the kind of person I am?

JEN: Well I –

From off-stage – a bang. Wood against a wall.

JEN: What was that?

LIAM: I um –

Another bang. And another. And another. Rhythmic now. Carrying on as they speak.

LIAM: I think that maybe –

Bang. Bang. Bang. Getting faster.

LIAM: Maybe Rick is home after all.

JEN: Right.

Bang. Bang. Bang.

LIAM: I might just go let him know we're here…

LIAM heads to the door. The banging louder and faster. As he reaches the door –

SUZE: *(From off.)* Oh that's it, that's it, that's what I want.…

LIAM stops just short of the door.

LIAM: That's Suze, his…

SUZE: *(From off.)* Oh you beautiful big bastard go *on*…

JEN: His?

LIAM: His really good mate.

SUZE: *(From off.)* Oh you are getting there. You are getting there. You are getting there.

LIAM: Right so they won't be long now.

SUZE: *(From off.)* You are getting there oh *FUCK*…

The banging peaks: subsides: stops.

JEN: Sounds like he got there.

LIAM: He usually does in the end.

The door opens. SUZE in a dark – coloured dressing gown – thrown around her, not done up. She's talking back into the room she's come from.

325

SUZE: – cos if it was you it was dripping out of, I don't think you'd be so fucking breezy about it –

LIAM: Right Suze?

SUZE: Fuck!

SUZE pulls the dressing gown tight. It has no belt so she has to hold it shut.

SUZE: Didn't realise you were back.

LIAM: Just walked in the door.

SUZE: Is it?

LIAM: Like one second ago. No more than that at all.

SUZE: *(To JEN.)* Alright, I'm Suze.

JEN: Jen.

SUZE: Like the wig.

JEN: Itches like buggery.

SUZE: Bet it does. I'm just gonna…

She darts over to where a roll of toilet paper sits on a table. Grabs the roll, heads back to the doorway.

SUZE: Won't be a sec now.

Into the bedroom, closes door behind her.

LIAM: So yeah…

LIAM and JEN look at each other.

LIAM: I think, with Suze and Rick, there is quite a strong sexual aspect, to their relationship.

JEN: Well that's nice. I've heard it promotes trust, and intimacy?

LIAM: Aw yeah it's all good stuff.

RICK appears in the door. Bare chest, doing up his belt. He looks at LIAM; at JEN.

RICK: Back alright then.

LIAM: Why wouldn't I be alright?

RICK: Must've been you woke us.

LIAM: Normal people are up by now.

RICK turns to JEN.

RICK: You must be Jen. Since my son hasn't done the introductions.

LIAM: Christ, I'm *so* sorry. Jen, this is my biological male parent, apparently. Though I don't see the resemblance, do you?

RICK: I'm Rick.

JEN: Alright?

LIAM: So that's 'Rick', starting with 'r', not another letter quite close to it in the alphabet.

RICK: Lovely to meet you. At last.

JEN: Yeah and you.

RICK: Good day was it?

JEN: Yeah okay.

RICK: Like the wig.

JEN: Everyone does.

SUZE emerges from the bedroom.

SUZE: Put yourself away love, you'll frighten the girl.

RICK: I'm not frightening anyone, am I?

SUZE finds RICK's top in the room, throws it at him, then finds her handbag, checks herself in a little mirror.

SUZE: Depress the shit out of her then, when she sees what she's got to look forward to in twenty years time.

LIAM smirks at this. RICK notices.

RICK: *(To LIAM.)* Whassat?

LIAM knows there's some piss-taking coming.

LIAM: What is what?

RICK: Round your neck.

LIAM: It's a bow tie.

RICK shakes his head, as if baffled.

LIAM: Are you telling me you've never seen a bow tie before?

RICK: Not in real life no.

LIAM: Bow ties are cool.

RICK: *(Beat.)* No they fucking are not.

LIAM: Well thanks for clearing that up.

SUZE finishes touching up her make-up.

SUZE: So where you been today then?

LIAM: Regenerations.

SUZE – blank.

JEN: It's a conference.

RICK looks to JEN when she speaks; his gaze lingers on her a little.

SUZE: Whassat, save the world sort of thing?

LIAM: Not exactly no.

JEN: It's about *Dr Who*.

SUZE: They have conferences, about *Dr Who?*

LIAM: And science fiction and fantasy more generally.

SUZE: What the fuck for?

LIAM: For fun?

Not immediately after RICK looks away from her, but not long after – and almost without being aware she's doing it – JEN tugs her skirt down a little.

SUZE: A conference: about *Dr Who?* It's wild, the stuff they got these days. *(To LIAM and JEN.)* And what people dress up do they?

LIAM: You don't have to, but it makes it –

SUZE: More fun?

LIAM: Yeah.

SUZE: Do they go as Daleks?

LIAM: That's like the number one thing. Even more than the Doctor.

SUZE: So then what d'they do when they get to stairs?

LIAM: Sorry?

SUZE: If they're a Dalek? And they get to stairs.

JEN: Well: it is just a costume. They've still got their actual legs.

RICK looks over at JEN when she speaks. His gaze lingers on her again.

SUZE: Yeah, course, Suze you twat…

LIAM: Plus Daleks can fly now.

SUZE: You are shitting me? How d'you stop 'em, if they can get up stairs?

LIAM: Madcap genius, or a very big gun.

JEN: 'S alright if I get changed?

LIAM: Yeah, sure.

She picks up her bag.

JEN: So…

…where does she do that?

LIAM: Aw yeah, my room's down there.

JEN: Won't be a sec.

JEN heads off.

SUZE: You're brave.

LIAM: What?

SUZE: You know what state your room's in?

LIAM doesn't, panics: but then remembers. It's fine.

LIAM: It's fine.

SUZE: Apart from all them scrunched up balls of bog roll, piled under the bed?

LIAM stares at her.

SUZE: Don't worry, I cleared them. I shouldn't bloody have to…

LIAM: I've got a cold.

SUZE: It's summer.

LIAM: It's a summer cold.

SUZE: Funny sort of cold makes your snot smell like jizz.

LIAM: Oh my God…

SUZE: Yeah. I said it. Now I don't mind clearing out the plates and the coffee cups with mould in them, but all these wads of tissue paper, all smelling, every so slightly, of bleach – I don't see why I gotta be dealing with that.

LIAM: Don't go in there then.

SUZE: Oh, right. Put 'em back shall I? Still in the black bag in the kitchen, I can if you want, just tip 'em all out in front of that girl of / yours

LIAM: Obviously no

RICK: So what d'you say, then?

LIAM: Cheers Suze, you're a lifesaver.

SUZE: That's better.

Satisfied the point is won, she turns to RICK.

SUZE: He's done well with her hasn't he?

RICK: Father's son.

LIAM: As fucking if.

RICK: How old's she then?

LIAM shrugs.

RICK: Don't gimme the fuckin shrug how old's she?

LIAM: Does it matter?

RICK: Obviously yes or why'd I ask.

LIAM: Eighteen I think.

RICK: Eighteen he thinks? Eighteen he knows.

RICK's smiling.

LIAM: What?

RICK: Older woman. She'll teach you a thing or two…

SUZE: You're embarrassing him…

But she's enjoying teasing him too.

RICK: He embarrasses me enough, going round the place in his paedo outfits. *(To LIAM.)* How'd it go today then? You seal the deal?

LIAM: And what would constitute sealing the deal, in your considered opinion?

RICK: Cop a squeeze?

LIAM: *(Beat.)* Fingered her on the bus.

RICK: You fuckin never? Put it there boy!

LIAM: Course I didn't, you – Jesus…

RICK: She bloody wants it. You know that dunnew.

LIAM: We're just friends.

SUZE: Serious? Nothing going on?

LIAM: We enjoy each other's company. As friends.

RICK: Like fuck.

LIAM: Yeah, I know that's hard for you to process, but, in the twenty-first century, we can manage it quite easily?

RICK: She wear a skirt like that for all her friends?

LIAM: She's not wearing it *for* me. It's a costume.

RICK looks at SUZE, laughs.

RICK: And that's the only costume she could've wore?

LIAM: No, but the Weeping Angel outfit's a bit of faff getting on the bus.

RICK: *(To SUZE.)* Fuck's a Weeping Angel?

SUZE: How the fuck'd I know?

RICK: *(Back to LIAM.)* I'm saying, does she wear stuff like that normally?

LIAM: What, a policewoman's outfit? Hardly ever.

RICK: Skirts like they're fucking belts.

LIAM: Well no –

RICK: There we are then. She fuckin wants it.

LIAM: – she's not normally going to a Dr Who conference, so –

RICK: *(To SUZE.)* Christ Almighty I give up…You have a go?

LIAM: *(Also to SUZE.)* Could you explain to him, not every relationship between a man and a woman is based around shagging.

RICK: You don't fancy her then?

LIAM: Sorry, I was talking to Suze, wasn't I?

SUZE: Lee, you know the summer?

LIAM: No. You're gonna have to remind me.

SUZE: The summer when it's hot.

LIAM: Ah right in theory yes.

SUZE: So it's hot, and you wear shorts. Or whatever you wear. And it's just, you're wearing it cos it suits?

LIAM: Not really a shorts kind of guy myself, I think there's something very sad about grown men dressing like toddlers.

SUZE stares at him, a little weary.

LIAM: But I take your point.

SUZE: When you're a girl, ever since you're ten years old, you put a pair of shorts on, you got blokes eyeing you up. You get to Jen's age, you show some skin, you know what you're doing. Course you do. So she chooses that skirt, on this day, when she's going off with you? That is no fucking accident no way.

LIAM: There is nothing going on between us. She's got a boyfriend.

SUZE: Why's he not taking her?

RICK: Cos he's not a fucking geek.

LIAM: No. He's not. Which is why she's gonna finish with him.

SUZE: So it *was* a bit of a date. Like a pre-date date.

LIAM: No because, she hasn't finished with him yet. But she wanted to go to this conference with me. So long's it's just friends.

SUZE: So she said to you, it had to be, just friends.

LIAM: Yeah.

A look between RICK and SUZE – what is he like?

SUZE: 'S nice of her…

RICK: The things you could learn from me, if you had half the wit…

LIAM: I love that you actually think that's true.

RICK: You know what you've done? You have sold yourself cheap. She wants to go to this thing, doesn't wanna go on her own – so she gets you to come. She gets what she wants. What d'you get? 'Friends'. You should've held out for more. Cos there's more to be had, believe you me.

LIAM: You know a lot about what's going on in the head of this girl you met for two minutes.

RICK turns to SUZE.

RICK: Am I right – or am I right?

SUZE: Sorry – he is, love. It's like – being really honest now – if there's a bloke, and you like him as friend… and you can have him as a friend, and get another bloke as like your bloke as well – you'll have the both. Course you will.

LIAM: No offence now Suze –

SUZE: That's never a good start…

LIAM: – I don't think Jen is like you? In that way? So I don't think what you think really / matters…

RICK: Tell her you won't go with her to any more of this geeky shit, unless it's a date. And if she really wants to go, and there's no – one else to go with her – she'll say yes. You get your date. And then it's everything to play for.

LIAM: I bully her, into going on a date with me? *(To SUZE.)* Was that how it was, with you two?

SUZE: No, it was a bet. And then this place is handy for the pub, so…

RICK: How the fuck's it bullying?

LIAM: Cos I'm telling her she has to do what I say or else.

RICK: No, it's like – you go into a shop. To get some of your fucking… dolls or whatever.

LIAM: Collectable action figures but let it pass.

RICK: And they've got the doll you want, and the price on it's a tenner. So you pay a tenner. Or not, if that's too much for you. 'S no fuckin bullying about it…

SUZE: Just be honest. Tell her what's on your mind.

RICK: He's a teenage boy: what's on his mind is filth.

SUZE: And what d'you think's on a teenage girl's mind, Vile – puppy dogs and ribbons? *(Back to LIAM.)* Don't pretend you're just being mates with her, if really you're not. Cos that's sort of a lie.

LIAM: Okay.

SUZE: Alright.

LIAM: So what exactly does that translate to as action, for me, now?

SUZE: Well I can't tell you what to do, / can I?

RICK: Tell her – that you like her too much to be just friends. You thought you could do it, but you can't. It hurts too much. So if that's all you can ever be to each other… then you can't be with her at all.

SUZE: Where the fuck'd that come from?

RICK gives her a wink.

SUZE: How come you never used the flowery shit on me?

RICK: Was never a need.

He turns to LIAM.

334

RICK: Just, this once, listen to your old man.

LIAM: I would rather exfoliate my own bollocks, with molten lead. That's not even hyperbole. Hyperbole means wild exaggeration. I'm saying I'd literally do it. I'm saying I'd prefer an agonising death, over listening / to you.

RICK: All I'm saying is, I'm the one getting it on tap twenty-four seven –

SUZE: Oi, you prick…

RICK: – you're the one with the mountain of wank rags under your bed. You think on.

SUZE: D'you have to talk about me like that?

RICK: Like what?

SUZE: Like I'm a hole for you to shoot it into.

RICK: Sweetheart. You are much more than a hole for me to shoot it into…

SUZE already knows where this is going.

RICK: ..you're three, at least.

SUZE: Fuck you – *(Changes tone.)* What d'you mean three at least? What's number four?

RICK: Bloke I knew on the rigs was very fond of an armpit.

SUZE: Armpit's not a hole.

RICK: No, it's… a hollow. You're on those rigs long enough a hollow's all you need.

LIAM picks up JEN approaching.

LIAM: Could you two *please* just –

He breaks off as JEN emerges from LIAM's room, back into civvies.

SUZE: By the way, Jen: it's mould it is. In the walls. Gutter's bust and the damp comes through.

JEN: What now?

SUZE: The smell. It's mould. Not, him.

JEN: Ah, okay. I did wonder.

RICK: So we won't be five minutes then. Suze?

She looks at him – what?

RICK: Off to get chips aren't we?

SUZE: I wish you'd fuckin said...

RICK: I am saying. This is me saying now.

SUZE: I'm sticky as fuck, aren't I.

SUZE is fiddling in her bag.

JEN: You're not getting for me are you?

RICK: Course we are.

JEN: I was just off –

RICK: I'm getting chips anyway. Saturday.

SUZE: But usually you find the way by yourself. With it being two doors down an' all…

SUZE pulls a tiny bottle of perfume from her bag.

SUZE: 'Scuse all.

Sticks it up her top, a burst in the direction of each armpit. Then slightly pulls her leggings away from her stomach, sprays towards her upper thighs. Winces.

RICK: You want anything with your chips Jen?

JEN: Honestly I'm fine.

RICK: Fish? Sausage? Burger? Chicken? Veggie burger? Kebab?

JEN: I'm alright.

RICK: …rissole?

JEN: I'll just be off I think.

RICK: Don't say I didn't ask.

JEN: I don't think I can.

RICK: Right. See you then.

JEN: Tara.

SUZE: Nice to meet you Jen.

JEN: Yeah and you.

SUZE is gone, RICK lingering. JEN turns away, distracted with some bit of business – check make-up, tie a shoe-lace, pull on a jumper. Anything that means she doesn't see –

RICK, nods at JEN, winks at LIAM.

LIAM shrugs – what the hell's that supposed to mean?

So RICK makes a circle from the index finger and thumb of one hand. Then jabs the index finger of the other hand through it.

LIAM is appalled.

Once RICK is definitely gone.

LIAM: It's actually a lovely story them getting together? They'd been going to the York, for years, getting hammered every Thursday Friday Saturday, but they never actually met? And when they got together they realised three separate times they'd been involved in the same mass brawls, but never met: twice they'd stolen each other's drinks off the bar, but never met; and once had sex in next door cubicles in the bogs – but never actually set eyes on each other?

JEN: Amazing.

LIAM: Isn't it?

JEN: How did they meet in the end then?

LIAM: Internet dating.

They look at each other.

JEN: I had a lovely day.

LIAM: Yeah me too.

She looks around the place.

JEN: I best be off then.

LIAM: If you want.

JEN: Well, just: Jordan'll be wondering.

LIAM: Probably.

JEN: Or maybe not. Maybe won't've noticed. Anyway…

She turns to go.

LIAM: I hope we can do it again. There's a good one in Bristol supposed to be.

JEN: Yeah well.

They look at each other.

JEN: T'ra then.

LIAM: See you.

JEN: See you Liam.

She's going.

LIAM: Is that it?

JEN: Is that what?

LIAM: Is that how our day ends?

JEN: T'ra, see you. Pretty standard.

LIAM shrugs.

JEN: So…

LIAM shrugs again, not looking at her.

JEN: But hasn't it been a lovely day?

LIAM: I said that.

JEN: So don't – you know.

LIAM: Don't what?

JEN: Don't get weird and spoil it.

LIAM: Maybe I am weird. Maybe I've been weird all along and I'm just hiding it. Maybe that's too much for you.

JEN: It's more it's too fuckin boring.

LIAM: Oh well that's me told.

JEN: I don't think you are weird. I don't think dressing up like the Doctor is weird, see. I think it's a laugh. So you're not weird. And don't make yourself be now. Just –

They look at each other.

JEN: Okay. I'll see you very soon.

She goes to leave.

LIAM: No I can't.

JEN: Oh.

LIAM: I can't pretend that's it all fine, and I can't pretend I'm not… feeling certain / things when

JEN: *(Cutting in.)* What then?

LIAM: If we go to another conference, it can't be just as friends. I can't do that.

JEN: So you're telling me, I have to go on a date with you.

LIAM: No, I'm not saying / that

JEN: You are –

LIAM: No!

JEN: You're saying I have to go out with you. On a date. When you know I've got a boyfriend.

LIAM: No!

JEN: How's that gonna work? You gonna tell Jordan for me? Cos I can't see him being too happy about it –

LIAM: I'm not saying you have to do anything, right?

JEN: Fuckin sounds like you are.

LIAM: I'm saying – *all* I'm saying – is about me. It's about what *I'm* gonna do. And I'm not going to be able to go out with you so anything else, and pretend I just wanna be your friend. Alright? Because *(Beat.)* I think I could love you, actually.

JEN just stares at him.

LIAM: Not now, that would be – that would be weird – I'm saying, if we gave it a chance –

JEN: So if I want to carry on being your friend, and nothing more: then I can fuck right off?

LIAM: That's obviously not how I'd put it.

JEN: That *is* how I'm putting it.

LIAM: Well if that's how you *want* to put it, the last thing I want to do is tell you how you can or cannot put things.

JEN: Well then.

She stares at him.

JEN: Okay. So this is me, fucking right off.

She's up and off.

LIAM: What?

And she's gone.

LIAM sits, gob-smacked.

LIAM: Shit.

He gets out his phone. Dials. It gets busied. Answerphone.

Tries again. It gets busied.

LIAM: Yeah Jen will you answer please.

He sits for a bit.

Tries her number again. Rings off as soon as he gets answerphone.

And again.

And again. This time he lets the answerphone finish his message.

LIAM: Everything I just said – pretend I didn't. Can we? Course we can be friends. That's all I want, really, just – to be with you. And then if anything happens, as and when you know – that's just a bonus. Yeah a brilliant bonus, like the bonus ball that makes the difference between a couple of grand and like a genuinely life changing sum of money – but still, you'd be an idiot to say no to that couple of grand. And I am not an idiot. Any more. I was, for a second, but – that can happen, can't it? You can be an idiot for a bit and then drop it and just be normal again. So just please pick up, please?

He ends the call.

LIAM: Shit…

Noise at the door. LIAM's hopes rise – but then RICK and SUZE bundle into the room. SUZE carrying a big bag of chips, RICK carrying a couple of six-packs of cans.

RICK: Well with a bucket like yours you probably do prefer it sideways –

SUZE: Vile…

SUZE looks round.

SUZE: Where's your little friend?

LIAM: Dunno.

RICK moves into the room; puts down his six-packs. Pulls free a can and opens it. Takes drink.

LIAM: So I told her, like you said.

He's talking to RICK. RICK says nothing.

SUZE: And?

LIAM: And what d'you think?

SUZE: She didn't go for it.

LIAM: Not really no.

RICK drinks. LIAM's looking at him.

RICK: So what you fuckin looking at me for?

LIAM: You told me / that if I

RICK: *(Over him.)* You didn't have to listen.

LIAM: And that's all you got to say?

RICK shrugs.

SUZE: C'mon on love, plenty other fish in the sea.

LIAM: Oh really? Oh are there? What a devastating insight that is. I feel loads better now.

SUZE: You can't make somebody like you, and maybe she just didn't. She's young, you know. That age, they see some rugby lad with thighs like concrete and that's all they can see. It's her loss.

LIAM: Doesn't feel like her loss…

341

SUZE: Well, not now, no, but in time...

LIAM: Oh fuck off will you...

SUZE: *(Calm.)* You fuck off yourself you little shit.

> *LIAM looks at her.*

SUZE: Oh yeah, he likes to chuck the swears about, doesn't like it so much when they start coming back...

> *LIAM sits down somewhere so he's not looking at .*
>
> *SUZE gets on with eating.*

RICK: Want some chips?

LIAM: Eff off with your chips.

> *RICK moves a little closer to LIAM.*

RICK: The thing is, with girls –

LIAM: More wisdom is it.

RICK: Say when Doctor Who, is trying to stop the Daleks.

> *LIAM looks over at him, but doesn't speak.*

RICK: And like the first thing he tries, doesn't work. So what then? Does he sit and sulk? Or does he / try something –

LIAM: *(Interrupting.)* Are you trying to use Doctor Who as a teaching tool for my romantic life?

RICK: I'm saying, does Doctor Who give up, at the first knock back?

LIAM: No he doesn't.

RICK: No he doesn't. Doctor Who keeps / on going.

LIAM: Please stop it now–

RICK: What?

LIAM: *(Beat.)* 'Doctor Who' is the show. The character is 'The Doctor'.

RICK: What's the fuckin difference?

LIAM: The damage it does my head hearing you say it wrong.

SUZE: Leave him stew, Vile.

LIAM: Yeah, leave me, why don't you.

Rick hesitates.

RICK: What I'm saying is, don't give up.

LIAM: So I have another go with Jen then and / what?

RICK: No no no no.

LIAM: No?

RICK: No, fuckin Jen's gone mate. You blew it. Forget her. She's like… *the Doctor's* –

He pauses, expecting congratulations for getting it right. LIAM is stony-faced.

RICK: – first plan. Now you need another plan.

LIAM: When you say, another plan, you mean –

RICK: Well like what other girls do you like?

LIAM: None.

RICK: None?

Liam shakes his head.

SUZE: Aw well there we are then.

RICK: So all the girls, your school –

LIAM: College.

RICK: – if they all tipped up here offering to shag you now – you'd send them on their way? Couldn't bear to stick it in even one of them?

LIAM: That's my standard? A girl I could bear to stick it in?

SUZE: Don't knock a good shag, Liam. Things grow from a good shag.

LIAM: Is that what you think, Suze? Explains a lot…

RICK: Hey. Cool it.

LIAM: Or what?

SUZE: Vile.

RICK: Bit of fuckin respect's all it takes.

SUZE: *Vile.*

RICK snaps out of it.

SUZE: He didn't mean nothing. Alright?

RICK drinks, says nothing.

LIAM: There's a girl called Emma. She's got this funny sort of… mouth but it's, you know. Cute.

SUZE: Alright, so what's this Emma into then?

LIAM: She's a bit… like she's not so full of herself as Jen? Like Jen's here slagging off her boyfriend to me: but in college she is a bit – oh, did I mention I'm going out with the captain of the rugby team?

RICK: Yeah her mum's a stuck-up bitch too.

SUZE: How d'you know her mum?

RICK: Got to know her years back. Couple of times. Not so much now…

SUZE: Jesus…

RICK: What?

SUZE turns away from RICK, back to LIAM.

SUZE: Emma, she's a bit more down to earth?

LIAM: S'pose yeah.

RICK: Bit more your sort of level like?

LIAM: Fuck's that mean?

RICK: So, this Emma. Monday morning, you find your moment –

LIAM: She's not in Mondays.

RICK: Tuesday morning then. You find your moment, and you chat to her. Just anything. Just start it off. But you have to do it. Alright.

LIAM: Yeah, whatever.

RICK: You swear now. You'll talk to her when you see her next. And we take it from there.

344

LIAM: Alright.

RICK: We gotta plan, then. We're set. Tuesday morning, you're gonna talk to her. And we take it from there. And if doesn't work out with this Emma girl, we'll try the next one, and the next one, and –

There's a knock at the outside door.

RICK holds LIAM's gaze a second.

Then he walks to the front door. Opens it.

RICK: *(Off.)* Alright.

RICK walks back in. JEN follows him. Soaked.

RICK: Raining a bit then.

JEN: Little bit.

SUZE gets up, heads to the bathroom.

RICK: Yeah, was drizzling on us the way back from the chip shop.

JEN: Then it got a bit worse than that. I started walking and it pissed down so I called for a taxi and they said absolutely fucking nothing going, give it an hour an ring 'em again so I thought –

RICK: Come back wait here.

JEN: Yeah, if you don't mind?

RICK: We don't mind at all, do we? Do we, Lee?

LIAM doesn't answer.

SUZE is back with a towel.

SUZE: There you go love.

JEN: Aw cheers.

SUZE: You're drenched, look at you.

JEN: Did piss down on me slightly.

RICK: She wants to wait for her taxi.

SUZE: Yeah, course you can.

RICK: Yeah I said.

SUZE: You can't wait in these though, you're soaked. I'd give you something of mine but Vile's a bit funny about me leaving stuff here.

JEN: I'll be fine.

RICK: Liam'll dig you out something of his. Lee?

JEN: I'm fine I am.

RICK: See what you can find for Jen. Clean, mind.

LIAM: She says she's fine.

RICK: Do's you're fuckin told for once, will you.

LIAM heads off to his bedroom.

JEN: Honestly, taxi'll be here in a bit.

RICK: Taxi? But we got you chips.

SUZE: Yeah, stay and have chips.

RICK: I thought you were staying so I got extra.

JEN: That's really nice of you. Although I did say I wasn't…

RICK: Just in case.

SUZE: You head home now they'll only go to waste.

JEN: Yeah. I would…

LIAM return with a shirt and tracksuit bottoms.

He offers them to JEN, without a word.

JEN: Just I get the feeling maybe someone doesn't want me.

SUZE: Liam'd love to have you. For tea.

SUZE absolutely means the double-entrendre implied by the pause between 'have you' and 'For tea', and LIAM knows she does. He gives her a look.

JEN: Or I could just go.

LIAM shrugs.

JEN looks at him, not sure what to do.

SUZE: Liam.

LIAM: Was you went running off.

346

RICK: Go on, stay for chips. Sod the taxi I'll run you home after.

JEN: I could give you some money for petrol?

RICK: *(Smiles.)* No, you're alright.

JEN: Aw thanks, that's really good of you.

SUZE: D'you wanna get out of those wet clothes love?

JEN: Please. *(To LIAM.)* Can I use your room? Again.

LIAM: Yeah, use what you like. Again.

JEN hears the dig, goes.

RICK waits till JEN is safely gone.

RICK: What'd I tell you?

LIAM: I dunno, most of the time I'm not really listening.

RICK: She stropped off trying to get you to back down. You stood your ground. And you won.

LIAM takes this on.

SUZE: Oi, shall we eat off plates, if we got a visitor?

RICK: Yeah, they're in the kitchen.

SUZE: I know where they fuckin are you twat, come and give me a hand.

RICK begins to move, after SUZE.

RICK: She's up for it. Only thing is, have you got the balls?

RICK leaves to the kitchen, after SUZE.

And left alone, LIAM allows himself to think that maybe, just maybe, he is genuinely in with a chance with JEN.

And then there's the noise of JEN returning from his bedroom and LIAM locks all those sorts of thoughts down.

JEN enters.

Smiles at him. He smiles back.

She sits near him.

JEN: Listen.

LIAM makes a showing of giving her his full attention. It knocks her off-course a bit.

JEN: Listen.

She doesn't know what to say.

LIAM: I thought there was more to come after that.

JEN: Yeah so did I.

They smile at each other.

JEN: Look.

LIAM: I'm listening, I'm looking, what do I sniff you next?

JEN: I knew you liked me. I knew when we started talking about going to Regenerations, and…I said yes. Because I quite liked the idea that you liked me.

She falls silent.

JEN: And I think about it and I can't see me being with Jordan in like a year's time. So I think…finish with him then.

LIAM: Yes, definitely, you absolutely should.

JEN: But it's just…

LIAM: He's captain of the rugby team and…

JEN: Yeah I am actually that shallow…

SUZE and RICK return with plates and cutlery and things.

SUZE: *(To LIAM.)* You don't like their veggie burgers, do you?

LIAM: It's not about like, it's about they're cooked on the same grill as the meat –

SUZE: Which is why I didn't get you any. So it's cheese and chips for you. Jen, I don't know what you like, but I'm guessing you can't be as much of a fussy bugger's this lot so I got large of everything and there's bound to be something you can have.

RICK starts unwrapping the parcels of chips. Throughout the next section, the actors can interrupt the scripted dialogue with requests for salt, vinegar, etc.

RICK: These are mine, are they?

348

SUZE: Reckon so. Get stuck in, love.

JEN: I will. Whiff of chips and I'm starving.

RICK: You wanna beer Jen?

JEN grabs a plate, loads some chips on.

JEN: Ah... alright then, yeah.

RICK: There you go. Don't tell your mum.

JEN: Cheers.

LIAM is obviously expecting to be offered a beer. None comes his way.

LIAM: Am I getting one?

RICK: You're underage.

LIAM: Can I have a beer please.

RICK: You'll get all silly and embarrass yourself.

SUZE: Give him one, Vile.

RICK hands over a beer. Watches LIAM as he opens it.

SUZE: Gotta say, these are bloody good chips.

RICK: Fresh on, he said. You can tell. End of the night they're all soggy. But then end of the night who gives a shit.

SUZE: Never's good though, are they, as years ago.

RICK: No, I know what you mean.

SUZE: The taste, is like different?

LIAM: It's the fat. They used to fry chips in animal fat. Not any more.

SUZE: Is it?

LIAM nods as he eats.

LIAM: So they're like six percent less heart-attacky than they were.

SUZE: When I was little, it used to be a treat we had fish and chips every Saturday tea, only I'd have chicken cos I didn't like the bones. And I used to stuff 'em down me and get hiccups and heartburn...

RICK: Greedy mare.

SUZE: No, it was cos um…

She so obviously dries up that people look.

RICK: What?

SUZE: I don't wanna say.

She's not frightened, more embarrassed.

RICK: *(Beat.)* Oh okay. Suze doesn't wanna say. She's led us in, but now she doesn't wanna say so let's talk about / something else –

SUZE: If I didn't eat 'em quick I'd be too scared to eat anything. Cos it was tea time. Saturday. In front of the telly.

LIAM puts it together first.

LIAM: *You* watched *Dr Who*?

SUZE: Well it was on wasn't it? And I'd be cwtched into my dad crapping myself…

LIAM: *(A chant.)* One of us, one of us…

JEN: 'S alright Suze, girls are allowed to be geeks nowadays.

SUZE: Is it?

JEN: No, not really. But we're working on it.

LIAM: So which Doctor was yours then?

SUZE: Well I dunno who they are do I.

LIAM: Well was it in black and white, / or…

SUZE: *(Cutting in.)* How fuckin old d'you think I am?

LIAM: I wouldn't even dare / begin to…

SUZE: *(Cutting in.)* It was the one with all the hair.

LIAM/JEN: Tom Baker.

SUZE: And he was proper scary, not like today where they're all cuddly and they snog. Chuck us the red sauce, Vile.

RICK passes her the ketchup.

SUZE: You want some more love?

JEN: I shouldn't…Christ I sound like my mum!

SUZE: Go on, help yourself.

JEN: I was gonna say, I remember having chips when we were little, cos mum'd always be on these stupid diets? Like black coffee and grapefruit?

SUZE: Christ I remember that one…

JEN: And all you would eat was –

SUZE: – black coffee and grapefruit!

JEN: And end of the day, she'd be in a foul mood, surprisingly.

RICK: *(To LIAM.)* All as daft as each other.

JEN: So like seven eight o'clock she'd give up, she'd have to eat. But to stick to the diet, she'd have nothing in the house. Like literally nothing. Spices and… out of date icing sugar. So she'd be stamping round the place waiting for Dad to come home to send him out for chips.

RICK: Why didn't she go out for chips?

SUZE: She had the kids didn't she.

JEN: No it was like – it was one of her things. She got funny going out at night?

RICK: Bit of a, tense lady your mum?

JEN: Used to be. Chilled out a lot now. Since she discovered pinot grigio comes in boxes.

RICK: You know what I remember? The test card. See you haven't got a clue what that is.

LIAM: Of course we do, it's on the net – like everything.

RICK: I remember seven eight, I hated school. And I hated dinners the worst dunno why.

SUZE: Cos they were so shit.

RICK: Probably yeah. And one day, going into the hall, Miss Williams grabs me. And I'm thinking, what've I done now? – and she says your dad's here. And he was. And he took me out of school, for my dinner. I didn't even know you could do that – but you could. And I remember – walking, holding his hand, walking down the high street, thinking all my friends stuck in school, and me out with my dad. And we went to the chip shop. I had chips and battered sausage. And in the chip shop there was a telly, and I wanted the telly on and they said there was nothing on, but Dad made them put it on anyway. And it was just the test card. Only then they kept it on for the music. *(Eats a chip.)* I was what five? And one second I'm in school hating it – and the next I'm having chips with my dad. Like magic. And he did it the next day. And the next day. Every day that week. *(Beat.)* And then the next week he moved out. And I hardly saw him after that.

RICK eats. A little silence.

SUZE: He was saying goodbye.

RICK looks at her. Smiles. Picks up his drink.

RICK: Cheers everyone.

SUZE and JEN raise their drinks in response.

SUZE: I wish I'd known him.

RICK: He was a prick he was.

RICK has said this and meant it: he doesn't now.

LIAM is looking at him. RICK notices. Holds LIAM's gaze. Not challenging, for once. Just not looking away.

Finally LIAM breaks it.

SUZE: Stuffed. You wanna finish these for me Vile?

RICK: Aye go on.

JEN: Why'd you call him that? Vile.

SUZE: It's like a nickname.

JEN: What, cos he's – vile?

RICK: I look vile to you?

SUZE: Don't tempt her, she's trying to be polite.

RICK: If you're trying so hard the effort shows, you might's well not bother.

SUZE: It's cos… when he was younger, like, he used to get into scrapes. Like a lot.

JEN: When you say scrapes?

SUZE: Like pub on a Saturday night. Or a Friday night. Or a Thursday night…

JEN: But scrapes, though: what, is that, exactly?

SUZE: Like silly stuff. You look at my bird, sort of thing.

JEN: D'you mean, fights?

SUZE: You know, like boys do.

LIAM: I don't.

RICK: I have never started a fight in my life. *(Beat.)* Finished a few though…

JEN: So he's called Vile cos…

SUZE: Like you get called by what you do. So Dai the Butcher, Steve the Post. And they called him – Violence.

JEN: Oh okay.

SUZE: As a joke.

JEN: Course.

SUZE: This is all donkey's years now. He's calmed down a lot. Haven't you?

RICK: You put that beer away Jen.

JEN: Did I? Christ I did.

RICK: It's the salt innit. Salt gives you a thirst. Have another.

SUZE: I was saying it's years ago, Vile. All that stuff. You haven't smacked anyone for ages.

RICK: Christ no. *(Beat.)* Apart from that retard I broke his jaw.

SUZE had not simply forgotten that incident.

SUZE: Well yeah. Apart from him.

RICK: Cos that was what, less than a twelvemonth?

SUZE: Yeah but I thought not to mention that –

LIAM: What was this?

SUZE: – not wanting to scare the girl, like?

RICK: No, fair play, but – truth's the truth. And I'm not ashamed of it. Plenty of the stuff I done when I was younger, yeah, I was a fucking cock. But not that. That needed doing.

JEN: Sorry what?

SUZE: What it was – you know the York? You know how it gets Friday Saturday night?

JEN: Rammed.

SUZE: And you know what happens?

LIAM: What?

SUZE: You dunno: she does. What happens, in the York, when it's rammed?

But JEN doesn't know.

SUZE: If you're a girl.

Instantly she does.

JEN: You get felt up.

SUZE: And a grope of the arse – well whatever you know. But there was this bloke. Nathan. And he's a bit – simple, like.

LIAM: You mean he's got learning difficulties?

SUZE: That sorta thing, yeah. And people'd had a word, but it didn't go in? I think, cos of the – learning difficulties? He didn't get it. So I'm in there one night, go to the bar – and he's behind me. Goes under my skirt. Rams his fingers, right up in me. And like I say I'm not the first. And they chuck him out and he's just giggling? So Vile goes out there and –

LIAM: And what?

RICK: Hit him.

JEN: And broke his jaw.

RICK: I didn't mean to.

JEN: Still you must've hit him pretty fucking hard to do that.

RICK: I meant to hit him pretty fucking hard. I meant to hit him hard enough it would hurt, for a long time.

SUZE: And – I know, I do – but the fact is he's not been in there since. Not touched anybody. Nothing.

LIAM: So he's learned his lesson then?

RICK: Looks like it, yeah.

JEN: Didn't think to go to the police?

SUZE: Has anybody ever stuck their hand up you?

JEN: *(Beat.)* Fucking obviously.

LIAM looks: that this is obvious is a surprise.

SUZE: You go the police?

JEN shakes her head.

SUZE: Yeah exactly. And people'd told him. His mum and dad, had told him. His brothers, had told him.

JEN: Yeah, well...

SUZE: What, I should just put up with it, should I?

JEN: I'm saying, there's ways.

SUZE: There weren't. And some of the girls he was going after were young. Really young, like fifteen.

JEN: What were they doing in the York then, they're that young?

RICK: And you were never in there that age...

JEN: You broke the jaw, of a man with learning difficulties. That is fucking psychotic.

RICK: Fair enough. I get why you don't like it. But I'll tell you this. Week after, the kid's dad comes round. And you know what he says to me?

They don't.

RICK: He says, thank you, Rick. He fucking *thanks* me. Cos he says, his boy's learned now. Says if he'd carried on the way he was going, he'd've ended up in jail. And what the fuck do you think happens to some simple little kid in jail? You think he has it easy? I wouldn't think so. I wouldn't think so at all. But that's where he was headed. Till I stopped him.

JEN: Yeah, well –

RICK: The dad says, he actually says to me, by rights he should've done it himself. And I get that. Your own son – you're fucking soft. So fine. You think I'm a bit of a cunt fair play. I'm not saying it's a nice thing I did. I'm not saying it's good. But the kid keeps to himself these days, no trouble to anybody. And his own dad, shakes my hand. *(Beat.)* But what the fuck, you got more exams'n I'll ever have, you know best.

JEN: Yeah well.

The fight goes out of her a little.

JEN: It's just fucking tragic that's how it is.

RICK: No fucking disagreement from me, love.

She relaxes.

RICK: So. Another beer?

JEN: Yeah…no I might be off.

SUZE: Aw is it? You don't have to.

JEN: No, I'm not being – look, I'm sorry alright, I still don't like it, what you did –

RICK: I don't like it.

JEN: – but, Christ, what the fuck're you supposed to do?

SUZE: Fucking put up with it, is what you're supposed to do…

JEN: S'pose yeah.

RICK: And you shouldn't have to.

JEN: No, course. It's just it's getting a bit, late, you know.

RICK: No worries, I said I'd give you a lift. Gimme till I've finished –

He stops.

RICK: I can't can I?

SUZE: What d'you mean you can't?

He's got a beer in his hand.

RICK: This is what my…

SUZE: Third?

RICK: Fifth now, if that. Christ, I'm sorry love.

JEN: That's alright. What now?

JEN hasn't quite understood.

RICK: Well I'll be over won't I. For driving you home.

JEN: Oh.

RICK: Yeah. Sorry, I didn't think –

JEN: No, that's alright –

RICK: – like cos for myself I bomb round the lanes all sorts of states and I know I'm safe but, passenger in the car – different thing, see.

JEN: 'S alright, I'll ring the taxi again.

JEN phones for a taxi. Waits for the number to answer.

SUZE: Where you live love?

JEN: Maesteg Road?

SUZE: Christ that is a way.

The number answers. JEN asks for a taxi to Maesteg Road.

RICK peers at SUZE's plate.

RICK: You eating that?

SUZE: Does it look like I am?

RICK: You might be having a break.

JEN: Okay thank you.

Ends the call.

JEN: They only got two cars out this way and one of them just crashed.

SUZE: What about your mum?

JEN: She's funny driving at night.

SUZE: And there's no buses that way are there?

JEN: Christ no. Though once Prince William came and they re-routed everything so they did go –

She stops.

JEN: No basically.

SUZE: What we gonna do then?

JEN: 'S alright. I'll walk.

SUZE: You'll get soaked.

JEN: I'll live.

SUZE: Late to be out walking alone.

LIAM: I'll come with.

JEN: I can't let you do that, it's miles. And raining.

LIAM: I don't know how you could stop me.

JEN: Break your legs?

RICK: Course. You know what you could do.

RICK waits till he has everyone's attention.

RICK: You could just crash here the night?

JEN: Well I –

RICK: If you're sure I'm not fucking psychotic!

He's making a point of being jovial.

JEN: Yeah alright fair play, I did go off on you a bit.

She looks to LIAM.

LIAM: I mean…if you want, whatever.

JEN: Whatever?

SUZE senses there is a negotiation that needs privacy.

SUZE: Gimme a hand clearing the plates, Vile.

RICK: You eat out the paper, it tastes better and you got fuck all to clear away.

SUZE: It's not fair is it – all the things people ask of you…

RICK follows SUZE off. JEN takes a moment to find what to say.

JEN: It's not that I don't want to stay.

LIAM: Right.

JEN: I mean…I could.

LIAM: Then definitely do!

JEN: It's just Jordan isn't it. Cos I haven't, like *officially* told him.

LIAM: But you are going to.

She doesn't say anything.

LIAM: Aren't you?

JEN: You know I am. *(Off his look.)* And don't look all chuffed with yourself, it's gonna break his fucking heart.

LIAM: No, I know. I'm sad for him, he seems like an alright bloke.

JEN: He is. As far as he goes.

A pause between them. LIAM fears to push the point might generate resistance.

LIAM: Does that really happen all the time?

JEN: …any sort of context?

LIAM: You get felt up in the pub.

JEN: Not *every* single time…

LIAM: Jesus Christ…

JEN: It's a tricky one cos – you wear jeans, you have at least got the protection of the thicker material but it means they can go straight in between the legs. You go with a skirt, they have to reach under it and then back up to get to your crotch which is a bit awkward, so they'll probably just make do with a knead of the arsecheek – but then if they *do* make the effort to get under and up and between, then you'll actually feel the fingernails scrape down the lips of your vagina.

LIAM: Jesus fucking Christ…

JEN: It's not super-fun.

LIAM: Someone should do something.

JEN: Yeah okay, what d'you think – petition? Awareness raising meme on social media?

LIAM: I am really, really sorry, you have to put up with that shit. On behalf of the male species.

JEN: Sometimes I feel like… there should be a fucking law against it.

LIAM: There should, let's try that.

JEN: My mate Katie, she's in the York, it's rammed, she's coming back from the bogs and – two fingers, right up her. So she turns round and this bloke, is just grinning. With his hand still, you know. And she's just had a-fucking-nough, of putting up with it. So she slaps him. And this bloke, takes his hand out of her crotch – and punches her in the face. And she goes straight down. She's sat there in the spilt beer, thick lip, bloody nose, people shoving past her. And the bloke just slips off.

LIAM: They get him?

JEN: They what? And now every time some random even… stares at her tits she's thinking where the fuck does this end up? She wishes she'd let the fucker just get on with it. Cos standing up to him just made everything worse.

LIAM: Seriously: how the fuck d'you cope with even going there?

JEN shrugs.

JEN: Pre-drinks are a girl's best friend. Plus it's where everyone goes. Where my mates go. Where Jordan goes…

LIAM: Is that where you're supposed to be going, tonight? Out with him to the York?

JEN: It is Saturday…

LIAM: I don't think you should. Cos it sounds horrible.

JEN: It really is…

She thinks about it.

JEN: That's it. I'm not going.

LIAM: And I'll be on the couch. Out here. You'll just be staying over. We don't have to do anything. If you don't want –

JEN: And you can calm it down too, I'm not staying here. I'm just gonna go home.

LIAM: Right. Okay.

JEN: Because I think – the first night we stay together, we should do it properly.

LIAM: Oh.

JEN: Not with me feeling all guilty about Jordan. So I'll go home. And tomorrow I'll finish with him. And then… you can whisk me away, in your magical blue box.

LIAM loves this idea.

But then –

LIAM: You know I haven't *really* got one, don't you?

SCENE TWO

LIAM in the living room. RICK enters.

RICK: Where's the lucky lady?

LIAM: Trying to talk her mum into coming picking her up. She said she didn't want me to hear her beg.

RICK: Reckon I could stand to hear her beg…

LIAM: That is… vile.

RICK: I can't believe I got her stuck here and you let her go. What is the point of you, honest to God…

LIAM: Yeah well actually, tomorrow she's going to see her
boyfriend and finish with him.

RICK: So she says...

LIAM: So she will.

RICK: Or she might go see her boyfriend... trip and fall gob
first on his cock.

LIAM: I don't know why I even bother listening / to you –

RICK: Well you might wanna start listening more. Cos what
did I say would happen? I said you stand your ground,
she'll come running back. And she fuckin did.

LIAM: She came back, to get out the rain.

RICK: You can get out the rain standing in a fucking bus stop.
She didn't do that. She came back here.

LIAM doesn't answer.

RICK: I said she would: and I was right.

LIAM: Stopped clock.

RICK looks at him.

LIAM: Is right twice a / day.

RICK: Old fuckin joke.

*RICK moves, to get another beer. This puts him standing behind
where LIAM is sitting.*

LIAM: I think it's an aphorism more than a joke. Is that what
an aphorism is?

LIAM's talking to himself.

RICK: How'd I fuckin know?

LIAM's getting out his phone, to look up 'aphorism'

LIAM: And, in a million years, why'd I be asking you?

RICK watches him.

LIAM finds something.

LIAM: Ah right. Maybe technically just a proverb.

RICK: Is it.

LIAM: Cos you were on tenterhooks, weren't you, to find out.

LIAM gets back to his phone, diverted by something else.

RICK watches him a little while.

RICK: So why then?

LIAM looks at him, not following?

RICK: Why's it a proverb, not a – whatcha/call

LIAM: *(Cutting in.)* An aphorism?

RICK: Yeah.

LIAM: D'you actually care.

RICK: I wanna know.

LIAM: How would it ever be of use to you?

RICK: I wanna know.

LIAM: A proverb is a saying, like any saying that's being around forever. An aphorism, it'd have to be something you made up yourself. Like, not something / you'd heard someone else –

RICK: *(Cutting in.)* No I get it.

LIAM gets back to his phone.

RICK: Clever little fucker aren't you. Knowing the difference.

LIAM: I just read it on my phone?

To which he returns, again.

RICK: No, you've done well with her though. Jen.

RICK gets the beer. Opens it. Takes a drink.

LIAM: Christ well your approval is, the *only* thing, really, I care about.

LIAM doesn't even look up.

RICK moves across the room, nearer LIAM. Finds something to fiddle with.

RICK: That girl had her kid next door?

LIAM: Fuck do I know.

RICK: Just asking.

Drinks.

Watching LIAM.

And then he reaches out, tousles LIAM's hair.

LIAM recoils.

LIAM: Get, the fuck off.

RICK: Just seeing what you got on your hair.

LIAM: Nothing.

RICK: Fucking greasy then. She'll get fucking acne running her hands through that.

LIAM: Piss off.

RICK: Joking mun.

LIAM: And how, is it funny?

RICK moves away.

RICK: Keep thinking I can hear a baby crying. Like, off, you know.

LIAM doesn't follow.

RICK: So I reckon she has had it: next door.

LIAM: Oh, d'you know what that is?

RICK: What?

LIAM: No cos I hear that.

RICK: At night like.

LIAM: All sorts of times. It's – you don't mind me saying?

RICK: How would I mind?

LIAM: I'm just trying to think how to put it.

RICK: Simplest's best.

LIAM: Yeah, absolutely, so, in the simplest possible terms: it's after you've fucked Suze?

He lets it hang a second.

LIAM: Cos afterwards, she goes off and has a little cry? I say little cry…she locks herself in the bog and screams a good five ten minutes?

RICK: Har-de-fuckin-har.

LIAM: Really not joking.

RICK drinks again.

RICK: All I'm saying is, I'm glad you got a girl round cos, I was ninety per cent you were a poof.

LIAM: Is that the best you've got? Because – in that case I definitely am a poof. If that's what was worrying you. I'm the biggest poof this valley's ever seen. I'm a massive cockingsucking poof. Even bigger… than your mate Trev. Because he is. Oh he is. No doubt about it.

LIAM smiles.

LIAM: 'Poof'. Seriously. Do you do that –

LIAM makes the limp-wristed, Larry Grayson gesture.

LIAM: When you think someone might be gay? Do you?

RICK: Showing off a bit.

LIAM: Who'm I showing off to?

RICK shrugs.

RICK: It's what kids do. Show how big they are.

LIAM: How the fuck'd you know what kids do?

RICK: Cocky now cos you got your girl round.

LIAM: Or maybe now I know I definitely definitely am a poof, now that nagging doubt about my sexuality's been dealt with, I just feel more confident, more assertive.

RICK: Think you can say what the fuck you like and there's no come back.

LIAM: I *can* say what the fuck I like.

RICK: Is it.

LIAM: I'm not scared of you.

RICK smiles.

LIAM: Alright. I am. I am scared.

RICK: Oh I know that.

LIAM: You proud of yourself? That a boy is scared of you?

RICK: You got no reason to be.

LIAM: Oh really. None at all.

RICK: Okay. I get wound up, I might *say* I'll chuck you out, but it's / pissed talk –

LIAM: Chuck me out?

RICK: But I'd never. This is your home.

LIAM doesn't answer immediately.

LIAM: Aw well, there we go.

RICK: What then?

LIAM looks at him.

RICK: What?

LIAM: Chuck me out. *That's* what I'm afraid of?

RICK doesn't answer immediately.

RICK: You see you're good with words. And that's fine. Lot of the time you can talk your way out of trouble. But's a bad thing too. Cos you think you're safe with words. You think can say what you like. And you can't. There are some things, you say them, you're in a heap of shit. *(Beat.)* Course if I'd brought you up, you'd know that.

LIAM: If you'd brought me up I'd've fucking killed myself by now.

RICK doesn't answer.

LIAM: Because she told me, before she went. What kind of bloke you are.

RICK: And what kind's that?

LIAM: I know why she ran away from you.

RICK: And she says it so it's true? Two sides to every story.

LIAM: Hers, yours. I know what I believe.

RICK: Course you do. Woman that ran off with you, never let me see you, never let me speak to you – course you believe her.

LIAM: I know what you are.

RICK: What?

LIAM doesn't speak.

RICK: You can't even fuckin say. Look at you. Mummy's boy.

LIAM: Well I had to be.

RICK: You turn up, and what do I do? Put a roof over your head, feed you. And who the fuck are you to me? Some kid I never met, that some pisshead says was mine. But in you come. And like that, this is your home. And where else you got would do that for you?

LIAM: Nowhere –

RICK: Exactly.

LIAM: – or I'd already be there.

RICK: Aw, clever.

LIAM: Not really.

RICK: I say your mum was a pisshead. She'd come home she wouldn't have a clue, where she'd been, what she'd been doing. So you could be mine. You could be half the blokes in town. Not just cos she was a fuckin slag. But she'd be out cold in the corner of the pub, anyone could've done anything, she'd never've had a fuckin clue. Except they knew fuckin better than to touch my girl.

LIAM: Wasn't she lucky you were there to look after her.

RICK: Aye, she fuckin was.

LIAM: Shall we actually get a DNA test done?

RICK: Fuck it why not.

LIAM: And then if I'm not yours, you can kick me out.

RICK: Suit me.

LIAM: Alright.

LIAM gets out his phone.

RICK drinks.

LIAM finds what he was looking for on his phone.

LIAM: Here we are. Ninety-nine quid. They send us swabs. We send 'em back special delivery, get the result the next day. I'll fill out the form, shall I?

RICK: If you want.

LIAM: Brilliant.

LIAM starts filling out a form on his phone.

RICK watches for a bit.

RICK: Oi.

LIAM: What?

RICK: Fuckin stop it.

LIAM's still filling out the form.

LIAM: Why?

RICK: Lee.

LIAM: Name's got two syllables. Just two. See if you can be arsed.

RICK: Liam. Joke's over, alright.

LIAM: Again: not joking. Tuesday… and we will know!

RICK: Fucked if I'm doing that.

LIAM: 'S alright. I'll wipe up your slobber when you pass out on the settee.

RICK: Gimme that phone.

LIAM: What, my phone? Don't think so.

RICK: Give it.

LIAM: Fuck off.

RICK snatches it off him.

LIAM: I'll just get it back when you're pissed.

RICK: You fuckin try it.

LIAM: I will.

> *RICK stares at him.*
>
> *LIAM grabs for the phone.*
>
> *RICK dumps the phone in a pint glass of water.*

LIAM: You prick.

RICK: I said stop.

LIAM: You absolute prick.

RICK: Now you'll know to listen.

LIAM: That was my phone.

RICK: And?

LIAM: Mum got me it.

> *RICK gets the phone out the glass.*

RICK: 'S probably alright.

LIAM: Just give it to me.…

RICK: Was only in there two seconds –

> *LIAM grabs the phone off him, begins taking it to bits.*

LIAM: You got any rice?

RICK: Rice?

LIAM: As in pudding.

RICK: Why the fuck'd I have rice pudding?

> *LIAM grabs a tea towel, lays it flat on a surface.*

LIAM: No, the rice, I want the rice. Have you got any?

RICK: No.

LIAM: Course you fucking haven't.

RICK: What's the rice for?

LIMA's putting all the components of the phone out on the tea towel.

LIAM: Because if you put the parts of a wet phone in a bag with rice, the rice absorbs the moisture and saves your phone. Supposedly.

RICK: Shall I get some?

LIAM: It's probably bollocks. Sounds like bollocks.

RICK: There's a shop, they fix phones, we'll take it / round there.

LIAM: And what'll they do, in this shop?

RICK: There's bound to be something they can do.

LIAM: Yes there is: the thing I'm doing now.

RICK: They don't just fix phones, they sell 'em. Get you a new one if you want. Newer one than that.

LIAM: I don't want a newer one, I want mine.

RICK: Don't be like that mun.

LIAM: What'm I being like, Vile?

RICK: It's just a fucking phone.

LIAM: It's not just a fucking phone.

RICK: And I've said I'll buy you new. Don't be a cunt about it.

LIAM: Is that what I'm being?

RICK: Okay, sorry, but – Christ, mun…

LIAM stops his fiddling with the phone. Looks at RICK.

RICK: Well, you are.

LIAM: After they sent her home from the hospital. She looked like she was a two hundred years old, oxygen tanks and drips in her arm. I wanted to remember her. I wanted to remember the last time she was with me. And I knew she wouldn't want any pictures taken, with her in that state. So I waited till she was asleep. Snuck a few on this.

Beat.

LIAM: It was the last thing I had of her. The last thing I had. And now I've got nothing.

RICK: C'mon mun.

LIAM: C'mon what?

Not immediately –

RICK: You can't say you got nothing.

LIAM: What've I got then? Huh?

They stare at each other.

LIAM: What've I got, in the world?

RICK: You know.

And then LIAM folds up.

Begins to cry.

RICK: Aw now…

LIAM tries to lock it down –

– but then can't. Is crying properly.

RICK: You want Jen seeing you like this?

LIAM: Couldn't give a toss.

RICK: Aye well you should. No – one wants to fuck a crybaby.

LIAM cries.

RICK: Yeah alright give it a rest.

LIAM cries.

RICK: Liam.

LIAM cries.

RICK: We've heard enough.

LIAM: I fucking hate you.

RICK: Yeah we know.

LIAM cries.

RICK: This is just showing off. This is showing off, again.

LIAM: I'm going to my room.

RICK: No you are not. You are gonna sit there, and shape up.

LIAM tries to get past him.

RICK won't let him.

LIAM: The fuck are you doing.

RICK: You're gonna sit there, and we're gonna cheer you up, before Jen comes back.

LIAM: Piss off.

LIAM tries to shove past RICK.

RICK holds him back.

LIAM: What the fuck?

LIAM tries, with all his might, to get past RICK.

RICK can't hold him, has to shove him away. It's a hard shove. LIAM staggers back, and then falls. Hits his head. Cries out in pain and shock.

RICK: Now see?

LIAM's getting up.

RICK: Now look what you done.

LIAM's back on his feet. He's bleeding a bit.

RICK: You alright?

They look at each other.

Something in RICK breaks – he moves towards LIAM.

RICK: Listen, now, listen to me –

LIAM backs off.

RICK: No, I know, I know –

SUZE enters.

SUZE: What the fuck's going on?

RICK: Nothing.

She looks at LIAM.

SUZE: How'd you do that?

He doesn't answer, just looks at her.

SUZE: Your head's bleeding.

LIAM: Pigs come, at night, with teeth, but then I'm fine later.

SUZE: You what?

LIAM: After they go I'm fine.

SUZE: Liam, are you okay?

LIAM: I said I'm fine!

LIAM touches his head – finds the blood.

LIAM: Oh shit.

SCENE THREE

JEN and LIAM.

LIAM is blowing on the bits of phone with a hair dryer.

He stops.

LIAM: What d'you reckon?

JEN: Give it another while. Better safe than sorry.

She looks at him.

JEN: Has he done this before?

LIAM: Done what.

JEN: Hit you.

LIAM: He didn't hit me.

JEN: You look like you got hit.

LIAM: I hit my head.

JEN: When he shoved you.

LIAM doesn't respond.

JEN: Has he?

LIAM: No he has not hit me.

JEN: But.

LIAM: I didn't say but.

JEN: Really cos I definitely heard one.

LIAM: It's just when he's had a bit.

JEN: Lucky he only drinks birthdays and Christmas then.

LIAM: Not every time he drinks, obviously. Just he gets wound up.

JEN: And unwinding involves putting you bleeding on the floor.

LIAM: Just, once or twice, he's… pushed past me.

JEN: And once or twice is that literally one time, or two times, or does it mean more like half a dozen times.

LIAM shrugs.

JEN: You've been here *six months.*

LIAM: We're getting used to each other.

JEN: D'you think it's gonna get better? It is not gonna get better Liam. That is not how these things go. How they go is, they get worse. He's knocked you about once or twice and what happens? Fuck all. So that's normal now. Normal, for him, is pushing you about so hard you smash your head open –

LIAM: I didn't smash anything.

JEN: What would you prefer, then?

LIAM: I think you're being a bit melodramatic is all.

She stares at him. Not immediately –

LIAM: When he loses it with me, he feels like absolute shit afterwards. Only for about five minutes but still.

JEN: What?

LIAM: I piss him off on purpose. So he'll lose it. Cos it's funny how it torments him.

JEN: So it's your fault?

LIAM: Well, you know.

JEN shrugs. She doesn't.

LIAM: Yes. I make him do it. So it's my fault.

JEN: Or…maybe you're just saying that. Cos you're embarrassed. You're embarrassed, that your dad knocks you about. Because it makes you feel pathetic and weak and you are, in the most non-stereotypical, twenty-first century way, pretty keen on looking the big man in front of me.

LIAM: Oh *that's* what I'm doing…

JEN: It's not you should be embarrassed. It's him. Jesus you could've died…

LIAM smiles at her – come off it…

JEN: If you'd've hit your head a bit harder, / then Christ knows –

LIAM: By that logic you could die any time you fall over.

JEN: You could.

LIAM: So best remain in a seated position at all times. In case I die.

JEN: Is it happening more or less often, Liam.

LIAM doesn't answer.

JEN: He doesn't answer.

LIAM: I don't keep count.

She comes to a stop.

JEN: This is what you should be embarrassed about. This. It's one thing him doing it, but you covering it up for him.

LIAM: There's nothing to / cover up –

JEN: Because that is actually a bit cowardly.

LIAM: I'm a coward am I?

JEN: I didn't say that.

LIAM: You just – obviously you just fucking did!

JEN: Alright, I'm sorry –

LIAM: My mum dies and I've got nowhere to go but this shithole, with that cunt – and I'm a coward?

JEN: It was – I didn't mean it like that. I'm sorry.

They look at each other.

LIAM looks away.

LIAM: More often.

JEN: More often?

LIAM: Like the first month it was all – not exactly sweetness and light but – and then it was just he'd barge past me getting out of the room. Cos he couldn't stand my fucking whining any more. Then… you remember when I came into college with stitches?

JEN: You are fucking kidding me.

LIAM: He meant to just give me a tap. Just playful.

JEN: What'd you tell 'em in A&E?

LIAM: That I fell. Cos I was pissed. *(Beat.)* And a couple of times since then.

JEN: So it's just normal now.

LIAM nods.

JEN: What's gonna happen when you really piss him off? Cos he can't just give you a shove, or a tap. Cos that's every day. What's he gonna do, next time he's really angry?

LIAM: Playful headbutt. Playful kick to the crotch.

JEN: Playful broken bottle in your face…

LIAM: He does feel bad. After.

JEN: Course he does. He's not a monster. He's just a prick. *(Beat.)* And how do you feel?

He thinks about it, properly.

LIAM: Nothing that prick does is as hard as losing my mum, so…

JEN: But he could kill you, Liam. He could kill you put you in a wheelchair fuck knows.

LIAM: S'pose.

JEN: You suppose?

LIAM: I'll be careful.

JEN: You'll be careful? Fuck off…

LIAM: What then?

JEN: You'll get out.

LIAM: Get out to where?

JEN: Anywhere.

LIAM: Oh yeah sure, just, yeah, just go –

JEN: You cannot stay here.

LIAM: It's six more months. I finish the year, I'm off to uni, I never see him again.

JEN: If you make it six months.

LIAM: What'm I supposed to do? I've got nowhere to *go*.

JEN: Get your own place.

LIAM: Oh yeah, why didn't I think of that…

JEN: People do. At your age.

LIAM: Who has. Who do you know, has set up on their own?

JEN: But you could.

LIAM: So – walk into a job, do I? Cos that's a piece of piss. Then get myself a place. Then – oh hold on. When do I do my A-levels.

JEN: Do them part-time.

LIAM: Oh yeah. In the evening maybe. When I get home from work. That would be it.

JEN: I'm not saying it would be easy.

LIAM: Oh okay. Oh that's fine then. Oh so it'd be hard, but tough fucking luck. *(Beat.)* Could you do that?

She doesn't answer.

LIAM: Course you fuckin couldn't.

JEN: This is your life's at stake. You're gonna risk that, so you can finish your A-levels?

LIAM: I've got no choice.

JEN: Yes you have. Yes you bloody have. Just you're too scared to take it.

377

LIAM: That's nice. Thanks.

JEN: Fuck being nice. This is your *life*.

They look at each other.

JEN: If it was me. If it was my dad, hurting me, what would you say? Tell me to just chance it? Cos never know he might *not* put me in hospital?

LIAM: I'd tell you to get the fuck out.

JEN: Well then.

LIAM: But I don't think I'd call you a coward if you stayed.

She doesn't say anything.

LIAM: Cos that's fuckin harsh Jen.

JEN: D'you know what I think? I think, when you start going out with someone, you think they're the best thing ever. So you're super-nice to them. Much better than you are to yourself. But as it goes on, they get to be part of the furniture. Part of you. So if you're good to yourself, you're good to them.

They look at each other.

JEN: So I think, if we were together. In the end. What you put up with for yourself, you'd put up with for me.

LIAM: That's right, cos this is all about you…

JEN: I'm saying it cos, I think you're the kind of person, you care more about other people than you do yourself.

LIAM: Yeah, well…that's what it is, being half-decent isn't it.

JEN: And it's lovely, but – it gets to a point, if you put up with shit for yourself, the people who care about you have to put up with it too.

She gets up.

JEN: I'm gonna start off for home.

She gets her things together.

JEN: Hope your phone's alright.

LIAM: Me too.

JEN: Said you should've backed it up.

LIAM: Yes, I know.

JEN: But you didn't.

LIAM: Yes, I know.

JEN: Even though apparently it was super-important to you.

LIAM: No, that's nice. Have one last go, why not.

JEN looks at him: makes a decision.

JEN: You should come.

LIAM: …for a walk?

JEN: Leave here, right now, and come with me, to my house. We've got fuck all room but you could stay for a bit. Coupla weeks at least. Get yourself sorted somewhere. You could.

LIAM: And then what?

JEN: I don't know. We'll find something.

LIAM: So I've got a week, and then –

JEN: I don't know but it's got to be better than some prick who's gonna –

She falls silent. Noise off.

JEN: Come on.

LIAM: To what?

JEN: You and me now. Come *on*, mun.

She holds out her hand to him.

LIAM: I can't.

SUZE sticks her head round the door.

SUZE: We alright?

JEN: Super-alright thanks Suze.

SUZE: Yeah fair play. Now, I got a big old idiot of a bloke here, and he's feeling a bit of a twat to be honest.

Neither JEN nor LIAM speak.

SUZE: So's it alright he comes in or what?

LIAM: His place.

SUZE: *(To off.)* Come on then.

SUZE moves into the room. RICK shuffles after her.

SUZE: And?

RICK: He knows I'm sorry.

SUZE: Ah well that's fine then.

RICK: I'm sorry, alright.

JEN: Tell it to the police. That's right, we called them.

RICK: Where are they then?

JEN: *(Beat.)* There's a wait.

LIAM: We didn't call the police.

RICK: Call 'em if you want.

JEN: We could've. That's assault that is.

RICK: What was?

JEN: Look at him!

SUZE: Vile.

RICK: Listen, I don't wanna argue…

JEN: You shoved him so hard he fell over.

SUZE: Sorry Jen – were you there?

JEN: He told me.

SUZE: Right so you weren't.

JEN: He said it, I believe him.

SUZE: I believe him too: just, be nice to hear what *he* thinks happened.

SUZE is staying calm.

LIAM: He shoved me, didn't he.

SUZE: Are you sure?

LIAM: Sure I ended up on the floor.

SUZE: No, no one's saying you didn't. Are you sure, that's cos Vile shoved you?

JEN: Just tripped, did he? Floor a bit slippy?

SUZE: Listen. Jen. You're a nice girl but – I swear to God love.

Unsaid: if you don't shut up…

JEN: Oh that's lovely.

LIAM: Yes, he shoved me. Definitely.

SUZE: Is it?

LIAM: Yes.

SUZE: Cos that's not what Vile says. Is it Vile?

They look at him.

RICK: What'm I gonna say?

SUZE: Say what you said to me.

RICK: He knows what he thinks.

SUZE: Yeah, but…

RICK: And he thinks that? He thinks I'd fuckin…

RICK looks at LIAM till LIAM looks back at him.

RICK: I never would.

LIAM: How'd I end up on the floor then?

RICK: You got pissed off with me, and you were off, you were out the door, and I didn't get out your way fast enough, and you crashed into me and sort of1… bounced off.

SUZE: So you didn't shove him at all.

RICK: I put out my hands, to try to sort of, steady him like.

SUZE: So it might've looked –

RICK: – exactly yeah –

SUZE: – like you were shoving him. But you weren't. You were trying, to stop him falling.

RICK: Course.

JEN: And what about the time he needed stitches?

SUZE: He fell.

JEN: Falls a lot, doesn't he.

RICK: Now, that was my fault.

JEN: Well. At least you're not fucking lying about it.

RICK: I should never've given him them last two beers.

JEN: Sorry?

SUZE: Time he got stitches. He fell cos he was pissed.

RICK: If I'd known he'd been drinking out with his mates, I never would've given him those cans when he come home. Never.

JEN looks to LIAM.

JEN: *Were* you pissed?

LIAM: I'd had a bit, yeah.

JEN: You didn't say.

LIAM: And?

JEN: But it was him gave you the stitches? Not an accident?

LIAM: Well what I can remember…

SUZE: Yeah but – it is easy, to get confused. When things get a bit het up. Like've you ever been in a proper fight?

LIAM nods. This surprises SUZE.

SUZE: Have you?

LIAM: Have you seen the way I dress?

SUZE: Aye, fair play. Myself, what I find is, getting hit – it scrambles your brains a bit? And all your hormones are going? All your adrenaline? Sometimes things get a bit mixed up. I've had it. Did that girl bump into you just trying to squeeze past, or did she spill your drink deliberate? And when you're riled up the bitch did it on purpose. But actually, maybe…

LIAM: I'm not talking about a girl, I'm talking about / him –

SUZE: And when you've been drinking, of course, that hardly helps keep things straight in your head.

LIAM: I know what happened. He got angry, and he punched me, and I ended up getting stitches. And tonight he shoved me, and I ended up on the floor.

SUZE: Course you been drinking tonight as well.

LIAM: One beer!

SUZE: And there's no way, at all, it could've happened different? No way, that you might've just fell cos you were pissed? And then – remembered it wrong? That's actually impossible is it?

LIAM: I suppose it's not actually impossible.

SUZE: Alright okay. So it is possible, then.

LIAM: In theory yes.

SUZE: Right so it might be just accidents. All of it.

JEN: I can't fuckin believe this…

SUZE: *(Controlled.)* You know what love? You remind me of me. Cos I needed a fuckin slap when I was your age.

She turns back to LIAM.

SUZE: Cos I think you should think about what you're saying Lee. You're saying your dad hits you – that's fuckin serious stuff love.

LIAM: Well she thinks I should go. Before he puts me in hospital.

RICK looks to JEN.

JEN: Well he should.

SUZE: You're not wrong love. Course he should. If he's getting hit, he should run for his fucking life.

LIAM: So I'll be off then? Jen says I can stay at hers.

SUZE: Well that's very nice of your mum, Jen. The only thing I would say, is – what if there's been a bit of a mix-up. What if we're sending a boy away from his dad – cos of a mix-up? Now, I wasn't there, when these things happened, / so I don't know

LIAM: Yeah well I was, and / I do.

RICK: You haven't got a fucking clue boy. I might be fucking raging with you. I might chuck things and punch the walls. But I could never lay a hand on you. Cos if I did – I couldn't fuckin live with myself. And you'll understand one day. I never would've. But I do now. Once you got your own child / then you –

LIAM: I am not your child.

RICK: No, fair play, you're a grown man, just about. I'm just / saying –

LIAM: Mum said, when you found out she was pregnant, you vanished. Didn't see you for weeks. And then you showed up. You sat her down. And you had five hundred quid, in twenties and tens. And you gave it to her. And you said, there you go love. That's for you. To get rid of it.

JEN: Fuckin hell...

LIAM: Is that true?

RICK turns away, starts another drink.

LIAM: So I was never your child. And that was your choice.

JEN: What a fucking cunt.

RICK looks at her.

JEN loses her nerve a little.

RICK pulls out a can from the pack, offers it to her.

RICK: Sorry love, rude of me.

JEN shakes her head. RICK turns back to LIAM.

RICK: You do stupid things when you're young.

LIAM: Is it.

RICK nods.

LIAM: You say stupid it's coming across just fucking nasty.

RICK: Sometimes you start out stupid you end up being nasty.

LIAM: Can't quite see how that works myself.

RICK: Give you time.

A silence. Which SUZE breaks.

SUZE: What we're saying is, you might've got things wrong Liam. Maybe, in the mix-up, you thought / your dad had done things –

RICK: Give it a rest Suze.

SUZE: Sorry, sod me for trying to help.

RICK: Thing is. Maybe your girl's right.

LIAM: Right how.

RICK: I get a bit rough. When I've had a few. And there's always the chance. You could piss me off.

LIAM: What d'you mean?

RICK: Cos you haven't got the wit to know, have you, when you should keep it shut. You'll wind me up when I'm not in the mood. You haven't got a clue.

LIAM: Are you serious?

RICK: If I laid a finger on you, I couldn't live with myself. So perhaps best you should. You know.

LIAM: Have the balls to fuckin say it.

RICK: You should go.

LIAM: Go where, exactly?

RICK: She said you could stay at hers.

LIAM: For *a week.*

RICK: There's bound to be places.

LIAM: What places? What places do think there are?

RICK: Somebody'll take you.

LIAM: No they – why do think I came to you? Cos there was *nowhere else.*

RICK: You'll sort yourself out.

LIAM: I know there are some people, some people are off at sixteen, standing on their own two feet, and they cope. I'm not like that. I'll be on the streets.

RICK doesn't answer.

LIAM: And I'm not – no – one's gonna be scared of me, are they – on the streets They'll all go for me. I won't last a month.

RICK: The thing is, boy…

RICK stops.

RICK: I think you'd make it.

LIAM: Not a chance.

RICK: There's a bit of steel in you I reckon.

LIAM: Not really.

RICK: There is if you're my son.

LIAM: I know I'm a dick. I know I shoot my mouth off. I won't. I won't anymore. Whenever you've had a drink, then I'll button it. I won't wind you up.

RICK: No.

LIAM: Please.

RICK: No.

LIAM: I'll be good.

RICK: It's not about you being good. It's about not leaving you in harm's way. I'm sorry, son.

LIAM: Fuck you.

JEN: Come on Liam, let's go.

LIAM doesn't respond to her.

SUZE: You sure about this, Vile.

JEN: I'll help you pack, yeah.

LIAM: My mum dies. I have to go live with a prick in the middle of nowhere. And now – you can't keep your fists to yourself once you've had a drink – so I have to go. But why's it me? Why's it always me's got to do the hard thing? Why can't it be you? You're supposed to be the grown – up. So if you can't control yourself when you're pissed – stop fucking drinking. Stop it. Do that one thing. Or is that too hard for you?

RICK: I've had a drink every day since I was fourteen.

LIAM: So stop! Just for a few months, till I'm gone. Then drink yourself to fucking death for all I care.

RICK doesn't answer.

LIAM: I've never asked you anything. I'm asking you this.

Still doesn't answer.

LIAM: Can you do this. For me. Please.

And RICK realises –

RICK: Course I fucking can.

They stare at each other.

RICK: Right then.

RICK offers his can to SUZE.

RICK: You want that?

She takes it.

SUZE: You actually serious?

RICK's moving.

SUZE: Vile?

RICK's moving round the place, collecting cans and bottles on the table.

SUZE: You're not gonna chuck it all, are you?

RICK: If it's around, I'll drink it. There's a skip down the road.

RICK races round the place, into the kitchen.

SUZE: What, the fuck, have you done?

LIAM: I don't know.

RICK comes back with bottles of vodka and whisky, and a cardboard box, and a bag for life.

Starts putting the bottles into the box and bag.

RICK: Gimme a hand with this?

SUZE: 'S a fuck've a lot of booze to waste, Vile.

RICK: Yeah you're right. That's dull.

Moving slower, thinking, he finds a bottle of sherry and some odd liquer tucked in a cupboard. Adds them to the collection.

RICK: We'll take it all to the park. Leave it for the kids. They'll go fucking mental.

RICK picks up the box.

RICK: C'mon, you take them.

Indicates the bag to SUZE. Heads out.

SUZE takes the bag. Makes to go. Stops at the threshold.

SUZE: You know what your dad's like, sober?

LIAM: No.

SUZE: No. Me neither.

SUZE goes.

JEN: You think he's serious?

LIAM: Christ knows.

JEN: He looked pretty serious.

LIAM: He actually did.

JEN: And do you think it would make a difference? If he wasn't pissed the whole time.

LIAM: It is only when he's pissed he gets… lively.

JEN: That's a really, a thing. If he stops drinking.

LIAM: No I know.

They look at each other.

LIAM: Fucking *hell.*

JEN: Liam that's brilliant. You were brilliant.

LIAM: Well you know.

JEN: Aw come on mun you stood up to him. And not like in a shit stupid way that just made everything worse. You just told him what he needed to hear.

LIAM: And he *listened* is the thing.

JEN: Cos you made him.

A little silence.

JEN: Shall I get these back to you Monday?

He takes a moment to realise: the clothes.

LIAM: I suppose yeah.

She goes over. Stands near him. Kisses him on the forehead.

JEN: I'm really proud of you, you know.

They look at each other.

And then JEN turns away to go.

LIAM: Cos we've had a great day, haven't we.

JEN: Yeah, course.

LIAM: And then it got a little bit weird. And a little bit scary. And then something amazing happened. I stood up to him. And he backed down.

JEN: It was amazing.

LIAM: And it only happened, cos of you. Cos of you being here with me.

She doesn't say anything.

LIAM: And I think, we'll look back, and this will be the first day we were together. Because you are going to finish with Jordan. You know you are. And yeah sure this day could end with you trudging back across town in the rain. But I just think. Looking back. It'll just seem silly, that we didn't finish this amazing day, together. Just curled up, holding each other, till we drift off to sleep. Cos I don't know about you but I get so lonely, going to sleep on my own.

JEN: Yeah me too.

LIAM: Yeah so… don't.

She thinks about it.

Then puts down her bag.

SCENE FOUR

RICK and LIAM.

RICK: It was like – Willy Wonka in the chocolate factory. The kids couldn't fuckin believe it. Like half of them wouldn't touch it cos they thought there was something dodgy?

LIAM: I wonder why that would be…

RICK: They did though, in the end. One girl, just started necking the vodka, I had to say, cool head now love, you'll put yourself in harm's way.

LIAM: Incredibly responsible of you.

RICK: Fuck 'em, they don't have to drink it.

LIAM: But they will, and what if –

RICK: Here we fuckin go…

LIAM: – what if one of them falls down in the road gets run over?

RICK: 'S not gonna happen is it.

LIAM: It could.

RICK: Those kids are in that park getting hammered every weekend: they know what they're doing.

LIAM: Yeah, every weekend they don't have the entirety of your stash to work through.

RICK considers.

RICK: Ah, fuck 'em.

LIAM: Nice.

A little pause.

RICK: She's alright, your girl.

LIAM: She's not mine.

RICK: Not yet. In the bag though, isn't it.

LIAM: I mean, you don't talk about people as belonging to other people.

RICK: Fuck me is there nothing you can't make a fucking drag.

LIAM: Ask me again on my deathbed.

RICK: I tell you what I was thinking – I remember my mum trying to give up smoking. Christ she was a miserable bitch then. D'you reckon it's the same with drink?

LIAM: You've honestly never been a day without a drink? Since you were fourteen.

RICK: Maybe thirteen. Could be twelve.

LIAM: Like not if you were ill or something and you just didn't feel like it?

RICK: Never get ill.

LIAM: You were all last Sunday chucking up.

RICK: That was hungover not ill.

LIAM: You've really not had a day where you didn't touch a drop? Not one? Ever? In all these years?

RICK: Not even one.

LIAM stares at him.

RICK: I'm probably bullshitting a bit there.

LIAM: Oh really?

RICK smiles at him.

LIAM doesn't quite smile back.

RICK: And I don't mind, truth be told. Probably do me good in the end, and / it's only a couple of months –

LIAM: Would you maybe not mind making yourself scarce.

RICK: Why's 'at?

LIAM: Cos she's still here. She's staying over.

RICK: Bloody hell, how'd you get her to do that?

LIAM: I didn't get her to anything: she decided to.

RICK: 'S hope for you yet. Where is she then?

LIAM: Bathroom.

RICK: Getting ready for action…

LIAM: She's in my bed, I'm on the couch. Nothing's going to happen.

RICK: She wears a skirt size of a belt. *Decides* to stay over at yours. And now she's gonna peel her clothes off, climb into your filthy pit… and she doesn't want nothing to happen. Course not.

LIAM: Nothing's going to happen, because she hasn't finished with her boyfriend yet. Not officially. I mean she's gonna. Definitely.

RICK: Well…

LIAM: Well what?

RICK: You know what this is? This little night with you?

LIAM: I know whatever you think, I don't need to hear it.

RICK: Course, what do I know.

RICK moves. Without really thinking about it, looks in a cupboard. Finds a six-pack (of bitter: everything else he's drunk has been lager). Pulls off a can, opens it and begins to drink.

LIAM: What the fuck are you doing?

RICK: What'd you mean?

LIAM: The can.

RICK looks at the can.

Then realises.

RICK: Aw, fuck…

LIAM: What's that – not even half an hour.

RICK: It was a fuckin – force of habit. Look.

He puts the can down.

LIAM: Pathetic.

RICK: Alright.

RICK takes the can out to the kitchen.

Comes back.

RICK: Poured it away. Satisfied now?

LIAM: I thought you got rid of it all?

RICK: I thought I had! I just forgot about them, they were a Christmas present. From like fuckin... two thousand and nine. I don't even like the stuff. That's how come it's still here. Come on, mun. It was one slip.

LIAM: Within – ten seconds of swearing blind you're off it for good.

RICK: You never said for good, you said, for / a few months –

LIAM: *(Cutting in.)* You know what I fucking mean.

RICK: What, you think I'm not gonna do it?

LIAM: What d'you reckon?

RICK: You think you're not fuckin safe here, with me?

LIAM: I think...you haven't got a clue what it is, to do something for somebody else.

RICK: I let you into my fucking house!

LIAM: I bet Suze talked you into that.

RICK: Why, what's she said?

LIAM: I knew it!

RICK: Look. You think you're not safe? You are fuckin safer with me than you've ever been.

LIAM: Yeah I really feel it.

RICK: How many times've people picked on you, since you been here?

LIAM: Picked on me how?

RICK: Like, going round the place dressed like a fucking paedo. You said, at home, people'd shout at you, take the piss.

LIAM: Yeah course.

RICK: 'S that happen here?

LIAM: Get the odd look.

RICK: You get the odd look? You go about the place with a fucking fez and bow tie and tweed jacket even when it's fucking baking hot? I bet you get the odd fucking look. But how often, does someone shout at you, and call you a wanker?

LIAM: Once in Cardiff.

RICK: How many times *here*.

LIAM thinks about it.

LIAM: Actually… none.

RICK: And why's that d'you think?

LIAM: I dunno – I suppose I thought Dr Who's the only thing that's happened here in basically, forever, so – you know. People are grateful.

RICK looks at him, smiling.

LIAM: What then?

RICK: People know, you're my boy. And they know better than to lay a fucking finger on you.

LIAM takes this in.

RICK: See? You are safer here with me, than you have ever been.

RICK calms a little.

RICK: But like I'd ever get a word of thanks for it.

RICK waits for LIAM to respond. But he doesn't.

RICK: Right I'll be off to bed then.

LIAM: Alright, alright – what?

RICK: What'd you mean what?

LIAM: You were dying to tell me. What it is, this night. Jen staying here.

RICK looks at him.

LIAM: Or don't, I don't care.

But clearly he does care.

RICK: She's testing the goods. Seeing how it would be, to be with you, instead of him. And if you don't measure up – off she trots back to Jordan the rugby lad. This is your shot at glory boy. You blow it tonight, and it's game over.

LIAM: Thanks, that's making me feel great, and, um, suddenly very nervous about something that felt very natural and easy, so thank you.

RICK: So what you gotta do is, you gotta make it so she can't go back to him.

LIAM: Remind me how I control the actions of another human being, exactly?

RICK: Is she a slag?

LIAM looks at him.

LIAM: What d'you think I'm gonna say to that?

RICK: Yes she is, or no she isn't.

LIAM: I absolutely refuse, to define her on those terms –

RICK: Cos it's a bit of a slag move dossing down here at yours when she's with another bloke, but still, by the letter of the law, like, it's no foul. Cos you know. You're 'just mates'. So maybe, she isn't a slag. In her heart of hearts.

LIAM: Um…okay. She is not a slag.

RICK: You're in then, aren't you.

LIAM: How exactly?

RICK: A slag could fuck you, wetwipe round the gash on the way home, and be back shagging her boyfriend in the morning. Jen's not like that.

LIAM: I wouldn't have thought she was the… wetwipe round the gash type, no.

RICK: So something happens with you, she's not gonna be able to lie to him. She's not gonna be able to pretend. She'll have to tell him. And that's it for her and Jordan. He'll dump her like a busted fucking fridge.

LIAM takes this in.

RICK: So there's your answer. You close the deal tonight… and that girl is yours for keeps.

SCENE FIVE

LIAM sitting on the couch. If not in a sleeping bag then one draped over him.

JEN comes in, face washed for bed. Wearing one of LIAM's T-shirts. Massive on her.

She has a toothbrush. It is pink.

JEN: Ta for the lend.

Offers him the toothbrush back.

LIAM: I generally keep it in the bathroom?

JEN: Yeah course.

He takes it.

JEN: It's pink.

LIAM: I know.

JEN: Deliberate choice.

LIAM: Smashing gender stereotypes everywhere I go. Even first thing in the morning.

JEN: And last thing at night.

LIAM: And often in the middle of the day, if I've got a bit of a manky mouth on.

They look at each other.

JEN: I'll be off to bed then.

LIAM: Enjoy it.

JEN: You'll be alright, on the settee.

LIAM: What's the worst that can happen?

JEN: *(Beat.)* You fall asleep with a lit cigarette, settee catches fire, you burn to death.

LIAM: I don't smoke.

JEN: Well it is very bad for your health. *(Beat.)* Jordan um, text me? When I was doing my teeth and everything.

LIAM: Oh yeah.

JEN: Asked where I was today?

LIAM: Okay.

JEN: And I am shit at lying.

LIAM: I don't believe you.

JEN: No, serious, I get all nervous and giggly.

LIAM: Even by text?

JEN: Absolutely yeah every text like a dozen giggly emojis to sign off. Can't help myself.

LIAM: *(Beat.)* Say it then.

JEN: I told Jordan. Where I'd been, today. And who with. And um –

She pauses.

LIAM: Do not fucking X-Factor me Jen, I don't deserve that.

JEN: He was, completely not bothered.

LIAM: That's good, isn't it.

JEN: I thought, if he knew I was friends with you, he'd just be furious?

LIAM: Why?

JEN: Cos – obviously. You're so different to him. And me being friends with you is sort of saying…I wish he was different to how he is?

LIAM: No. It's saying, you want him, and maybe you thought you wanted me, and maybe you thought you had to make a choice: and now maybe you don't. You can keep him as boyfriend, and be friends with me. Best of both worlds.

JEN: No!

LIAM: It is though.

JEN: It just sounds fucking horrible when you put it like that.

LIAM: D'you think?

JEN: Makes me sound a horrible person.

LIAM: You're not a horrible person.

JEN: Thank you. Cos I think – we've got a real connection? And maybe I'm just not – maybe I'm just this stupid little teenage girl still and when I've grown up a bit, I really think, maybe, you and me might end up together, like in the long run. I know that sounds weird / saying it now –

LIAM: *(Cutting in.)* I don't think you're a stupid teenage girl at all.

JEN: Well you're very nice.

LIAM: I think… you're just out for as much as you can get. Like all humans.

JEN: D'you know, when I have guests at my house, I'm super-nice to them. Like if they fart, I blame it on the dog.

LIAM: You haven't got a dog.

JEN: That's the lengths I go to, I invent imaginary pets to avoid pointing out, my guests' failings.

LIAM: I've got a suggestion.

JEN: Okay.

LIAM: Why not have me as boyfriend, and be friends with Jordan? I wouldn't mind. I'm not the jealous type.

JEN: Yeah…

LIAM: Just think about. Try it out a week or two?

JEN: The problem would be – being friends with Jordan. What would that – what would that even *be?*

LIAM: It's mostly a physical thing, with you two.

JEN: He does try to talk to me sometimes. I just pick up my phone and look at… anything. And then after about twenty seconds so does he. *(Beat.)* Or in private I find him something better to do with his mouth.

She looks at him – he's not smiling.

398

JEN: Sorry.

LIAM: You say sorry. But know what you're doing, when you say things like that.

JEN: It was just a joke…

LIAM: You know what's happening in my head, don't you, when you say stuff like that.

JEN: And you quite like it. Don't / pretend you don't –

LIAM: *(Cutting in.)* Jen. Seriously. Get over yourself. If you scurry back to Jordan, it won't be the worst thing that's happened to me.

JEN: You sure? I'm quite a catch.

LIAM: It won't be the worst thing that's happened to me this year, even.

She looks at him.

JEN: Oh shit I'm so sorry…

LIAM: 'S alright.

JEN: It really is not.

LIAM: No. It's not. But what's wrong is not you forgetting about it. You forgetting about it is nice, actually.

JEN: It doesn't feel nice.

LIAM: Does to me. Feels like a relief. Like Rick. If he was less of a twat, he'd be asking about it all the time, or maybe occasionally, or ever. But he doesn't. He doesn't, ever, say a thing and actually – that's easiest.

JEN: So you don't think about it.

LIAM: I think about it all the time. I think – how long now till she comes through the door and takes me home?

JEN: Shit, Lee…

LIAM: You know you get pins and needles? Say in your leg. And you can't walk. But you don't really worry about it because, you know it'll go and you'll be fine in a minute?

This is like that. I'm not worried cos, it'll be fine, in a minute.

They sit.

JEN: Was she nice?

LIAM looks at her. And then smiles.

JEN: I'm so sorry…

LIAM: Yeah cos like, if my mum died but she was a bitch, I wouldn't mind so much?

JEN: I'm a fucking idiot aren't I.

LIAM: She was nice. I mean, probably since I was thirteen I slightly thought she was a twat but, after getting the diagnosis and then the surgery and the chemo and then, when it became clear she was really going to die, I probably, some point in that process, started to see her good points, quite a lot more than I had.

JEN: Do you –

LIAM: No I don't miss her. Why would I miss her? She's coming to get me any second. Listen, that's her. Here she is –

And he points at the door.

LIAM: Now!

The door does not open.

LIAM: Or any time in the next ten minutes.

JEN: I'm trying to decide is it brave or weird you're sort of smiling about it the whole time.

LIAM: It is so, so brave.

JEN: I think it is.

LIAM: Which means you don't need to worry about me. Or feel guilty. Or make an effort to be nice, or do anything. You definitely don't have to be with me, if actually you want to be with your boyfriend.

JEN: Okay.

LIAM: Alright.

They look at each other.

LIAM: Alright then.

JEN: Night then, Liam.

He smiles.

And she turns away, reaches for the door –

– and as she turns, LIAM makes a decision.

LIAM: You know you're supposed to go through these stages.

JEN stops.

LIAM: When you know you're gonna die? Like… anger, denial, pathetic last minute embrace of religion, then acceptance.

JEN: I've never understood what that is.

LIAM: Acceptance?

JEN: Yeah.

LIAM: You accept you're gonna die.

JEN: That's it?

LIAM: Yeah.

JEN: I always thought it'd be more.

LIAM: More how?

JEN: Like… you know how if you believed in heaven? Really believed? Then dying –

LIAM: Would not fucking worry you at all.

JEN: – because you weren't going to, really. I thought when you 'accepted' you were going to die, something happened, so it was like you felt you weren't going to die, really. Except without all the embarrassment of having to believe in God.

LIAM: No, it's nothing like that.

JEN: Jesus.

LIAM: It just means you, accept that you're dying. You accept, the life you got, was what you got, and you stop wishing there was more. You're just grateful for what there was. There's not a trick. It's just literally, accepting. And stopping fighting. And stopping struggling. And when you stop struggling, you can find a bit of peace. *(Beat.)* My mum never got to there. Because of me. Because she knew she was leaving me, with no-one. So she kept fighting, right to the end.

JEN: That's something isn't it? To never give up?

LIAM: She hated herself for dying. D'you see? Her last seconds. There was no peace. No calm. None of that for her. Just – despair. Because of me. Because she was leaving me behind. *(Beat.)* So you see I've been loved. I know what it is. And you –

He breaks off.

After a little while.

JEN: I think, if I was her –

JEN comes to a stop.

LIAM: What?

JEN doesn't know what to say.

LIAM: See? Nothing. You haven't got a clue.

JEN gets up, goes to LIAM's bedroom door.

Stops.

JEN: Maybe, you could just come give me a cwtch before you go to sleep.

LIAM: Don't think I need one, thanks.

JEN: No. But I do.

She goes.

LIAM sits there for a bit. He's thinking about following her in.

A tension drops away from him as he gives up on that thought.

He sits, shifts a few times.

RICK comes in.

RICK: 'Right.

RICK heads into the kitchen.

LIAM sits.

RICK comes back, with a pint glass of water.

Sips from it, looking at LIAM.

LIAM looks round.

LIAM: What?

RICK: Nervous?

LIAM: No.

RICK: You weren't nervous, you'd be in there already.

RICK sips again. Smiles.

RICK: Well this is one thing I can't do for you. Not that I'd mind… Goodnight, and God bless.

RICK makes to go.

LIAM: Rick.

RICK stops.

RICK: What?

LIAM looks at him.

RICK: There's no shame coming to your old man for help. If that's what you're doing.

LIAM: Forget it…

RICK: You don't want my advice?

RICK watches him a moment.

LIAM: Please.

A victory. RICK moves closer to him.

RICK: How can you be nervous going in there? How can you be nervous, climbing in that bed? It's your room. You go in there every night. It's your bed. You get in it every night.

LIAM: Except tonight now she's in it too.

RICK: That's where she's put herself. Your bed. Your room. Poor fucking girl, she couldn't be making it any fucking clearer – and here you are, fiddling with yourself on the fucking settee!

LIAM: It's not as easy as that, alright?

RICK: You know they say girls like bastards. You think that's right?

LIAM: Obviously it's a ridiculous stereotype.

RICK: Well, course.

LIAM: But having said that… it does seem…

RICK: Like girls like bastards.

LIAM: Yeah.

RICK: No they fucking don't. What a fucking stupid thing to say. Who likes a bastard? A bastard's a cunt, who wants a cunt in their lives?

LIAM: Very damaged people, with self-esteem / issues?

RICK: *(Cutting in.)* So why do girls go out with bastards? Cos no one wants to have to do everything themselves. No one wants to make all the running. You look at Jen. Don't you think she's nervous? Course she fuckin is. And every minute you don't go in there, she's wondering what the fuck is wrong with you. Or what the fuck is wrong with her. And if she was with some bastard – he'd be in there like a shot. Wouldn't he?

LIAM: Yes.

RICK: Yes he fucking would. And she would be glad, he had the fuckin balls to do that. And you think Suze. You think she likes, the way I am?

LIAM: Dunno.

RICK: Lot of the time she fuckin doesn't. But that bloke felt her up in the York and I wanted to break his face and I fuckin did it. And Suze was fuckin glad. And you.

LIAM: What about me?

RICK: You wanted me to stop drinking and you told me I had to do it and fuck me if I didn't.

LIAM: It's not the same though, is it –

RICK: And I did what you said. And I was glad you said it.

They look at each other.

RICK: She is offering herself to you. So get in there. Do what you want to. And make her yours.

RICK puts down his glass, goes.

LIAM left alone.

He thinks about it.

Isn't sure.

Then gets up.

Goes to the door.

Hesitates.

LIAM: *(Quietly.)* Fuck…

Heads back towards the sofa.

Stops. Comes back to the door.

Breathes.

Raises his hand, forms a fist to knock on the door.

Stops. Lowers his hand.

Breathes.

Opens the door and goes in.

SCENE SIX

Next morning.

LIAM enters from the kitchen, in T-shirt and pants, balancing two mugs and a plate of toast.

He thinks about trying to open the bedroom door with his hands full. Thinks better of it. Goes to the table to put down the mugs and plate.

JEN enters from the bedroom. Fully dressed.

LIAM: I couldn't remember if you said sugar or no sugar, so I guessed no sugar.

JEN: It was sugar. Two.

LIAM: See I thought – girls don't really, do they, sugar. Never mind, I'll get you another.

JEN: Don't worry about it.

LIAM: Take me two secs.

JEN: Nah my mum's coming now to pick me up.

LIAM: Yeah?

JEN: Just phoned.

LIAM: Oh okay. *(Beat.)* Didn't think you were heading straight off.

JEN: Yeah think so.

A little silence. LIAM drinks some tea.

LIAM: Was it… alright?

JEN: Alright?

LIAM: Last night. I haven't got much to compare it to.

JEN: What and I have?

LIAM: Well you know with Jordan.

She doesn't answer.

LIAM: Jen?

JEN: It was fine.

LIAM: Fine? Okay. I get the message. Not so great.

406

LIAM watches her.

LIAM: You want this toast?

JEN shakes her head.

LIAM: Mind if I do?

He eats.

LIAM: Bit quiet.

JEN: Bit of a hangover I think.

LIAM: You didn't have much.

JEN: You know how it gets you sometimes.

LIAM: Yeah sure.

He hesitates, then –

LIAM: Fuck was it that bad? Have I just blown it by being completely shit?

JEN: No…

LIAM: Can you just not imagine a relationship with someone who's so epically bad at shagging? I will get better, I promise. With a bit of practise.

JEN: Yeah, I'm sure you will.

LIAM: We could even… practise now a bit, if you want?

JEN: Nah I don't think so.

LIAM: No that's fine.

JEN: My mum'll be here soon, anyway.

LIAM: Yeah sure.

He stops.

LIAM: Jen?

She says nothing.

LIAM: What?

She looks at him.

LIAM: Are you feeling guilty about Jordan?

JEN: No.

407

LIAM: No?

JEN: Yes. Yes I am, but –

LIAM: But what?

JEN: But nothing.

LIAM: Yes you are – but it's not that?

She looks at him.

LIAM: Say.

She doesn't.

LIAM: Just spit it out.

She doesn't.

LIAM: *(Her accent.)* Come on, mun.

The mimicry makes her smile, a little.

He smiles back.

JEN: It was not, what I thought was gonna happen.

LIAM: Well, if you'd told me, a week ago, you and me'd be in that bed, you know. I mean – yeah. I get what you're saying.

JEN: It was not what I planned to happen.

LIAM: Well no Christ no.

JEN: So I'm just a bit –

She dries.

LIAM: You're a bit what?

She doesn't say.

LIAM: I mean I'm a bit. I'm a bit – fucking over the moon.

Beat.

LIAM: But you're not.

She shrugs.

LIAM: Are you alright?

JEN: I'm fine.

Beat.

LIAM: When you say, it's not what you planned. So did you then, did you think I was gonna sleep on the couch?

JEN: No, I didn't want that.

LIAM: What then?

JEN: I thought you'd sneak in with me and we'd be all cwtched up together.

LIAM: Just that?

JEN: Well, kiss and a cuddle.

LIAM: Well we had, a kiss and a cuddle.

JEN: And then… more.

LIAM: Yes.

JEN: And that… wasn't what I thought we'd do.

LIAM: Yeah cos I felt, when we were all curled up, I felt, you, grinding, just a little bit, against my leg.

JEN looks at him.

LIAM: But you didn't want – you weren't up for it?

JEN: Course, yeah, I *wanted* it.

LIAM: So what then?

JEN: I thought – we'd be all curled up together. And wanting it. But not doing it. Till it was the right time. Till I'd finished with Jordan properly and we… *(Stops.)* I thought we'd do it, I didn't think we'd do it then. But it's fine.

LIAM: How's it fine? It is not fine. What the fuck are you saying, Jen?

JEN: I've said.

LIAM: What've you said.

JEN: I just said. I just said – it isn't what I thought we'd do.

He takes a while to get to his next thought.

LIAM: Are you saying, you didn't want, what we did?

She doesn't answer.

LIAM: Jen.

JEN: I'm saying… I didn't think we'd do it, last night.

LIAM: And when you realised we *were* doing it. I didn't notice you saying stop.

JEN: I didn't want to spoil things.

LIAM: I'm sorry?

JEN: Cos we were having a lovely night. And we were. We really – we were.

LIAM: So you're saying – sorry – you're saying, you didn't want, what we did, last night.

JEN: I'm saying, it's alright.

LIAM: If you didn't want it you should've stopped me.

JEN: Well, yeah probably. But – it doesn't –

She hesitates.

JEN: Yeah okay probably I should. Sorry.

LIAM: Yeah you should. Jesus…

JEN: …I did say no.

LIAM: You did not.

JEN: I did.

LIAM: When?

She looks at him.

LIAM: At what point, exactly, did you say no?

JEN: When you were taking my knickers down.

LIAM: Well I didn't hear you.

JEN: I said it, twice.

LIAM: I didn't – really? – cos I didn't hear *anything* like that.

JEN: Are you saying I'm lying?

LIAM: No. But maybe…

JEN: What?

LIAM: Maybe, you thought you said it. But you actually /
   didn't.

JEN: *(Cutting in.)* I said it, alright –

LIAM: Not very loud.

JEN: I said it twice. I said no. Then I said no, stop.

LIAM: And when I didn't stop you should have maybe said it
   again. And maybe a bit louder?

JEN: I didn't want to make it a whole big thing.

LIAM: It wouldn't've been.

JEN: If I'd tried to stop you? You'd've just tucked yourself
   away? Been alright with that would you?

LIAM: Yes!

JEN: Wouldn't've got all moody and called me a cunt and
   Christ knows what?

LIAM: Not a chance.

JEN: Say that now…

LIAM: I'd say that always!

   She looks at him.

JEN: Thing is I think you did hear me. I thought you heard
   me. Like maybe you stopped what you were doing, just a
   second – and then you carried on. I said no, and I was sure
   you heard me say no. But you still carried on. So then I
   said no, stop. And you *still* carried on. And then I thought,
   well first I said no and then I said no, *stop*, and he's still
   carrying on so what now, what if I try and stand up to him
   then maybe it just gets much fucking worse – but it was just
   a misunderstanding. If you really didn't hear. So let's leave
   it / at that shall we?

LIAM: *(Cutting in.)* Hold on hold on hold on. You let me do it
   to you, cos you thought I'd – what? Hit you, if you didn't?

JEN: I dunno.

LIAM: You do! Course you fucking do! You know I'm not like
   that!

411

JEN: How do I know? All I know is I said stop, and you carried on.

LIAM: Oh come on, that is… how can you even say, I'm like that?

JEN: I don't know what you're like. Until you show me.

LIAM can't answer.

JEN: I didn't mind, alright. It wasn't / what I wanted

LIAM: You didn't *mind?*

JEN: But that's what you did, that's what happened, so let's just leave it be.

He looks at her.

LIAM: Would you have done that with Jordan? Gone to bed with him, wrapped yourself round him, and thought that's all it would be?

JEN: No chance.

LIAM: But you did with me.

JEN: Yeah.

LIAM: Cos I'm safe?

JEN: I thought you were, yeah.

LIAM takes this in.

LIAM: Have I done something horrible to you?

JEN: D'you feel like you have?

LIAM: Because I never –

JEN: Well then just leave it.

LIAM: Leave it how?

JEN: Chalk it up to experience.

They look at each other.

LIAM: Okay.

JEN: And just be a bit more careful next time.

LIAM: Okay yeah.

JEN: Just be a bit more fuckin respectful, alright?

LIAM: Yeah alright.

JEN: Okay. Good. There's enough pricks in the world, we don't need you turning into one.

LIAM: 'Kay.

JEN: And it would –

She hesitates.

LIAM: What?

JEN: It would mean a lot to me, if you would say you're sorry, for what you did.

He looks at her.

JEN: Cos if I knew you didn't mean, to do that, then it'd make me feel not so bad about it.

LIAM: What did I do?

JEN doesn't answer.

LIAM: What did I do?

Not immediately.

JEN: Please just tell me you didn't mean to.

LIAM looks at her.

LIAM: D'you know what I think? I think you wanted me to fuck you. So you climbed into my bed, and let me fuck you. And now you feel like a slag. And why is that, d'you think?

Not immediately –

JEN: D'you know, yeah you have done something horrible to me. And that was it, just there. *(Beat.)* I'm gonna go wait on the street.

She moves.

LIAM: Look, Jen –

She stops. Waits for him to continue.

He doesn't.

She goes.

LIAM left alone.

SCENE SEVEN

LIAM sitting.

RICK and SUZE enter.

RICK: Lemme see.

> *LIAM gets out his phone, swipes through a few screens. Hands it to RICK.*

> *RICK reads, scrolls, reads some more.*

RICK: Not good.

> *RICK gives the phone to SUZE.*

> *She reads.*

SUZE: Is this right?

LIAM: No.

SUZE: Liam…

LIAM: Not at all. No way. You know, she was here. Just then… the next morning. She started saying all this stuff.

> *SUZE puts the phone down.*

SUZE: You stupid, stupid little / shit –

RICK: Oi.

> *SUZE looks at him.*

RICK: Not helping. *(To LIAM.)* You heard from her since?

LIAM: No. But her mate text me, saying, she's gonna go to the police.

> *RICK looks at him.*

SUZE: Did you?

LIAM: Did I what?

SUZE: Force her?

LIAM: Course I didn't!

SUZE *looks at him.*

LIAM: You're seriously asking me? *Me?*

RICK: This is all her mum. You know her mum?

LIAM shakes his head.

RICK: She sees this Jordan bloke Jen's with now. He's signed with the Ospreys hasn't he?

LIAM: I mean… I think.

RICK: You know how much they earn? Top players like?

LIAM: Not a fucking clue.

RICK: She's looking at him, you know what she's seeing? Dollar signs.

He looks at LIAM.

LIAM: You think she will go to the police?

RICK: You come between her mum, and a bunch of posh hand bags? Absolutely no doubt.

LIAM: Jesus Christ…

SUZE: Vile.

RICK: What?

SUZE: Fuckin hand bags?

RICK: You know what she's like.

SUZE: This is serious.

They look at each other. SUZE turns on LIAM.

SUZE: How could you be such a fucking little prick?

LIAM: I didn't do – it wasn't like she's saying.

SUZE: Did you, make her.

LIAM: Absolutely not, no way, not at all.

SUZE stares him out.

LIAM: She let me.

SUZE: She let you?

LIAM: Well like I was doing things and she –

RICK: She let you.

LIAM: Yes…

SUZE: Did she tell you to stop?

LIAM: No!

SUZE: Not, at all.

LIAM doesn't answer.

SUZE: Lee…

LIAM: Well she says *now* she told me to stop. But she never.

SUZE: And you're sure.

LIAM: Not even – no. I swear.

SUZE looks at him.

SUZE: Alright. Alright. *(Gathers herself.)* I knew there was something about her, little tart.

LIAM: I think she's just / confused –

SUZE: Fuck that! You are too fuckin soft you are…

RICK: I tell you what though. Cos sometimes… a girl will say no. And it's just, a thing to say. And you think, well, if she means it, she'll say it again. So you carry on. You know – just to see whether she means it, or not. And maybe she says it again. And you think, well. If she *really* means it, she'll stop me. So you carry on. Just to see.

RICK's looking at LIAM.

RICK: Maybe it was a bit like that.

LIAM: No.

RICK: They say no, cos they have to, but they don't do fuck all to stop you. They say no – but then they let you. And letting you, is saying yes. Isn't it.

LIAM doesn't answer.

RICK: Isn't it.

SUZE: Liam?

LIAM nods.

SUZE: What?

LIAM: And we curled up, went to sleep, next morning – she said it was fine, you know? Not what she planned, yeah she said that, not what she planned – but it was *fine*. And she –

He stops.

LIAM: How is she saying no, if she lets me?

RICK: She's not. She's fucking not.

SUZE: She's saying no, when she says no.

LIAM: She gets in my bed, kisses me, gets me going, and she's like, she's gagging to do it – and then she can just say no, after all that?

SUZE: Yeah.

LIAM: How is that fair?

SUZE: Say it's you buying one of your dolls. And you're in the shop. You pick the one you want. You're at the till. You've got your tenner in your hand, like you're gagging to buy it. And right there, last second, you decide you don't want to – but the bloke snatches the tenner off you. Has he stolen from you, or has he not?

LIAM says nothing.

SUZE: You fuckin know he has.

LIAM: But why wouldn't she just *stop me*?

SUZE: Cos she's scared!

LIAM: Of me? Me? I'd never – I'm not like that. *(To RICK.)* Am I?

RICK: Say she does go to the police. Say the police bring you in. Just a few questions like. You know what they'll be thinking? They'll be thinking, their daughters. And fair play to them. And I gotta say, even talking to me now, you look nervous as fuck.

LIAM: Course I'm nervous!

RICK: Why'd you be nervous, if you haven't done nothing?

LIAM: What's gonna happen to me?

RICK: Well you say to the police, what you said to me now – and they are gonna fucking go for you. And you will not come back from it.

LIAM: Aw Jesus Christ…

SUZE: Yeah pity you weren't thinking about that a bit more when you had your dick in your hand.

RICK: And you had it all planned. A-levels, university…

LIAM: What'm I gonna do?

RICK looks at him.

LIAM: What am I going to do?

RICK: Get used to having a very different kind of life to what you thought.

LIAM: I thought she liked me.

RICK: She did. A bit. She liked hanging round you. She liked knowing you wanted her. Got off on that, didn't she. And fair play. Who wouldn't. And then you put one foot wrong. And where d'you end up? I'll tell you. You'll end up hanging off the end of your belt, son.

LIAM takes this in.

SUZE: Vile…

RICK: What, you think that's wrong? You think he could take prison? Are you fucking shitting me? *(To LIAM.)* D'you think you can take it?

LIAM: No.

RICK: No. Not a chance. Not for a second. So this is it for you. This is the end. Now tell me – look at me. Fucking look at me boy.

LIAM looks at him.

RICK: This is the rest of your life, gone. Even if you get through prison, you're on some register. And everyone you ever meet. Every job. Every girl. All they gotta do is put your name in their phone – and they know. Do you deserve that? For one mistake?

RICK pauses.

RICK: Cos this is all me this is.

LIAM: This is you how?

RICK: This is me, telling you – go and take what you want. All my fault.

LIAM doesn't know what to say.

RICK: It is, isn't it.

LIAM nods.

RICK: Say it.

LIAM: This is you.

RICK: I know.

LIAM: This is your fault, if I hadn't listened to you…

SUZE: What did you tell him, Vile?

RICK: To have a bit of fucking gumption.

LIAM: He told me, to take what I wanted.

SUZE: Jesus Christ…

RICK: I said, to take what was being offered you.

LIAM: And I that's all I *did*.

RICK: I know, I know. And everything you been through. Mum gets sick. You nurse her, alone. And then you watch her die. *(Beat.)* And then cunt like me is all you got. So is it fair, you have to take this as well?

LIAM shakes his head.

RICK: Say it.

LIAM: No it is not.

RICK: Even if you made a mistake.

LIAM: It's not fucking fair…

RICK: No. And it's my fault. I'm gonna fix it.

SUZE: What the fuck are you talking about?

LIAM: Fix it how?

RICK: I'll have a word with her.

SUZE: Vile…

LIAM: What, and she'll listen?

RICK: In the end.

LIAM: But you said her mum –

RICK: Her mum can't do nothing if Jen won't.

SUZE: Don't go making this any worse, alright.

RICK: How's it gonna be fuckin worse?

LIAM: But why would –

He stops.

LIAM: Why would Jen stop, cos you say so.

RICK: Why'd you think.

LIAM doesn't answer.

RICK: There are things I could do to her, she couldn't live with.

SUZE: What the fuck are you talking about?

RICK: And I will make her understand she's safe from those things. So long as she never says another word against you.

SUZE: You're gonna threaten her? This is fuckin – come *on*.

RICK: I'm not saying it's good. I'm saying it's what's gotta be.

SUZE: It's fuckin evil.

RICK: *(To LIAM.)* Do you want me to stop her?

SUZE: *(To LIAM.)* You can't do this. You've been stupid, you've been a fucking prick but this is –

RICK: Liam.

SUZE: Alright. Alright. Just think. Say she goes to the police. She came here, she had a few drinks, she got in your bed – the police aren't gonna do a thing, are they? Nothing's

420

gonna happen to you. So just – ride it out. I'll come with you. I'll be there. I'll hold your hand –

RICK: How will you hold his hand when he's in a cell?

SUZE: *(To LIAM.)* That is not gonna happen, I swear.

RICK: Course it is.

SUZE: Cos you can make a mistake. You can do something stupid. But this isn't a mistake. This is you doing this on purpose.

RICK: Do you know what happens to kids like him inside?

She steps towards LIAM.

SUZE: Come with me. Come with me now.

LIAM: I dunno…

SUZE: It'll be alright, I swear, we'll just face it, and get through it –

RICK shoves her back.

RICK: Get the fuck away from him.

She stumbles, hurts herself a bit.

SUZE: You bastard…

RICK: You fuckin say one more word and I will end you. He goes inside, he'll end up hanging from his sheets. And that's what you're saying. You're saying, my boy, can die, cos of some fuckin slag.

He picks up SUZE's bag – throws it at her.

RICK: Get the fuck out. And you never come back here again.

She goes to leave. Stops at the door.

SUZE: Liam.

He looks away from her.

SUZE: It won't work. She's a tough little thing, you threaten her it'll just make it worse –

RICK moves fast to the door. He stops, hand raised to strike.

SUZE, scared, but stares him out.

SUZE: Fuck you. Fuck the both of you.

SUZE goes.

RICK stands a second. Then goes to where he found the secret six-pack of cans in scene four, pulls out a new can. Takes a big drink.

He turns to LIAM. Looks at him.

RICK: Is this what you want?

LIAM doesn't respond.

RICK: Is this what you want me to do? You want me to stop her.

LIAM doesn't respond.

RICK: I am not doing this, unless you say. Is this, what you want me to do?

LIAM looks at him: nods.

RICK: Say it.

LIAM: Yes.

RICK: Alright.

LIAM: Say you threaten her. And it doesn't work. And she goes to the police. Will you really hurt her?

RICK puts down his can.

RICK: Why the fuck would you even ask me that?

LIAM begins to crack. RICK moves towards him. LIAM doesn't move away.

RICK throws his arms round his son.

RICK: It's alright. It's alright, son.

Kisses his head.

RICK: Daddy's got you.

The End.

MUM & DAD

Mum was first performed at the Sherman Theatre, Cardiff on November 18th 2005.

Performed by Nickie Rainsford

Directed by Gary Owen

Dad was first performed at the Tristan Bates Theatre, London on September 29th 2007.

Performed by Danny Sapani

Directed by George Perrin

1. Dad: Returno Farm

I told you about what I seen in the lane at Returno?

I have told you.

This was when father was in hospital,

After he'd had his brain haemorrhage.

I was at home on my own doing the milking

And

We had the two outside lights, one

On the end of the house exactly the same as they are now,

One up on the sheds.

And I'd put all the lights out in the sheds.

I was coming down.

And as you walk you know from the sheds down to the house

You pass the entrance to the lane.

I had the dog with me, Jack Russell,

Can't remember if it was a he or a she now, we had a few.

The dog was standing, looking down the lane, growling.

I got there I could see a shape: I thought,

God is that – a cow or something that's got out?

The dog was growling, getting agitated.

I was looking at this shape

And it wasn't on the ground.

You could see space between the shape and the...

It was floating.

And it was coming slowly up the lane.

I was looking at it, I thought –

427

I had no idea, I couldn't make it out

I was beginning to get a bit you know

Nervous.

And when I looked down,

The dog had gone.

He was disappearing round the back, trying to get into the house,

And animals have got – you know, they're sensible things.

And by this time now I was crapping my pants

This...   was getting closer and closer

And I still couldn't make out what it was.

It looked like

A small cloud of mist, that was moving,

It looked like

Say you'd put a couple of cats in a big white sheet

There was that sort of

Movement to it.

As I say I was crapping myself by this time.

Course when the dog disappeared that was enough for me.

I was gone, in the house, into the dairy.

Shotgun, two cartridges down the barrels,

And I went upstairs and was looking out the window

Expecting to see whatever this was coming up, you know, the lane.

But I never seen it again.

I don't know what happened.

It never came past the house, and

I never went out to see what it was.

I told you about it later, I know I did, but I didn't tell anyone then.

Once you've calmed down you think

Well that was a bit fucking silly.

So when everyone came home from the hospital I didn't
say a thing.

Just asked how father was.

And mother said,

Wandering.

2. Mum: Llanybydder Mart

I hated being a kid.

Any moment, any day, the ground could disappear underneath you.

You'd be carrying on quite happily and suddenly – you were in trouble.

You had no idea why.

And no idea what you could do, to get out of trouble.

I remember one time me and Moira.

We had these great big bikes, three-wheeled bikes, we'd seen something or found something and we were riding back to the house to tell mum and dad.

We got to the house ran in going mum, dad.

Dad was there in the kitchen.

Did you just ride across that field, he goes.

What've I told you, he goes.

How many times've I told you?

You ride along the side of the field.

You ride by the hedge.

I've told you. I've told you both.

And what did I just see you both do?

And that was it for us.

Bed with no supper.

And I can't even remember now, what it was me and Moira were so excited about.

I just remember all that excitement going cold in my throat.

And marching upstairs to bed.

And getting undressed.

And making a point of not crying, not even a bit.

Once dad'd gone out, Ninnie crept up the stairs with a few slices of bread and butter, and milky tea for the two of us.

Then the tears came, of course.

    Pause.

Back then I used to get thirty pounds for breaking in a pony.

Dad would let me keep every penny.

Which was amazing because everything with Dad was about money.

That sounds horrible. But it was sort of true.

It sort of, became true.

The house where we lived, wasn't ours. We rented it.

We'd rented it for years, and the landlady was a nice enough old woman but my dad.

It was like he couldn't settle.

He'd always be on that she could have us out anytime she wanted.

Then all the work he'd done on the house and the land would go to nothing.

In the end he decided was gonna have the house off her.

For that he was gonna need money.

More money than he had, and more money than he could make off our land.

So he started scrimping and saving.

Some bloke down the road from us went bankrupt, Dad had enough to pick up his couple of fields that bordered onto ours.

With the extra land, we were bringing in extra money.

Dad kept on saving, and before too long he bought a few more acres.

And then a few more.

And then a few more again.

And he carried on like that. Working every hour he could, saving every penny he could, buying every scrap of land he could till we had a decent sized farm, making decent enough money.

Bit of an achievement.

He didn't take much pleasure in it.

Because the heart of the farm, the house we lived in, was not ours.

It could be snatched from under us at any time. It could all just disappear.

Any moment. Any day.

But whatever Dad offered the landlady to sell up, she always thought he could offer a little bit more.

And he would offer more, six months later. And she would still say no.

And so it went on.

The horses I think he felt guilty about.

It was like they were – a distraction.

Cause though they were there to make money, he loved them.

Not like the farm work: he was good at the farm work, but he did it cause it paid.

With the horses, he properly loved them.

It started cause Teddy Bishop down the Mason's Arms had bought his daughter a pony, and needed a field to put it in.

And we had this field out the front of the house that was boggy most of the year, and good for nothing.

So we took in this pony, Trigger, and Dad built a little lean-to.

Then Teddy Bishop's daughter loses interest in Trigger. Stops coming up to feed him and muck him out.

So I start Trigger, and grooming him, and mucking him out. Dad starts charging this bloke an extra few bob a week for my efforts.

And like everything Dad did, it just sort of took off.

All we really had was this field, this lean-to, and this grumpy dapple grey mountain pony. But down the pub, the legend grew, and word got round the district we had this thriving business, stabling and breaking in ponies.

People started coming to us, wanting them to stable their horses and break in their ponies.

Thing was Dad didn't have time to be breaking in ponies.

I was gonna have to do it.

I wasn't sure, but Dad said I'd be fine. He told me I had good hands, I could feel what a horse was up to, when it was thinking about having a bolt.

He said he'd tell me the secret of breaking in ponies, if I'd let him whisper in my ear.

He was smiling, and it made me nervous, cause he was such a crotchety old sod usually if he smiled you'd look up to see what was about to hit you.

But I said oh all right then and he came up close and put his mouth to my ear, and he whispered – the secret is, when you take a pony out to ride her for the very first time, make sure you do it just after heavy rain, when the ground's all nice and muddy.

I said why's that Dad, does it calm the pony down, or what?

And he said no not a bit of it, but at least you'll get a soft landing when she chucks you.

He laughed liked anything.

And that was something you'd hardly ever see.

Like I say, he properly loved the horses.

But he was always a bit on guard about them.

As if they might lead him astray.

Pause.

We had some beautiful horses stabled with us in the end.

I'd be riding point-to-pointers in the off season, galloping them round the Rhos and Llys-y-fran.

But my favourite was always our first little pony, Trigger.

We had him for years and Teddy Bishop's daughter'd came up to ride him maybe half a dozen times.

I couldn't blame her, though. Nobody could ride Trigger. Not my dad, not Moira.

Nobody but me.

Anyone but me got on him, he'd be a little bugger, rearing and bolting, all his tricks to get you off.

But for me he'd behave. Mostly.

I don't know why he'd behave for me, he just –

She stops.

I got to thinking of him as being my pony.

At first just my pony in that if we took people out for a hack, then of course Trigger would have to be my pony cause no-one else could ride him.

But after a while, he was just – mine.

For years, he was mine.

Then Dad told me Teddy Bishop'd decided to sell Trigger, and I'd have to get him ready to take to Llanybydder mart.

I remember the feeling, of the ground being gone.

I didn't argue, of course.

You didn't so much argue with your parents, in those days.

But I tried to think, what could I do, how could I stop it.

At first I asked Dad if we could buy Trigger.

Dad said, what for? He's no use to anyone. No-one can ride him.

I can ride him, I said.

Dad said what, you'd rather trot round on some grumpy little pony, when there's proper horses you could be riding?

If I'd've said yes, I would rather be trotting on my grumpy little pony that would've been answering back. And you didn't, in those days.

On the way to the mart, me and Dad talked about – birds we saw out the window, cows we saw in the fields, cars we saw on the roads. We talked about what tractors were value for money, what tractors were expensive foreign rubbish. We talked about anything we could.

And then we got to Llanybydder.

And I said I would just stay in the Landrover.

And Dad said, who d'you think's gonna show Trigger? I can't show him, he'll play up with me and no-one'll touch him.

I said Dad, you're gonna make me show my own horse to be sold?

And he said, no love. I'm gonna make you show Teddy Bishop's horse to be sold.

And you're gonna show Trigger as best you can.

And we'll get the best price we can.

And then we'll go home.

So we get Trigger out of the box.

We walk him to the ring.

We get our number.

We wait for our turn.

And our turn comes.

Dad says to me, right.

You show them what they'll be getting.

And he turns, and hops up into the stalls.

And the auctioneer is calling my number.

I head into the ring. I take Trigger round for a first lap.

And I catch my Dad's eye.

He is, very gently, smiling at me.

And so I, very gently, give Trigger a squeeze.

He bolts across the ring. He rears up and whinnies.

I make a show of getting him back under control.

And then I give him another little squeeze and, away he goes again.

And I catch Dad's eye. He is smiling still.

I hear the auctioneer asking for bids.

Not a peep.

The auctioneer lowers his opening price.

Still no takers.

I'm doing one final circuit of the ring.

The auctioneer is saying that if there are no bids at all, he'll move on to the next lot.

I'm turning to take Trigger out of the ring.

And someone waves. Someone makes a bid.

I look to my dad.

The bid is nothing, a couple of quid.

I look to my dad and.

He's just about to raise his arm.

He's just about to raise his arm and make a bid of his own. A bid for me.

I see his fingers stretch and his arm start to lift.

And he turns away.

Walks off.

And Trigger gets sold. For a couple of quid.

In the Landrover on the way back Dad turns on the radio, puts it onto the news.

He makes conversation about wars and people starving in foreign countries and how lucky we are.

I stay quiet.

That night he comes and sits on the edge of the bed, makes sure I've said my prayers.

Tells me things'll be different once he's bought the house.

Once we own our own home there'll be firm ground to stand on.

A bit of money to spare.

But not till then.

Till then we all have to put up with things we don't like.

My dad dies in that house, ten or twelve years later.

And he still doesn't own it, even then.

He dies carrying bales of hay out to some horses, one freezing January.

Fifty-two. Heart attack.

He falls in the field, and dies there.

He loved those horses. Properly.

www.ingramcontent.com/pod-product-compliance
Ingram Content Group UK Ltd.
Pitfield, Milton Keynes, MK11 3LW, UK
UKHW031251020325
455689UK00008B/103